IMPERFECT UNION

REPRESENTATION AND TAXATION IN
MULTILEVEL GOVERNMENTS

This book offers the first political theory of special-purpose jurisdictions, including 35,000 special districts and 13,500 school districts, which constitute the most common form of local government in the United States today. Collectively, special-purpose governments have more civilian employees than the federal government and spend more than all city governments combined. The proliferation of special-purpose jurisdictions has fundamentally altered the nature of representation and taxation in local government. Citizens today are commonly represented by dozens—in some cases hundreds—of local officials in multiple layers of government. As a result, political participation in local elections is low, and special interest groups associated with each function exert disproportionate influence. With multiple special interest governments tapping the same tax base, it takes on the character of a common-pool resource, leading to familiar problems of overexploitation. Strong political parties can often mitigate the common-pool problem by informally coordinating the policies of multiple overlapping governments.

Christopher R. Berry is an assistant professor in the Harris School of Public Policy Studies at the University of Chicago. sly, he was a postdoctoral Fellow at Harvard University in the De overnment. Professor Berry received his B.A. from Vassar C Regional Planning (M.R.P.) from Cornell University, an nt of Political Science at the University of Chicago. Fellow at the University of Chicago.

For my grandparents
Howard and Helen Bullock
Robert and Patricia Berry

POLITICAL ECONOMY OF INSTITUTIONS AND DECISIONS

Series Editors

Stephen Ansolabehere, Harvard University
Jeffry Frieden, Harvard University

Founding Editors

James E. Alt, Harvard University
Douglass C. North, Washington University of St. Louis

Other Books in the Series

Alberto Alesina and Howard Rosenthal, *Partisan Politics, Divided Government and the Economy*

Lee J. Alston, Thrainn Eggertsson, and Douglass C. North, eds., *Empirical Studies in Institutional Change*

Lee J. Alston and Joseph P. Ferrie, *Southern Paternalism and the Rise of the American Welfare State: Economics, Politics, and Institutions, 1865–1965*

James E. Alt and Kenneth Shepsle, eds., *Perspectives on Positive Political Economy*

Josephine T. Andrews, *When Majorities Fail: The Russian Parliament, 1990–1993*

Jeffrey S. Banks and Eric A. Hanushek, eds., *Modern Political Economy: Old Topics, New Directions*

Yoram Barzel, *Economic Analysis of Property Rights*, 2nd edition

Yoram Barzel, *A Theory of the State: Economic Rights, Legal Rights, and the Scope of the State*

Robert Bates, *Beyond the Miracle of the Market: The Political Economy of Agrarian Development in Kenya*, 2nd edition

Jenna Bednar, *The Robust Federation: Principles of Design*

Charles M. Cameron, *Veto Bargaining: Presidents and the Politics of Negative Power*

Kelly H. Chang, *Appointing Central Bankers: The Politics of Monetary Policy in the United States and the European Monetary Union*

Peter Cowhey and Mathew McCubbins, eds., *Structure and Policy in Japan and the United States: An Institutionalist Approach*

Gary W. Cox, *The Efficient Secret: The Cabinet and the Development of Political Parties in Victorian England*

Gary W. Cox, *Making Votes Count: Strategic Coordination in the World's Electoral System*

Gary W. Cox and Jonathan N. Katz, *Elbridge Gerry's Salamander: The Electoral Consequences of the Reapportionment Revolution*

Continued following index

IMPERFECT UNION

*Representation and Taxation in
Multilevel Governments*

CHRISTOPHER R. BERRY

The University of Chicago

CAMBRIDGE
UNIVERSITY PRESS

CAMBRIDGE
UNIVERSITY PRESS

32 Avenue of the Americas, New York NY 10013-2473, USA

Cambridge University Press is part of the University of Cambridge.

It furthers the University's mission by disseminating knowledge in the pursuit of education, learning and research at the highest international levels of excellence.

www.cambridge.org
Information on this title: www.cambridge.org/9780521758352

First published 2009

A catalogue record for this publication is available from the British Library

Library of Congress Cataloguing in Publication data
Berry, Christopher R.
Imperfect union : representation and taxation in multilevel governments / Christopher R. Berry.
p.   cm. – (Political economy of institutions and decisions)
Includes bibliographical references and index.
ISBN 978-0-521-76473-5 (hardback)
ISBN 978-0-521-75835-2 (pbk.)
1. Special districts – United States.   2. Local finance – United States.
I. Title.   II. Series.
JS425.B47 2009
352.4'2190973–dc22   2009011591

ISBN 978-0-521-76473-5 Hardback
ISBN 978-0-521-75835-2 Paperback

Contents

Preface

This book was influenced by statements from two eminent political scientists who have shaped my approach to the study of urban politics. The first statement is Paul Peterson's preface to *City Limits* (1981), in particular its first five paragraphs. Although it was not a statement made specifically to me—I was only to meet Peterson years later—it spoke to me quite directly. Therein, Peterson submits a trenchant indictment of the "loss of intellectual vitality" in the study of urban politics. He had the courage to say what most knew then and all must surely realize by now, namely, that while urban politics as a field of human endeavor remains exciting, fascinating, and central to modern life, urban politics as a field of academic study is an intellectual backwater. The reason, according to Peterson, is that urban scholars have stopped asking questions of first-order importance. Ironically, his accusation is vindicated most powerfully by the fact that *City Limits* remains the only book on urban politics written in the past 30 years that is still widely read by nonspecialists.

The second statement was made to me by Ken Shepsle over drinks in Harvard Square, just as I was beginning to form the ideas that became my dissertation and ultimately this book. I had met Ken at a conference the summer before, and we stayed in touch as a result of his generosity in mentoring a young student who had taken an interest in some of his work. When I described to him my ideas and asked his opinion on the prospect of writing a dissertation in the area of urban politics, he became pensive. "The essential thing," he said finally, "is that it not be sui generis." I nodded gravely in agreement and went home directly thereafter to look up the meaning of *sui generis*.

What both Peterson and Shepsle were saying, I came to realize, was that urban politics had become a moribund field by becoming disengaged from the intellectually lively debates of the discipline. It was asking questions that few outsiders cared about and whose answers had no implications for the rest of the field. Too often, the answers were being pursued using methods that would not have been state-of-the-art two generations ago. As the rest of the discipline discovered the "new" institutionalism, formal theory, and modern econometrics, too many urban politics scholars continued to produce case studies, ad hoc theorizing, and cross-sectional correlations. For the field to regain its former stature and vigor, urbanists must again work on issues that are central to the discipline of political science as whole.

On first blush, this book does not appear to be a step in the right direction. It is, after all, centrally concerned with special-purpose governments, distinctly local political institutions. Yet, I hope to convince the reader, special-purpose local governments are not sui generis. In fact, instances of specialized jurisdiction are ubiquitous in modern political systems, whether in the form of congressional committees, parliamentary ministries, or international organizations. Moreover, at a very general level, differences between policymaking in single-dimensional and multi-dimensional settings have been the subject of intense debate among political theorists. Local governments, therefore, provide an ideal laboratory for studying universal questions about the politics of specialized jurisdictions. While some of the institutional details differ from, say, congressional committees, the central issues are the same. Indeed, I expect that the average student of Congress will find the material and methods in this book more familiar than will the average student of urban politics. If so, then I will have succeeded, though at the risk of pleasing neither one.

Acknowledgments

This book grew out of my dissertation, and I owe an immeasurable debt of gratitude to my committee. I thank Mark Hansen, my chair, for allowing me the freedom to work outside the mainstream, but not too far, for his near-encyclopedic knowledge of the literature (on almost anything), for providing the basic ideas that ultimately became Chapter 6, and, above all, for teaching by example what it means to be a professional scholar. Sven Feldmann went far beyond the call of duty in his participation, and I thank him for never accepting anything less than the best I could produce. I am indebted to Sam Peltzman for injecting a healthy dose of common sense into the project, for encouraging me to let the data speak for themselves, and for being the only one to care more than I did about getting it finished. Finally, I thank Richard Posner for never letting me ask small questions, for encouraging me not to shy away from saying controversial things, and for making it all look so easy. I could not have asked for a more talented, committed group, and if this book makes even a small contribution, their influence will be obvious.

Although not on my committee, others at the University of Chicago during my student days lent their support in various ways to this project and to my intellectual development. I am especially grateful to John Brehm, Michael Dawson, Jeff Milyo, Gerald Rosenberg, and Lisa Wedeen.

After leaving Chicago, I had the good fortune to spend two years at Harvard in the Program on Education Policy and Governance (PEPG), run by Paul Peterson. I thank Paul for his supportive and generous mentoring, and his friendship. The cadre of young scholars whom Paul has helped shape through PEPG is truly remarkable and will stand as one of his great contributions, alongside his own seminal scholarship. I hope my membership will not detract too much from that otherwise superlative group.

I later had the even greater fortune to return to the University of Chicago, this time as a faculty member at the Harris School of Public Policy Studies. My scholarship has benefited tremendously from my colleagues at Harris—all of them. I thank in particular Duncan Snidal, for convincing me to return to this project and transform it into a book rather than a series of articles, and Marcos Rangel for detailed comments on an early draft. Disciplinary boundaries are especially porous at Chicago, and this book has been improved as a result of my interactions with colleagues throughout the university, especially Jacob Gersen, Roger Myerson, and Francesco Trebbi. Terry Clark deserves special mention for his generous support and for sharing data on party organizational strength that greatly enhanced Chapter 6.

Jeff Lewis, Terry Moe, Eric Oliver, and Ken Shepsle were the invited participants at a conference devoted to this book, and they provided extensive comments and lively discussion of the draft manuscript. Anyone who was at that conference can attest that the book has been dramatically improved as a result of their efforts. I thank them and the Harris School's Program on Political Institutions for sponsoring the conference.

Conversations with Brandice Canes-Wrone, Sanford Gordon, John Matsusaka, Michael Munger, Jonathan Rodden, Andrew Rutten, Koleman Strumpf, Nick Weller, and Martin West were important in the development of this project. Craig Volden was the discussant of a paper based on an early version of one of the chapters and, in addition to providing insightful comments, has been a consistent booster of this work ever since. John Curry at the U.S. Census Bureau helped me assemble, and comprehend, much of the data used in my analyses. I thank them all.

Sarah Anzia, C. C. DuBois, Sarah Lee, and Lindsay Wilhelm were outstanding research assistants. Sarah Anzia, in particular, went beyond the call of duty in collecting data on special district election timing and turnout, and helped write a section on the history of library districts for Chapter 5.

A few individuals must be singled out for extraordinary gratitude. As long as I have known him, Will Howell has been a great colleague and a better friend. Ethan Bueno de Mesquita is an intellectual force of nature, and his passion and seriousness of purpose are infectious. He also makes the best cup of hot chocolate the world has ever known. Mat McCubbins, whom I had never met before, extended to me an extraordinary act of professional generosity. All of them read the manuscript and provided indispensable comments, but that is beside the point.

I received funding that contributed to this project as a Charles Merriam Fellow of the University of Chicago, as a Daniel Levin Fellow of the Harris School, and as a Domestic Public Policy Fellow of the Smith Richardson Foundation. A grant from the Searle Foundation provided resources for me to complete the book.

Acknowledgments

At Cambridge University Press, Scott Parris, Lewis Bateman, and Adam Levine have been a terrific team. From the first submission to the final proofs, they have been encouraging, careful, and professional. Steven Ansolabehere, one of the editors of the Political Economy of Institutions and Decisions series, took an energetic role in the project, acting as reviewer, editor, and mentor. The prospect of Steve's involvement was what lured me to Cambridge, and I have not been disappointed.

Of course, no project as intense and long-term as writing a book can succeed without the support of friends and family. Mark Schindler and Alf Estberg are like brothers to me. A person is lucky to have one great friend in a lifetime. I do not deserve two such as these. I also thank D. Wayne and Larry Love for inspiration on Cold Harbour Lane.

Eric Tyrrell Knott, more than anyone I know, takes pleasure in the success of his friends, and he took an early interest in my project. He is perhaps the only layperson who can use the phrase "à la Tiebout" in dinner conversation (correctly). It is pretty boring dinner conversation, mind you, but still an impressive feat.

My parents, Robert and Joy, gave me every opportunity to succeed and, more importantly, the belief that I could. Together with Lynn, Colleen, Connor, and K.C., they have made my family life a great source of warmth and stability.

Saving the best for last, I thank my wife, Ané, whose love is the one true thing I know. I am privileged to share my life with such a beautiful person.

As I was finishing this book, I was blessed with the birth of my first child, Diego, who is five months old as it goes to press. It will be a long time before he can read this book and longer still before he will want to. So, let me explain it in the simplest possible terms. Daddy wrote this book so the mean people won't fire him. And also for the love of knowledge.

I

Introduction

American Politics in 3D

Over the past 50 years, a new government was created somewhere in the United States roughly every 18 hours. From cities and counties to school districts and transit authorities, there are now nearly 90,000 governments in the United States. The vast majority of them have the power to tax.

The proliferation of local governments has resulted largely from the layering of jurisdictions on top of one another. Territorially overlapping, single-function jurisdictions, including 35,000 special districts and 13,500 school districts, today constitute the majority of local governments. Collectively, these single-function jurisdictions have more civilian employees than the federal government and spend more than all city governments combined. As overlapping jurisdictions pile up, citizens increasingly receive services from—and pay taxes to—a multiplicity of independent governments.

The vertical layering of governments with independent tax authority raises fundamental issues of representation and taxation, which form the two major themes of this book. Representation in single-function governments operates through elected governing boards, which together employ a total of 173,000 local officials. Because these jurisdictions overlap, individual citizens today are represented by dozens—in some cases even hundreds—of local elected officers. Participating in so many elections places unprecedented demands on citizens. A citizen of Cook County, Illinois, for instance, would have to go to the polls on six separate dates over the course of four years in order to vote for each of the 70 different local officials that represent her. It is little surprise, then, that voter turnout in local single-function elections is usually in the range of 2 to 10 percent. Perversely, therefore, the proliferation of governments and elected officials may actually undermine democratic participation and accountability.

I will argue that the narrow scope of participation in single-function elections has important implications for the policies enacted by local governments. Each overlapping jurisdiction shares the same tax base but serves a different special interest constituency. Parents care more about school spending than other residents do, for instance, and bookworms care more about libraries, and nature lovers care more about parks, and so on. Rather than engaging with each other in the push-and-pull pluralism that characterizes a general-purpose government, however, the jurisdictional fragmentation of specialized government encourages each group to focus its attention, and concentrate its influence, on its own narrow policy domain. As a result, because the benefits of a single-function jurisdiction's spending accrue disproportionately to a particular group but the costs of taxation are spread over all groups, a problem arises that is analytically similar to the *overfishing* problem seen in environmental economics. That is, just as each individual fisherman has an incentive to overexploit the shared resources of the sea because he receives all the benefits of the increased catch but suffers only a small fraction of the adverse consequences, so too, I contend, each government has an incentive to overexploit the shared tax base to provide benefits to its special-interest constituency. The *fiscal common-pool problem* is the major issue analyzed in this book.

1.1 COOK COUNTY'S 10.25 PERCENT SOLUTION

In March 2008, Chicago attained the ignominious distinction of having the highest sales tax of any major American city, at 10.25 percent.[1] To understand how this milestone came to pass, one must first understand that, within the Chicago city limits, sales taxes are imposed by no fewer than six different governments: the state, city, county, transit authority, parks and recreation district, and water commission.[2] In fact, the feat that put Chicago's sales tax rate over the top was a 1 percentage point increase levied by Cook County. The simultaneous 0.25 percentage point bump by the regional transit authority was only icing on the layer cake.

As an overlapping jurisdiction in a densely developed county where most services are provided by incorporated municipalities, the Cook County government has become a specialized provider of two major services, public safety and hospitals, that together account for 90 percent

---

1 My discussion of this case is drawn from several news accounts, including Olmstead (2008), Ford and Keilman (2008), and the *Chicago Tribune* editorial board (2008), as well as the Cook County *Citizens' Budget Summary* for 2008.
2 The Metropolitan Pier and Exposition Authority levies an additional sales tax on restaurants and hotels.

of its $2.2 billion operating budget. Facing a $230 million deficit from 2007, the county board threatened service reductions and job cuts in the Cook County Health Facilities, the second-largest public health system in the nation. The outcry was immediate and predictable, coming from employees and from constituents who depended on the county for heavily subsidized health care.[3] At a midnight meeting, the county board responded by raising its sales tax levy from 0.75 percent to 1.75 percent.[4] The tax increase was projected to yield $430 million in new revenue for the county each year. Rather than cutting jobs, the new budget planned for 1,100 new positions, boosting the county's workforce to nearly 25,000. Critics of the board's decision to use a $430 million tax increase to cover a $230 million deficit could take solace in the fact that the board president's original proposal to raise the county's sales tax to 2.75 percent was defeated (by one vote).

While the late-night tax vote spared the county board from having to make tough budget cuts, and won it the admiration of employees and patients of the county health system, some other local governments were less pleased. Municipalities within the county worried about balancing their own budgets, as well as the health of their local businesses, if consumers crossed the border to shop, where in some cases the sales tax rate would now be 3 percentage points lower. Among some municipalities near the border, there was talk of secession. In the words of Palatine Village Council member Scott Lamerand, "What really gets me most is it's not only us: It's going to be the schools along with the village, the park district, any taxing body—the dollars are going to shift from our area" (Ford and Keilman 2008, p. 1). The Civic Federation, a local budget watchdog group, warned of the detrimental effects that the county's tax increase would have on overlapping jurisdictions. "The county, in its arrogance to grab so much tax revenue, has really thumbed its nose at other local governments," said Laurence Msall, the group's president (Ford and Keilman 2008, p. 2).

If Chicago now stands out for the loftiness of its accumulated sales taxes, there is nothing at all unusual about the basic problem it faces: common taxation by multiple governments. Nor is the issue restricted to sales taxes; indeed, concurrent property taxes may be even more ubiquitous. In the pages that follow, I will show that virtually every locality in the United States has multiple layers of taxing jurisdictions.

---

3 In addition to the intended subsidies, the county health system is regularly criticized for failing to collect even the patient fees it is owed (Olmstead 2008).
4 Countless news reports described that tax hike as a *1 percent* increase rather than a *1 percentage point* increase. In fact, this was a 133 percent increase in Cook County's sales tax.

Chicago's tax escalation cannot easily be explained by traditional theories of local political economy. Beginning with Tiebout (1956), conventional wisdom has been that when there are many local governments, competition among them will keep taxes low, maybe even too low (Oates 1972). So, then, why does the county with the most local governments also have the highest taxes? The governments in this example do not appear to be competing with one another, unless it is competition for sales tax revenue. The familiar theories do not have an answer, nor do they provide a useful framework for understanding the common taxation of shared resources by overlapping, functionally specialized governments that is now the rule rather than the exception for U.S. localities. This is because the standard theories are missing two critical ingredients: institutions and politics. Put differently, the conventional theories inhabit a two-dimensional world where competition takes place through mobility. This book is about a three-dimensional world where competition takes place through politics.

I.2 COMPETITION IN 2-D: VOTING WITH YOUR FEET

Fiscal common-pool problems have received scant attention from scholars of local politics. Indeed, problems of institutional design and accountability more generally have received relatively little attention. Scholars of local political economy have been fairly sanguine about the correspondence between citizen desires and government performance even as a growing body of scholarship questions the institutional foundations of democratic government.[5] In large part, the relative unconcern with classic problems of preference aggregation, information asymmetries, and electoral accountability at the local level reflects the belief that residential mobility is sufficient to keep governments informed, efficient, and honest. Voting with the feet seems to make voting at the ballot box superfluous. Thus, many who would be uncomfortable accepting the argument

5 Social choice problems inherent in democratic politics have become the subject of a vast literature demonstrating that voting mechanisms are subject to inconsistent aggregation, cycling and instability, and other such difficulties (Arrow 1951; Plott 1967). In the legislature, the possibility of vote trading may lead to outcomes that are collectively undesirable (Tullock 1959; Weingast, Shepsle and Johnsen 1981). Budget-maximizing bureaucrats may exploit information asymmetries to opt for and likely to receive excessive budgets (Niskanen 1971). A clever agenda setter can lead the median voter to support an undesirable policy by offering an even less preferred outcome as a reversion point (Romer and Rosenthal 1978, 1979; Rosenthal 1990). Even well-intentioned representatives have at best incomplete information about the preferences of their constituents and may inadvertently produce policies that the electorate does not favor (Matsusaka 1992). This line of research is encapsulated in Mueller (2003).

that electoral competition ensures government fidelity to citizens' interests at the national level nevertheless accept the notion that interjurisdictional competition achieves just such an outcome at the local level (e.g., Brennan and Buchanan 1980; Weingast 1995). In this respect, Qian and Weingast are typical in their conclusion that "Competition among jurisdictions forces governments to represent citizen interests and preserve markets" (1997, p. 88).

The widely held belief that a local government is less likely than the national government to deviate from citizens' interests is inspired by Tiebout's (1956) classic article "A Pure Theory of Local Government Expenditures." In it, Tiebout sketched a view of the local public sector as the governmental analogue to the private marketplace, with competition among local governments leading to marketlike efficiency in the production of local public goods and services. It is difficult to imagine any area of political science or economics in which one model—indeed, one article—has had as profound an influence as the Tiebout model has had in the study of local political economy.[6]

Tiebout's (1956) model is largely a response to Samuelson's (1954) argument that nonexcludability and jointness of supply in public goods promote free riding and provide incentives for citizens to misrepresent their preferences. While Samuelson's analysis holds, Tiebout acknowledged, at the federal level, it need not apply to local expenditures. For whereas there is only one central service provider at the federal level, at the local level the citizen may choose from many municipalities offering different bundles of taxes and public goods. In making her choice of residential location, Tiebout argued, the citizen indirectly reveals her preferences for public goods. In other words,

Just as the consumer may be visualized as walking to a private marketplace to buy his goods, the prices of which are set, we place him in the position of walking to a community where the prices (taxes) of community services are set. Both trips take the consumer to market. There is no way in which the consumer can avoid revealing his preferences in a spatial economy. Spatial mobility provides the local public-goods counterpart to the private market's shopping trip. (Tiebout, 1956, p. 422)

In the Tiebout model, with a large number of competing governments a citizen-taxpayer can find perfect substitutes for the services of any particular local government, meaning that demand for that government's services is infinitely elastic, as in a competitive market. Local governments,

---

6 Rhode and Strumpf (2003) estimate that more than 1,000 articles have been written about the Tiebout model.

like competitive firms, thus become price-takers in their tax rates. Given such competition, each government will produce its output at the point of minimum average cost relative to population. All taxes become benefits taxes. In this setting, each resident chooses the locality whose bundle of taxes and services best matches her preferences, and all the messy issues of majority cycling, logrolling, agenda-setting, and the like are averted.

In fact, Tiebout competition has been seen as such a panacea that even Brennan and Buchanan (1980, ch. 9), whose "Leviathan" is perhaps the most extreme model of a disjuncture between citizens' interests and government behavior, have suggested interjurisdictional competition as a sufficient constraint on government excess. Specifically, they suggest that Tiebout sorting and competition are "partial or possibly complete substitutes for explicit fiscal constraints on the taxing power" (1980, p. 184). In a perfect Tiebout world, even a revenue-maximizing government will behave like a competitive firm.[7]

Tiebout's disciples have relatively uncritically adapted the competitive model of government to explain special-purpose jurisdictions. If interjurisdictional competition is good, the argument seems to be, then more jurisdictions must be better. Tiebout's shopping analogy is extended to encompass special-purpose jurisdictions by Ostrom, Bish, and Ostrom, who write that "In the United States, in fact, several hundred separate local governments in a metropolitan area is not unusual—with each citizen generally participating in a city, county, school district, and several other special districts. ... Being a member of several local governments may seem complicated, but it is no more complicated than shopping in several establishments—some of which are general purpose stores and others of which are specialized" (1988, p. 97). The work of the Ostroms and their colleagues and students has come to be known as the *Indiana School* of local political economy, whose guiding idea is *polycentricity*, or the desirability of having many centers of local government decision making that are independent of each other.[8]

1.3 POLITICS IN 3-D: TERRITORIAL OVERLAP AND CONCURRENT TAXATION

I do not doubt that competition among local governments for mobile residents and capital is a powerful, efficiency-enhancing force. But I do

---

7 Empirical evidence for the *competition-constrains-Leviathan* hypothesis, however, has been mixed. See Oates (1989) for a review.
8 The contributions to McGinnis (1999) provide a useful sampling of the polycentricity literature.

doubt that the competitive model of government applies well to most special-purpose jurisdictions. In fact, I contend that the multiplication of single-function governments undermines, rather than enhances, interjuris-dictional competition. The reality is that the proliferation of governments in the United States has resulted largely from the vertical layering of juris-dictions on top of one another rather than the horizontal partitioning of territory into competing units. Jurisdictions that share the same borders do not compete for mobile resources. Rather, they possess the authority to provide services to, and levy taxes on, the same people. Seen from this perspective, the two defining characteristics of single-function govern-ment are territorial overlap and concurrent taxation.

By *territorial overlap*, I mean a situation in which two or more gov-ernments co-occupy the same piece of land and, by implication, the same tax base. The territorial overlap of governments is plainly illustrated in Figure 1.1, which shows the various jurisdictions in the vicinity of Sheridan, Colorado, a small suburb in the Denver metropolitan area.[9] The city is overlaid by school, fire, recreation, and sanitation districts. The school, fire, and recreation districts roughly follow the municipal boundaries, while the city is carved into six separate sanitation districts. In fact, there are several additional jurisdictions overlapping Sheridan for which I was unable to attain boundary maps. In other words, Figure 1.1 actually understates the extent of jurisdictional overlap in this case. A gallery of maps for other areas of the country can be found on my Web site.[10]

The two-dimensional Tiebout model proceeds as though only the city layer of government exists, and proposes that competition among Sheridan and other cities in the Denver region will guarantee efficient policy outcomes. While it may be reasonable to think that Sheridan is competing for residents and businesses with other cities in the region, it is wholly implausible to think that the city and its overlapping juris-dictions are in competition with one another. The city cannot compete for residents with a school district or a recreation district, for example. From the citizens' perspective, the locational choice is a choice among composite bundles of services provided by combinations of overlapping jurisdictions. In other words, while the *provision* of services is unbun-dled, *consumption* of the services is not. Even when jurisdictions overlap in more complex patterns than those in Sheridan, the citizen's choice is ultimately of a single location rather than an à la carte assortment of

---

9 I produced the figure using GIS shapefiles downloaded from the county's Web site: http://gis.co.arapahoe.co.us/, accessed December, 26 2008.
10 The URL is http://harrisschool.uchicago.edu/faculty/web-pages/christopher-berry.asp.

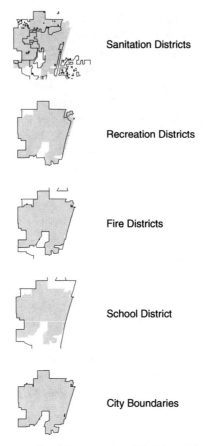

Figure 1.1. Local Governments of Sheridan, Colorado

jurisdictions. The location carries with it the imposed choice of a particular set of special district and municipal services.[11]

As a composite territorial unit, Sheridan and its overlapping special districts can be seen as a competitor with other jurisdictional composites in the region. However, the overlapping governments do not compete with each other. Instead, the various overlapping governments all have the authority to tax and provide services in the same territory.

This leads to the second defining characteristic of special-function government: concurrent taxation. When jurisdictions overlap, the most common scenario is that several governments independently tax the same property and economic activities within their shared territory, with

---

11 An exception might be a system like school vouchers, although in practice these systems usually allow a choice of schools within, rather than across, districts.

each government controlling its own budget. Returning to Cook County, Figure 1.2 shows an actual residential property tax bill from the city of Evanston. While it is just an ordinary tax bill, the striking point is that the property owner is paying taxes to 14 different overlapping jurisdictions. The taxing jurisdictions include three general-purpose governments—the city of Evanston, the town of Evanston, and Cook County—as well as a host of special districts—two school districts (elementary and high school), a mass transit district, a water reclamation district, a community college district, a forest preserve district, a mosquito abatement district, and a tuberculosis sanitarium district.[12] Nor is concurrent taxation limited to property taxation, as was made clear in the preceding example of Cook County's sales tax increase.

While Cook County is certainly above average in its degree of jurisdictional overlap, it is hardly an outlier. Although I do not have access to a property tax bill from every county in the country, Figure 1.3 shows a national map of an approximate measure of jurisdictional overlap: the number of territorially overlapping jurisdictions per municipality. The numerator is the number of jurisdictions that have the area flexibility to overlap the territory of a city. These jurisdictions include school districts and other special districts. The denominator is the number of municipalities.[13] The resulting ratio of overlapping jurisdictions to municipalities gives an indication of the extent of concurrent taxation in a county. Figure 1.3 shows that concurrent taxation is seen throughout the nation to varying degrees and is most extensive in the West and Midwest.

Together, territorial overlap and concurrent taxation transform the local tax base into a fiscal common-pool resource. Seen from this vantage point, the relevant literature from which to begin forging theories of special-purpose local government comes not from the Tiebout tradition, but from the modern study of distributive politics and comparative fiscal institutions.

1.4 THE FISCAL COMMON POOL

While the essence of the problem was recognized at least as early as Aristotle—in his observation that "what is common to the greatest number has the least care bestowed upon it" (*Politics*, Book II, ch. 3)—Garret Hardin (1968) coined the phrase *tragedy of the commons* and hence became the intellectual figurehead for a large subsequent literature on the

12 Not all of these jurisdictions satisfy the requirements of fiscal and administrative autonomy necessary to be counted as independent governments by the Census Bureau, as explained in the next chapter.

13 Town and township governments are counted either as overlapping districts or as municipalities in different states, as will be explained in the next chapter.

2000 Second Installment Property Tax Bill

Amount due if paid 11/01/2001:
$ 3,446.81

Property Index Number (PIN) — Volume **052** — Code **17001** — Tax Year (Payable in) **2000** **(2001)** — (Township) **EVANSTON**

1362-000396030

AVOID LATE PAYMETN PENAL TIES

If received:	Amount due is:
(on time) 11/01/2001	3,446.81
(late) 11/02/2001 – 12/01/2001	3,498.51
(late) 12/02/2001 – 1/01/2002	3,550.21

Do not double pay. Pay only one amount.
Late payment penalty is 1.5% per month.

	1st Installment		2nd Installment	
	Tax due 3/1/2001	Penalty	Tax due 11/1/2001	Penalty
	0.00	0.00	3,446.81	0.00
	0.00	0.00	3,446.81	51.70
	0.00	**0.00**	**3,446.81**	**103.40**

Thank you for your 1st Installment payment of 3,322.69
Last payment received on 03-01-01

Through 1/15/2002, you may at any LaSalle Bank.

Property Location (To update, please contact the Cook County Assessor's Office at 312-603-7509.)
EVASTON IL 60201 1115

www.cookcountytreasurer.com

How was my tax calculated?

199 Equalized Assessed Value (EAV)   **63,097**

Property Value	175,231
Assessment Level	× 16%
2000 Assessed Value =	28,037
2000 State Equalization Factor ×	2.2235
2000 Equalized Assessed Value (EAV) =	**62,340**
2000 Local Tax Rate ×	10.859%
2000 Tax Before Exemptions =	6,769.50
Less Homeowner Exemption –	0.00
Less Senior Citizen Exemption –	0.00
Less Senior Freeze Exemption –	0.00

Taxing District	2000 Tax	2000 Rate	Pension	1999 Tax	1999 Rate
SCHOOL DISTRICT C C 65	2,638.23	4.232	89.14	2,569.94	4.073
N SUBURB MASS TRANSIT DIST	0.00	0.000		0.00	0.000
CITY OF EVANSTON	1,267.37	2.033	231.28	1,220.30	1.934
OAKTON COLLEGE DISTRICT	132.78	0.213	1.24	128.09	0.203
HIGH SCHOOL DISTRICT 202	1855.86	2.977	77.92	1007.73	2.865
N SHORE MOSQUITO ABATEMENT	6.86	0.011		6.94	0.011
WATER RECLAMATION DIST	258.71	0.415	16.20	264.38	0.419
EVANSTON GEN. ASSISTANCE	34.91	0.056		32.81	0.052
TOWN OF EVANSTON	13.09	0.021		12.62	0.020
CONSOLIDATED ELECTIONS	0.00	0.000		14.51	0.023
SUBURBAN T B SANITARIUM	4.99	0.008		5.05	0.008
FOREST PRESERVE DISTRICT	43.01	0.069	1.87	44.17	0.070
COUNTY OF COOK	377.17	0.605	102.23	389.93	0.618
COOK COUNTY HEALTH FACIL.	136.52	0.219		148.91	0.236
DO NOT PAY THESE TOTALS	6,769.50	10.859		6,645.38	10.532

Figure 1.2. Property Tax Bill, 14 Taxing Jurisdictions

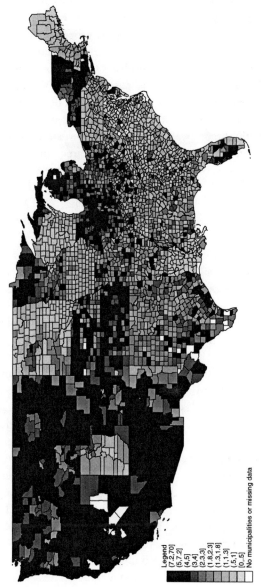

Figure 1.3. Territorially Overlapping Jurisdictions per Municipality, 2002

exploitation of shared resources. Hardin illustrated the tragedy through the eyes of a herdsman grazing his sheep in an open pasture. In deciding whether to enlarge his herd by one sheep, the shepherd faces a trade-off. On one hand, he receives the additional benefits from the sale of one more animal. On the other hand, overgrazing the pasture will strain its carrying capacity and reduce its ability to support other animals. The individual herdsman gains all the proceeds from the additional animal, while he suffers only a fraction of the costs resulting from overgrazing, which are borne by all the herdsmen using the pasture. Thus, the herdsman concludes that it is beneficial—to him—to increase his flock. However, when every other herdsman follows the same logic, the pasture is destroyed. "Ruin is the destination toward which all men rush, each pursuing his own best interest in a society that believes in the freedom of the commons. Freedom in a commons brings ruin to all" (Hardin 1968, p. 1244).

Following Hardin, the basic common-pool theory was formalized in environmental economics by, among others, Levhari and Mirman (1980) and Benhabib and Radner (1992) and has been applied to the study of a wide range of natural resource issues, including the use of oil fields and fishing grounds, air and water pollution, climate change, and even the allocation of radio wave frequencies.

While Hardin obviously had in mind environmental issues when he penned his famous article, the basic framework has been extended to characterize a broad class of collective action problems involving shared resources (see Cornes and Sandler 1996). Most notably, for present purposes, the common-pool framework has infiltrated the study of distributive politics.[14] An early discussion of the tax base as a fiscal common-pool resource is found in the congressional "gains from trade" literature associated with Weingast et al. (1981). These models portray a geographically districted legislature in which individual representatives fully value the benefits of projects for their district but internalize only a fraction of the costs, which are financed from a common pool of national tax revenue. Because individual legislators do not internalize the full social costs of spending for projects in their district, there is excessive demand for public goods with geographically concentrated benefits financed by nationwide taxes. Combined with a legislative norm of *universalism*, such fiscal externalities lead to overspending in the aggregate budget.

Empirical studies of legislative budgeting have generally found support for the common-pool model. Using data on U.S. states, Gilligan and Matsusaka (1995) find the model's predicted positive relationship

---

14 For a review of the literature on common-pool tax problems in legislatures, see Knight (2006).

between government spending and legislature size. Langbein, Crewson, and Brasher (1996) and Baqir (2002) both find a positive relationship between the size of a city council and local tax rates, which they relate to Weingast et al.'s (1981) "law of $1/n$." Bradbury and Crain (2001) also find a positive correlation between the number of seats in a legislature and per capita spending using cross-national data. On the other hand, Pettersson-Lidbom (2006) finds that an increase in council size results in a *reduction* in spending in a sample of Swedish municipalities.

Other studies have tested the common-pool model by examining the behavior of individual legislators. DelRossi and Inman (1999) find that members of Congress requested smaller water-related projects for their districts following an administrative change that increased the fraction of project costs borne by local jurisdictions. Knight (2003) finds that individual legislators respond to common-pool incentives when voting on transportation projects funded by a gasoline tax: The probability that a representative supports a project is increasing in its spending for her district and decreasing in expected gas tax payments.

Recently, scholars of comparative political economy have come to rely on fiscal common-pool models to explain persistent deficits in many countries (e.g., Alesina and Perotti 1999; Ricciuti 2004; Rodden 2005). In their summary of this literature, Poterba and von Hagen explain that "Deficits arise because the government's general tax fund is a 'common property resource' from which projects of public policy are being financed. ... This induces a 'common-pool problem' in which competing political groups vie for government expenditures that are financed using broad-based tax instruments" (1999, p. 3). A common theme in this literature is that more "fragmented" budgetary institutions generate a bias toward higher spending and deficits. In different contexts, fragmentation has been measured in terms of the number of representatives, the number of legislative committees, the number of spending ministers, and the number of lower-tier governments. The basic common-pool framework has been applied in a variety of institutional settings ranging from American states to Organization for Economic Cooperation and Development (OECD) countries and Argentine provinces.[15]

Seen from this comparative institutional perspective, special-purpose jurisdictions in local politics resemble spending ministries in parliamentary cabinets as portrayed by Hallerberg (2000), Hallerberg and von

---

15 The contributions to Poterba and von Hagen (1999) provide a good representation of research in this area. In the same volume, Alesina and Perotti (1999) provide a useful literature review. Rodden (2005) provides the most fully developed analysis of common-pool debt problems in federations.

Hagen (1999), and von Hagen and Harden (1995). In these models, although each minister nominally serves the nation as a whole, each is in fact beholden to special interests in the domain governed by the ministry (e.g., labor, education, defense). In setting the budget for her department, each minister fully values spending on programs she considers important for her policy goals but considers only the tax burden that her constituency must bear. Because she does not internalize the full tax burden of additional spending, each minister proposes a budget that is larger than what is socially optimal. Unless subsequent negotiations within the government lead to spending reductions, the aggregate budget will be larger than a single spending minister who represented all groups would propose. Kontopolous and Perotti (1999) and Ricciuti (2004) find empirical support for the prediction that the aggregate size of the budget deficit increases with the number of spending ministers in OECD countries. The mechanisms at work in these parliamentary models are quite similar to those in Weingast et al.'s (1981) model of a geographically districted legislature, but here the "districting" is determined by policy domain rather than geography. Special purpose local governments represent a similar form of districting by policy domain.

There are reasons to expect the common-pool problems of overlapping special-purpose jurisdictions to be even more severe than those of legislatures or parliamentary governments. Most notably, district officials have more fiscal independence than either legislators or ministers and need not negotiate with one another to produce a collectively approved budget. Thus, whereas the legislative budgeting process requires (at least) a majority of members to recognize and agree upon an aggregate level of taxes and spending, there is no unifying process that forces independent local governments to jointly approve the cumulative tax bill; in fact, there is no guarantee that each jurisdiction is even aware of the taxes imposed by the others that overlap its territory.

Independent taxation by two or more levels of government—known as *concurrent taxation* in the public finance literature—is not a new problem. It was a concern to the American founders, especially Alexander Hamilton, who worried about granting "the power of the purse" to both the federal and state governments (see Rodden 2005, ch. 2).[16] One of the

---

16 Among the antifederalists, Patrick Henry was a leading opponent of concurrent taxation. His speech before the Virginia ratifying convention is worth quoting, if only for its colorful phrasing: "In this scheme of energetic government, the people will find two sets of taxgatherers—the state and the federal sheriffs. This, it seems to me, will produce such dreadful oppression as the people cannot possibly bear. The federal sheriff may commit what oppression, make what distresses, he pleases, and ruin you with impunity; for how are you to tie his hands? Have you

earliest and most famous examples of concurrent taxation was the system of medieval Rhine tolls.[17] The Rhine River was the most important shipping route in Western Europe throughout the Middle Ages. Commercial river traffic flowed through many cities and principalities on its way down the Rhine, each of which was eager to impose a toll. The Holy Roman Empire relied on river taxes as an important source of revenue and controlled the right of localities to collect tolls. In siting tolling stations, the emperor faced a complex optimization problem. More tolling stations allowed the collection of additional revenue, but having too many tolling stations would discourage river traffic by raising the aggregate costs of shipping, which ultimately could reduce the empire's revenue.[18]

Throughout much of the history of the empire, emperors allowed few tolling stations and kept overall customs relatively low. However, during the Interregnum (1250–1273) there was no emperor, and the number of tolling stations on the Rhine more than doubled. From that point on, the proliferation of tolling stations appears to have proceeded unabated. According to Postan's (1966, p. 184) analysis of river tolls in the Middle Ages:

> The most advertised, the most bitterly resented and, from the point of view of trade, the most damaging, were the tolls on the Rhine. ... There were about 19 toll stations along the Rhine at the end of the twelfth century, about 35 or more at the end of the thirteenth century, nearly 50 at the end of the fourteenth, and more than 60 at the end of the fifteenth century; mostly belonging to the great ecclesiastical princes of western Germany. Writing in the middle of the thirteenth century,

any sufficiently decided means of preventing him from sucking your blood by speculations, commissions, and fees? Thus thousands of your people will be most shamefully robbed: our state sheriffs, those unfeeling blood-suckers, have, under the watchful eye of our legislature, committed the most horrid and barbarous ravages on our people. It has required the most constant vigilance of the legislature to keep them from totally ruining the people; a repeated succession of laws has been made to suppress their iniquitous speculations and cruel extortions; and as often has their nefarious ingenuity devised methods of evading the force of those laws: in the struggle they have generally triumphed over the legislature. ... When these harpies are aided by excisemen, who may search, at any time, your houses, and most secret recesses, will the people bear it? If you think so, you differ from me. Where I thought there was a possibility of such mischiefs, I would grant power with a niggardly hand; and here there is a strong probability that these oppressions shall actually happen. I may be told that it is safe to err on that side, because such regulations may be made by Congress as shall restrain these officers, and because laws are made by our representatives, and judged by righteous judges: but, Sir, as these regulations may be made, so they may not; and many reasons there are to induce a belief that they will not, I shall therefore be an infidel on that point till the day of my death." Patrick Henry, "The Problem of Concurrent Taxation," delivered to the Virginia ratifying convention, June 5, 1788.

17 My discussion of the Rhine tolls is based Gardner, Gaston, and Masson (2003).
18 The *Laffer curve* strikes again (see Laffer 2004).

an English chronicler, Thomas Wykes, could find no other way of describing the system on the Rhine than 'the raving madness of the Teutons.'

Thompson (1931) estimated that tolls could consume as much as 60 percent of the value of shipments during this period, and Postan (1966, pp. 198–199) went on to add that "if, in spite of the greater economy of water carriage, traffic was apt to desert the great waterways, the fault lay with the owners of the tolls who preyed upon them.... At times some rivers, mainly German, came near to being deserted by the merchant and the barge-man."

The proliferation of toll stations during the era of decentralized river tolling is an early example of a fiscal common-pool problem. Each additional toll station reduces the traffic willing to travel on the river, thus diminishing the revenue of all the other toll collectors. The collective revenue drawn from the river could be increased if there were fewer toll stations, but no locality has an incentive to unilaterally lift its toll.[19] The analogy of river tolls to overlapping local government jurisdictions is straightforward. Local homeowners involved in choosing a locality of residence, like the medieval bargemen involved in choosing a shipping route, respond to the sum of all the taxes levied upon them. Yet, overlapping special-purpose jurisdictions, like the Rhine toll collectors, each control only a fraction of the tax bill and have little to gain by reigning in their own levies regardless of what the other toll collectors do.

Scholars of industrial organization will recognize the Rhine tolls as a special class of the *double-marginalization* or *chain-of-monopolies* problem (Spengler 1950; Tirole 1988, ch. 4). In the typical setup, there is an upstream firm, called a *manufacturer*, that produces an intermediate good, which is sold to a downstream firm, a *retailer*. The retailer resells the product to a consumer. The total quantity of goods sold depends on, and is declining in, the retail price. If both the retailer and the manufacturer have market power, then their relationship involves *vertical externalities*: The pricing decisions of one affect the profits of the other. If the retailer gets to set the retail price, she has an incentive to set a price that maximizes her own profit. Thus, the retailer will raise her price whenever the increase in her own revenue due to the higher price outweighs the loss due to selling fewer units. When considering this price hike, however, the retailer will not take into account the manufacturer's profit, which also declines when fewer units are sold. The manufacturer's loss

---

19 Eventually, according to Gardner et al. (2003), the Rhine League, an informal cooperative of Rhine toll collectors, was created to manage toll collections along the river, preventing overexploitation of the shared tax base. I will return to the Rhine League later.

may outweigh the retailer's gain, resulting in a net drop in total profit. The manufacturer faces a similar incentive in setting the price that he charges to the retailer. Because of two consecutive markups, or double marginalization, the price will be higher but the profit lower when pricing is done independently by the upstream and downstream firms than if the two were integrated. While the upstream–downstream relationship is merely figurative for the retailer and the manufacturer, the underlying logic recalls the rival river princes of the Rhine.

Vertical externalities thus have a long pedigree and wide applicability. Surprisingly, although the essence of federalism is multilevel government, the fiscal federalism literature has devoted relatively little attention to vertical fiscal externalities apart from the issue of intergovernmental grants.[20] Rather, following the seminal work of Oates (1972), the literature has focused primarily on horizontal competition, or competition among multiple nonoverlapping governments for a mobile tax base, where the concern is that a "race to the bottom" may lead to taxes that are too low.[21]

Scholars of fiscal federalism have only recently begun to devote sustained attention to the vertical fiscal externalities arising from co-occupation of a common tax base by two layers of government in a federation. Following early contributions by Flowers (1988) and Johnson (1988), a growing theoretical literature suggests that lower-level jurisdictions in a federation have incentives to overtax relative to the social optimum.[22] Most of the vertical tax competition models are similar in spirit to the double-marginalization model explained previously, and are built on the idea that state governments underestimate the costs of their tax increases because they do not fully internalize the costs imposed upon the federal government––and, by implication, upon the other states—from lost taxable activity.[23]

With horizontal externalities in a federation pointing to state taxes that are too low and vertical externalities pointing to state taxes that are too high, what is likely to be the net outcome? There appears to be no general answer. Keen and Kotsogiannis (2002) provide the most ambitious theoretical examination of the question. Superimposing a

---

20 See Mueller (2003) for a review of the literature on intergovernmental grants.
21 The contents of Oates (1998) represent many of the most influential contributions to this literature. Wilson (1999) provides a useful literature review. Gordon (1983) is a seminal contribution on the subject of horizontal fiscal externalities.
22 More recent theoretical contributions include Keen (1998), Wrede (1997, 1999), Flochel and Thierry (2002), and Volden (2005).
23 Some have argued that the federal government can correct for the vertical externalities with a properly structured system of intergovernmental transfers (e.g., Hoyte 2001). However, such arguments rest on rather heroic assumptions about the central government's access to fiscal instruments and information about the states. See Keen (1998) for a discussion.

federal government on the well-known horizontal tax competition model of Zodrow and Mieszkowski (1986), they find no clear theoretical prediction as to whether vertical or horizontal externalities will dominate. The outcome depends on assumptions of the models as well as empirical values of key variables, such as the elasticity of the base with respect to the tax rate and the relative size of the federal government.[24] That is, either the horizontal or the vertical externality may dominate under different, but similarly plausible, conditions. The authors are left to conclude that whether horizontal or empirical externalities dominate—that is, whether taxes in a federation are too high or too low—is a question to be answered empirically.

If existing theory is inconclusive, what does the evidence indicate? Brulhart and Jametti (2006) is the first—and, to date, only—study to try to disentangle vertical and horizontal fiscal externalities empirically. Studying local taxation in a panel of Swiss municipalities, they find that vertical externalities dominate overall. Whether these findings generalize to other fiscal settings remains to be seen.[25]

A somewhat larger empirical literature has investigated the responsiveness of local to federal tax rates when both layers of government tax the same underlying base, such as income or commodities. Although these studies do not assess the question of whether vertical or horizontal externalities dominate, they look for evidence that vertical externalities produce interdependencies in the tax policies of overlapping governments. The first study to address the issue was Besley and Rosen (1998). Looking at gasoline and cigarette taxes in the United States, they find that when the federal government increases taxes, there is a significant positive response in state taxes. Esteller-More and Sole-Olle find a similar positive reaction of state tax rates to changes in the federal tax rate for personal income taxes in the United States (2001) and Canada (2002). In contrast, Hayashi and Boadway (2001), examining corporate taxation in Canada, find that provincial tax rates respond

24 Keen (1998) contains a more expansive discussion of these issues, concluding that "theory admits no unambiguous answer to the question of whether federal structures create an inherent tendency toward excessively high tax rates" (p. 470).

25 At a more general level, it does not appear that federations charge higher tax rates than nonfederal countries. Keen (1998) examines OECD countries in 1990 and finds that federations have lower taxes as a share of gross domestic product (GDP) than nonfederal countries. However, there are only five federations in his sample, and the result appears to be driven largely by Switzerland and the United States (Keen 1998, p. 470). More recently, Persson and Tabellini (2003) studied a sample of 80 democracies in the 1990s. Using a richer set of control variables than Keen (1998), they find that spending is lower in federal countries, by about 5 percent of GDP (2003, p. 41). It is unclear whether this relationship is causal or coincidental.

negatively to the federal tax rate. In a related cross-national study, Goodspeed (2000) finds that local tax rates are lower where national tax rates are higher in a sample of 13 OECD countries from 1975 to 1984, although he does not attempt to assess the reaction of lower-level government to *changes* in national taxes. Given the underlying theoretical ambiguity, more empirical work is needed to make sense of these divergent findings.

In summary, fiscal common-pool problems have a long history and general applicability. The fiscal common-pool model has become a workhorse in distributive politics, with relevance in both American and comparative politics. Scholars of fiscal federalism have demonstrated increasing interest in vertical fiscal externalities in recent years, although many theoretical and empirical issues remain unresolved in this context. In the next section, I explain how ideas about fiscal common-pool problems can be applied to overlapping local governments, and how studying the U.S. experience with special-purpose jurisdictions can be instrumental in advancing related research agendas in areas such as distributive politics, comparative institutions, and fiscal federalism.

I.5 PUTTING POLITICS BACK INTO LOCAL POLITICAL ECONOMY

If the existing literature provides a number of precedents for thinking about the influence of special-purpose governments on local politics, my argument nevertheless departs from the familiar models in several important directions. Most notably, all of the models of concurrent taxation discussed previously assume that governments are either Leviathans, who care exclusively about maximizing the size of their budgets, or benevolent social planners, who single-mindedly devote themselves to enhancing the welfare of the citizenry. There is no role for politics in either of these extreme views. There are no elections, nor any other form of action on the part of citizens other than moving from one jurisdiction to another. Governments are like machines, pursuing preprogrammed objectives without regard for the political implications of their actions—because there are no political implications.

By contrast, my theory puts politics front and center, arguing that the nature and extent of local fiscal common-pool problems depend on the (endogenous) political interactions between citizens and their elected representatives. Specifically, I assume that local governments are run by politicians whose primary goal is to be reelected. Reelection-minded politicians do not care directly about the size of their budgets or the value of the local tax base; they care about such things only to the extent that they influence voters' decisions at election time. Voters, for their part, are heterogeneous in their preferences concerning the government's spending priorities, with some groups desiring more spending on particular publicly provided goods than other groups do, while all dislike paying taxes to finance services that are not important to them. In this setting, the creation of special-purpose governments leads to fiscal common-pool problems by altering the electoral incentives for voters and politicians.

When there is one general-purpose government, all interest groups lobby the same politicians and compete for a share of the collective spending pie. Strategic politicians distribute spending among the competing priorities in the way that maximizes their chances of reelection. The resulting budget allocation favors groups that are more politically active or whose voting decisions are particularly sensitive to the government's taxing and spending policies.

When a specialized jurisdiction is created with independent tax authority and a separately elected board, groups with a particular stake in the jurisdiction's policy domain have a disproportionate incentive to become informed about the board's policies and to participate in its election. As I will show in the pages to follow, elections for special-purpose jurisdictions are typically held on different days from major statewide or national elections and even in different locations. As a result, only a small fraction of those who vote for general-purpose government offices turn out to vote for specialized offices, and those who do turn out are not representative of the wider electorate. For example, Terry Moe (2006) has shown that teachers' union members are two to seven times more likely to vote in school board elections than are other registered voters. When each specialized jurisdiction faces an electorate composed of self-selected voters who care more than others do about its services, the resulting policies will reflect their preferences.

Whereas a general-purpose government must trade off the benefits of pleasing one group against another, a special-purpose board is more likely to find itself facing a dominant interest group and relative disinterest from the groups that care more about other policies. Thus, a special-purpose governing board, guided by the desire for reelection, will seek to please policy-relevant interest groups to a greater extent than a general-purpose official would. The common-pool problem arises when the special-purpose board can levy a general tax on all citizens but the voters active in its election are disproportionately high demanders of its services. The severity of the special-purpose government's overfishing from the shared tax base is constrained by the threat that, as its tax levy increases, otherwise disengaged general-interest voters will be induced to turn out at the next election to oust the spendthrift board.

The fiscal externalities in this institutional setting are more complex than those in the literature reviewed previously. In the case of a geographically districted legislature, the representative of district A does not internalize the costs of taxes paid by residents in other districts because those outside district A cannot vote in that representative's reelection. Similarly, in the two-layer fiscal federalism model, politicians from state B do not internalize the full costs of their actions on the federal government because most of those costs are ultimately borne by residents of other states. In the case of overlapping local governments, however, all the politicians ostensibly serve the same constituents. If each politician internalized the costs of her jurisdiction's policies on all those constituents, there would be no externalities; hence, jurisdictional overlap would not lead to a fiscal common-pool problem. Externalities arise only because of *selective participation*: Groups that care more about a special-purpose jurisdiction's policies are more likely to vote in its elections. If there is selective participation, and if politicians seek to please *voters* rather than citizens per se, externalities arise because the politician can provide benefits to her voting base funded through generalized taxation. In the absence of selective participation, however, jurisdictional overlap would have no effect on the provision of services, ceteris paribus. Thus, in my theory, the fiscal common-pool problem is a product of, and cannot be understood apart from, the *politics* of local special-purpose government.

My story does not end with the fiscal common-pool problems arising from selective participation in special-purpose jurisdictions, however. For while tragedies of the commons are widespread and familiar, so too are instances in which users of shared resources have created institutions to successfully "govern the commons" (Ostrom 1990). In medieval times, the Rhine League—a coalition of merchants and toll collectors— emerged to prevent overexploitation of river shipping (Gardner et al. 2003). Students of industrial organization point to various forms of vertical integration across firms that can enhance both industry profits and consumer welfare by mitigating double marginalization (Tirole 1988, sec. 4.2.2). A strong independent executive, who is not beholden to any particular district and hence internalizes the full costs of tax and spending decisions, can rein in the overspending bias due to fiscal common-pool problems in the legislature (Alesina and Perotti 1999; Baqir 2002; Holtz-Eakin 1988).

I argue that a strong local political party can enforce fiscal discipline on overlapping special-purpose jurisdictions. My theory builds on the work of Riker (1964), who contends that parties are the key determinant of the level of decentralization in a federal system, and of Filippov, Ordeshook, and Shvetsova (2004) and Rodden (2005), who expand Riker's argument and apply it to contemporary comparative federalism. The core idea is that if a strong party controls the multiple governments in a given locality, it can serve to informally coordinate their policies and induce their officials to internalize the full social costs of their fiscal decisions. The motivation for a party to fulfill this role, I will argue, is that the vote-maximizing platform of a party involves lower total spending than the amalgamation of the vote-maximizing platforms of independent candidates. Through control of candidate slating, a party can run a group of candidates for local office who are better off cooperating to avoid overfishing their shared tax base.

1.6 CONTRIBUTIONS

Together, the theoretical and empirical analyses contained in this book produce several important contributions. First, problems of concurrent taxation in *local* government have been essentially unrecognized before now. My results demonstrate that concurrent taxation is an issue of first-order importance, which should be front and center in any discussion of local government organization.

Second, I provide the first systematic theory of politics and policy-making in special-purpose local governments. My common-pool, selective participation model of special-interest politics provides a new lens for viewing a wide range of policy problems in local government. For instance, while I focus on taxation, the same basic model applies to other situations where vertical interjurisdictional externalities affect policy-making, such as environmental regulation, transportation, crime, collective bargaining, and the municipal bond market, to name only a few.

Third, I demonstrate a novel role for local political parties. Following Peterson (1981), the scholarly community has tended to view local parties as hollow shells of their national counterparts because local politics is thought to be nonpartisan and to a large extent even nonideological. I show that parties serve a crucial function in coordinating policymaking in a fragmented jurisdictional landscape.

Fourth, I extend the scope of fiscal common-pool models generally. Existing studies that estimate the reaction functions between federal and state taxes deal with just two layers of government. With multiple levels of government within counties, I am able to examine the relationship between the number of overlapping taxing jurisdictions and the aggregate tax rate, a question that heretofore has received little empirical attention. At the same time, because I analyze data from 3,000 counties observed over 30 years, my degrees of freedom are greatly increased relative to those of prior studies based on states or countries. In so doing, I hope to enrich the knowledge of both specialized jurisdictions and concurrent taxation generally.

Finally, the project yields a variety of direct, practical policy implications. Fundamental institutional design recommendations are to limit the concurrent taxation of the same tax base by multiple governments and to encourage broad-based voter participation in special-purpose governments. More speculatively, even seemingly mundane changes, such as holding special district elections on the same day as municipal elections, may have significant fiscal effects by weakening special interest influence in district policymaking.

I.7   PLAN OF THE BOOK

The next chapter provides a detailed introduction to special-purpose local government institutions. I trace their evolution from colonial times to the present day, giving special emphasis to the proliferation of special districts since World War II. I describe their functions, governance, and finances and explain their connection to the problem of jurisdictional overlap. In addition, I review prior theoretical and empirical literature on special-purpose governments.

In Chapter 3, I offer the first formal theory of special district politics. My theory is built on microfoundations of utility maximization by voters and politicians. I begin with a basic theory of interest groups, link this to common-pool problems in distributive politics, and incorporate probabilistic voting and electoral competition. I model the decision by a reelection-minded politician of how much to spend on each component of a set of multiple public goods. I contrast policymaking by one general-purpose government with that undertaken by a set of single-purpose jurisdictions. All spending is financed from a uniform tax on property in the jurisdiction. There is a special interest group that benefits disproportionately from each public good and whose members vote according to the tax-spending platforms offered by competing candidates. First, I show that electoral competition can mitigate the common-pool tax problem when there is a single government. This is a noteworthy result in its own right. More important, I show that, due to the political transaction costs of participating in multiple elections, when there are several jurisdictions, each interest group focuses its attention on the policymaker who controls its own preferred good. Because each group fully values the public service that benefits its members but only internalizes its own fraction of the tax price, the result is overfishing from the shared tax base. The important prediction is that the aggregate size of the public sector increases with the number of overlapping specialized governments. Thus, I provide a theory of special district politics that yields clear, empirically testable predictions. While the theoretical model is embedded in the institutional context of special districts, it applies broadly to specialized governments, such as congressional committees or spending ministries.

The central prediction from Chapter 3 is that aggregate taxes and spending rise as specialized jurisdictions with independent tax authority pile on top of one another. In Chapter 4, I test that hypothesis using a panel data set of counties from 1972 to 2002. I compute the number of overlapping taxing jurisdictions in each county and relate this measure to aggregate taxes and spending. I use fixed effects panel models, in addition to instrumental variables techniques. In all cases, I find strong support for the common-pool model. I estimate that the *overlap effect* is on the order of 10 to 15 percent of the total budget. I show that the results are *not* due to changes in the bundle of public services provided when special-purpose jurisdictions are created. The results are robust to controlling for infrastructure investment, tax and expenditure limitations, and economies of scale.

The main argument of the first four chapters is that interest groups dominate special district governments, leading to overexploitation of the common-pool tax base. An important related question is whether the increased spending produces higher-quality public goods. In other words, interest groups concerned with a particular policy may effectively force other citizens to pay for higher-quality services than they would otherwise like. On the other hand, if the relevant interest groups prefer wasteful or particularistic spending, then larger budgets may not translate into higher-quality services. I explore such ideas in Chapter 5.

While measuring the quality of public services can be a formidable challenge, I focus on a domain where the task is relatively straightforward: libraries. Using a panel data set of 8,100 library systems observed annually from 1992 to 2004, I find that special district libraries have larger budgets but fewer books. District employees are less likely to actually be librarians. Special district libraries are less efficient on a cost-per-circulation-transaction basis as well. I also review the secondary literature on government organization and service quality. Overall, I find little support for the proposition that special district governments provide higher-quality services. Rather, the evidence suggests that interest groups use special districts to obtain particularistic benefits.

Chapters 4 and 5 amass evidence of overfishing from the shared tax base by multiple overlapping jurisdictions. In Chapter 6, I analyze how political parties can serve to govern the fiscal commons of the local public sector. I argue that if a strong party controls multiple governments, it can improve coordination among them. Consistent with these theories, I find that areas with strong political parties do not suffer from common-pool overexploitation due to concurrent taxation. Specifically, I estimate an interaction between party strength and jurisdictional overlap in the models introduced in Chapter 4. I find that party strength offsets jurisdictional overlap so that the common-pool effect exists specifically in weak party areas.

I conclude the book by arguing that the Tiebout (1956) model, which has dominated studies of the local public sector for decades, must be brought up-to-date. Local government today is dominated by territorially overlapping, concurrently taxing, single-function jurisdictions, not the general-purpose territorial monopolies that inhabit economic theory. The old Tiebout-inspired logic that more governments lead to more competition, which leads to more efficiency, does not comport with contemporary political institutions. I argue that the theoretical framework and empirical results of *Imperfect Union* provide the beginnings of a modern alternative view of local government. I emphasize that the two views are not necessarily in conflict. Where real government institutions approximate the general-purpose territorial monopolies of Tiebout's world, the competitive model applies. But in the more common cases where local institutions are specialized, overlapping, and concurrently taxing, the common-pool theory presented in this book provides a more appropriate framework for analyzing local political economy. I also examine the policy implications that arise from my model of local government. Finally, I discuss how the ideas raised in this book apply broadly in different institutional contexts, including the U.S. Congress, the European Union, and other governments with multiple layers or functionally specialized jurisdictions.

2

What's Special about Special-Purpose Governments?

While virtually every U.S. citizen pays taxes to one or more special-purpose jurisdictions, these institutions remain obscure even to many specialists in local government. In this chapter, I will provide an overview of the recent history, functions, governance, and finances of special districts. Several excellent scholars have provided thorough treatments of these issues, and I do not intend the present discussion to be comprehensive.[1] I focus on those aspects of special-purpose government that will be central in the remainder of the book, namely, representation and taxation.

2.1 WHAT IS A SPECIAL DISTRICT?

According to the *Census of Governments*, "Special district governments are independent, special-purpose governmental units ... that exist as separate entities with substantial administrative and fiscal independence from general-purpose local governments" (1994 p. vii). Most special districts perform a single function, although some provide a few related services. Almost any service provided by a municipality can be provided by a special district government. The special district familiar to most Americans is the school district. Although school districts are the most numerous, they represent less than one-third of all special districts. Among the 35,000 nonschool special districts in existence as of 2002, some of the most common functions included providing fire protection, water, sanitation,

---

1 Bollens (1957) is the classic reference on special districts and remains indispensable. Foster (1997) is the most comprehensive recent treatment of special districts. Burns (1994) specifically addresses the growth in the number of special districts in the 20th century. Stetzer (1975) provides a fascinating description of the history of special districts in one locality, Cook County, Illinois. Teaford (1979) offers an historian's perspective on local government institutions, with significant attention to the development of special districts.

parks, and libraries, although this list hardly begins to convey the variety of special district functions (more on this later).

The twin pillars of fiscal and administrative autonomy are especially important in distinguishing special districts as *governments* from mere agencies or departments. The Census Bureau's summary definition of an independent government is "an organized entity which, in addition to having governmental character, has sufficient discretion in the management of its own affairs to distinguish it as a separate unit from the administrative structure of any other governmental unit" (Bureau of the Census, 1994, p. ix). In other words, to be counted as an independent government, an entity must meet the three criteria of *existence as an organized entity*, *governmental character*, and *substantial autonomy*.

Because autonomy is such an important criterion here, it is worth elaborating on how a governmental entity passes the test. The Census Bureau (1994, p. x) states:

This requirement is met where ... an entity has considerable fiscal and administrative independence. Fiscal independence generally derives from the power of an entity to determine its budget without review and detailed modification by other local officials or governments, to determine taxes to be levied for its support, to fix and collect charges for its services, or to issue debt without review by another local government.

In addition to fiscal independence, administrative independence requires that the government has a popularly elected governing body or, if appointed, not appointed by a single parent government. Districts governed by appointed boards must perform functions that are "essentially different from those of, and are not subject to specification by, its creating government(s)" (Census Bureau, 1994, p. x). Furthermore, the Bureau (1994, x) specifies seven additional criteria (not detailed here) to ensure that an entity is not indirectly controlled by another government (e.g., through control of the governing board). Entities not meeting the criteria for fiscal and administrative autonomy are classified as dependent agencies rather than special district governments. For instance, a parks *district* is an independent government, whereas a parks *department* is a dependent agency of a city or county, whose activities are attributed to its parent government.

When I refer to *governments*, *special districts*, and *municipalities* in the pages that follow, I mean independent governments as classified in the *Census of Governments* (COG). By tradition, the Census Bureau does not classify school districts as a type of special district, and it reports statistics separately for the two entities. However, for my purposes, school districts and special districts are more alike than different, and when

I wish to refer to these two groups of governments collectively I will use the terms *single-function governments* or *special-purpose governments.*[2] Meanwhile, cities and counties will be collectively termed *general-purpose governments.* Town and township governments, which exist in only about half of the states, have a special status, which will be explained later.

While most of the special districts currently in existence were created within the past 50 years, it is worth noting that the institution of special-purpose local government has a longer lineage. Private and public corporations existed as early as the 1600s to supplement the activities of colonial governments (Frug 1980). The early districts were often created to finance construction of major public works, such as canals, railroads, bridges, and harbors, whose scale was beyond the capacity of contemporary local governments (Wallis and Weingast 2005). In the late 1800s, an economic downturn triggered a wave of fiscal crises and defaults among cities that were overextended in the bond market, which prompted state legislatures to place limits on the ability of cities to issue debt (Teaford 1984). Special districts, which were deemed to be exempt from such fiscal constraints, became a popular alternative vehicle for municipal borrowing. The appeal of special districts was not lost on the Progressives of the 1920s and 1930s, who saw in districts' corporate structure a model of "good government." The result was growth in the number of professionally run, nonelected public authorities (Foster 1997). The suburbanization of the post–World War II era ushered in the modern use of special districts as core local service providers, as newly developing areas turned to districts to supplement the services provided by counties and cities, or in some cases rejected incorporation altogether in favor of contracting with multiple special-purpose governments (Bollens and Schmandt 1970; Miller 1981).

Nearly all of the growth in the number of local governments over the past 50 years has been due to the proliferation of special districts. Figure 2.1 shows that the number of nonschool special districts nearly tripled between 1952 and 2002, from roughly 12,000 to 35,000 units.[3] Over the same period, the number of municipalities increased modestly

---

2 Technically speaking, not all special districts are single-function governments. But about 90 percent of them are, and to avoid a morass of jargon I shall take the liberty of referring to all special districts and school districts as *single-function governments.*

3 If anything, these numbers actually understate the propagation of special-purpose jurisdictions because they do not reflect the increase in special assessment districts, which are formally under the control of general-purpose governments but able to levy separate taxes (see Kogan and McCubbins 2008).

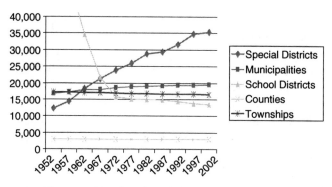

Figure 2.1. Number of Local Governments, 1952–2002

from 16,000 to 19,000, while the numbers of townships and counties were essentially unchanged. A second trend evident from Figure 2.1 is that the number of school districts dropped precipitously over this period. In fact, Figure 2.1 portrays merely the tail end of a longer process in which the number of school districts fell from more than 100,000 as of 1930 to about 15,000 in 1970. The success of the school consolidation movement represents one of the great institutional transformations of American government in the twentieth century (Berry and West forthcoming). However, I do not pursue that issue here, as most of the analysis in this book is focused on the post-1970 period, by which point school consolidation had largely run its course.

2.2 WHAT DO SPECIAL DISTRICTS DO?

Special districts have inherited the *corporate* powers of cities but not the *police* powers (Foster 1997). This means that special districts generally can levy taxes, issue bonds, enter into contracts, hire employees, own property, deliver services, construct public works, and so on. However, except in unusual cases, districts do not have the power of zoning, regulation, or law enforcement. Within these fairly broad parameters, special districts can, and do, perform virtually any function of a general-purpose government.

Before presenting more detailed information about district functional performance, I should introduce one of the data sources that will be used throughout this book. The COG was conducted first in 1942 and then every five years starting in 1952. It includes extensive data on the finances, employment, and organization of state and local governments. In 1967, 1977, 1987, and 1992, the COG also executed a census of publicly elected officials at all levels of government. While the COG is an invaluable resource for researchers, it has two limitations: nonresponse and noncomparability across time.[4] The COG, as the name suggests, is intended as a census of local governments, not a sample. However, nonresponse is an issue, and it is highest among special districts, averaging about 16 percent. While an 84 percent response rate would be enviable for a survey, it is less so for a census. The Census Bureau is often able to fill in financial data from secondary sources, but other pieces of information remain missing for nonrespondents. The second limitation is that the content of the COG has changed over time, and some data elements may not be comparable across years. This is particularly true for censuses conducted before and after 1972; the later editions have more comprehensive and consistent coverage. For the purposes of this introductory survey, I will largely gloss over these limitations and attempt to glean patterns from all the available data. In later chapters, when I engage in more rigorous statistical analysis, I will use only the post-1972 data.

With these caveats in mind, Table 2.1 shows the number of special districts and the functions they perform, traced from 1942 to 2002. Aside from school districts, the most common function of special districts is fire protection, followed by water supply and housing and community development. More notable than any particular functional category is the sheer range of services provided by single-function districts. No specific function constitutes *the* dominant type of district. Rather, districts are active in all the major functions of local government, including social services, transportation, housing, natural resources, utilities, industrial development, education, and beyond. And remember that Table 2.1 does not even include school districts.

Just as significant as the variation in the number and type of districts over time is the variation in the types of districts that are used from state to state. Table 2.2 tabulates, for each district type and year, the number of states in which the district was in use, that is, the number of states in which at least one district performed the specified function. The most striking finding is that no single type of district is present in every state. The most widespread district type is the catchall category, multifunction district, followed by water supply and housing and community development. On the other hand, special districts operate parking facilities in 6 states, provide education services—that is, services that augment the services of school districts—in 6 states, and supply gas in 11 states. The robustness of districts as an institution is evidenced by the fact that every

---

4 See Foster (1997, pp. 81–84) for a discussion. COG data issues are discussed further in the Methodological Appendix, Section A.1.1.

Table 2.1. *Number of Special Districts, by Function, 1942–2002*

	2002	1997	1992	1987	1982	1977	1972	1967	1962	1957	1952	1942
Total districts	35,052	34,683	31,555	29,532	28,588	25,962	23,885	21,264	18,323	14,424	12,340	8,299
Total single-function districts	31,877	31,965	29,036	27,481	25,991	24,242	22,981	20,811	18,013	13,761	12,273	8,299
Education services												
Education services	518	755	757	713	960	1,020	1,085	956	915	—	—	—
Libraries	1,580	1,496	1,043	830	638	586	498	410	349	322	269	207
Social services												
Health and hospital total	1,464	1,449	1,321	1,267	1,226	1,065	914	771	649	568	371	52
Hospitals	711	763	737	783	775	715	657	537	418	345	143	—
Health	753	686	584	484	451	350	257	234	231	223	228	—
Public welfare	57	59	52	—	—	—	—	—	—	—	—	—
Transportation												
Highways	743	721	636	621	598	652	698	774	773	782	774	1,331
Air transp.	510	476	435	369	357	299	247	—	—	29	23	—
Water transport	159	138	135	172	156	166	162	—	—	105	136	96
Parking facilities	46	69	100	103	120	122	110	—	—	—	—	—
Environment and housing												
Drainage	2,600	2,703	2,049	2,104	2,112	2,255	2,192	2,193	2,240	2,132	2,174	1,955
Flood control	647	666	660	668	593	681	684	662	500	209	206	200
Soil and water conservation	2,506	2,449	2,428	2,469	2,409	2,431	2,561	2,571	2,461	2,300	1,989	92

(continued)

Table 2.1. *(continued)*

	2002	1997	1992	1987	1982	1977	1972	1967	1962	1957	1952	1942
Other	1,226	1,165	1,091	1,119	1,118	1,228	1,202	1,113	957	917	863	909
Irrigation	837	808	792	854	829	934	971	904	781	564	641	523
Parks and recreation	1,287	1,253	1,156	1,004	924	829	750	613	488	316	194	128
Housing and community development	3,399	3,469	3,470	3,464	3,296	2,408	2,271	1,565	1,099	972	866	543
Sewerage	2,004	2,004	1,710	1,607	1,631	1,610	1,411	1,233	937	—	—	401
Solid waste mgmt.	455	482	395	154	101	71	44	—	—	—	—	—
Utilities												
Water supply	3,405	3,409	3,302	3,060	2,637	2,480	2,333	2,140	1,502	787	665	357
Electric power	150	139	156	143	88	82	74	75	—	73	99	—
Gas supply	50	49	52	56	57	46	48	37	—	19	2	—
Transit systems	285	282	253	212	172	96	33	14	—	7	4	—
Fire protection	5,725	5,601	5,260	5,070	4,560	4,187	3,872	3,665	3,229	2,624	2,272	1,189
Cemeteries	1,666	1,655	1,628	1,627	1,577	1,615	1,494	1,397	1,283	1,107	911	490
Industrial development and mortgage revenue	234	215	155	92	—	—	—	—	—	—	—	—
Other single-function	1,161	1,261	792	557	661	313	298	622	515	146	162	295
Multiple-function districts	3,175	2,718	2,519	2,051	2,597	1,720	904	453	310	663	67	—

Source: Census of Governments, Government Organization Historical Database.

Table 2.2. *Number of States Where District Type Exists, 1942–2002*

	2002	1997	1992	1987	1982	1977	1972	1967	1962	1957	1952	1942
Education services	6	6	7	5	6	3	3	3	3	0	0	0
Libraries	27	27	18	16	14	13	12	11	10	10	8	5
Health and Hospital total	38	37	36	34	34	34	31	32	30	26	16	5
Hospitals	32	32	31	30	30	30	29	29	26	22	12	0
Health	34	31	29	25	22	18	17	16	14	9	9	0
Public welfare	14	12	14	0	0	0	0	0	0	0	0	0
Highways	31	29	28	28	25	25	27	25	23	24	21	20
Air transport	31	29	29	29	29	25	24	0	0	9	6	0
Water transport	21	20	20	23	18	16	15	0	0	14	15	12
Parking facilities	6	6	8	6	6	3	3	0	0	0	0	0
Drainage	27	28	27	31	27	30	33	35	34	32	33	26
Flood control	34	35	37	32	31	33	32	30	31	23	19	14
Soil and water conservation	45	41	41	41	41	40	41	41	41	40	40	5
Other	35	31	27	24	21	27	31	31	28	32	21	26
Irrigation	26	22	20	20	19	24	30	28	25	21	17	17
Parks and recreation	39	36	33	30	31	27	29	28	25	19	15	12
Housing and community development	44	44	44	44	44	41	44	41	38	38	40	40
Sewerage	42	42	43	43	41	40	41	40	39	0	0	22
Solid waste mgmt.	41	41	41	30	19	16	9	0	0	0	0	0
Water supply	48	47	47	46	44	41	40	39	37	34	34	20

(continued)

Table 2.2. (*continued*)

	2002	1997	1992	1987	1982	1977	1972	1967	1962	1957	1952	1942
Electric power	35	32	32	30	23	16	11	10	0	12	15	0
Gas supply	11	13	13	11	9	7	8	8	0	7	3	0
Transit systems	36	36	36	32	31	23	12	6	0	4	4	0
Fire protection	36	35	35	36	32	31	30	30	30	24	22	18
Cemeteries	14	14	14	14	14	14	14	13	13	12	9	4
Industrial development and mortgage revenue	26	23	20	13	0	0	0	0	0	0	0	0
Other single-function districts	41	38	31	27	25	25	33	38	35	18	18	24
Multiple-function districts	49	49	49	46	46	43	42	32	34	44	9	0

Source: Author's calculations from the Census of Governments, Government Organization Historical Database.

Table 2.3. *Special Districts by Type of Operation*

	1992	1987
Total Special Districts	31,555	29,532
Directly provides program or service with own employees	14,437	11,537
Indirectly provides program or service by contractual arrangements	7,196	5,719
Constructs public facilities by contract or with own employees	5,297	4,049
Finances public facilities or services by issuing public debt	7,377	5,901
Not answered	7,687	9,857
Percent of Valid Responses		
Directly provides program or service with own employees	60%	59%
Indirectly provides program or service by contractual arrangements	30%	29%
Constructs public facilities by contract or with own employees	22%	21%
Finances public facilities or services by issuing public debt	31%	30%

Note: A district may engage in one or more of the activities listed.
Source: Author's calculations from the Census of Governments, Government Organization Historical Database.

category has been increasing its geographic scope over time or at least holding steady. There are relatively few cases in which a state, once having utilized a type of special district, subsequently decides to jettison it. Moreover, new functions for special districts are emerging almost constantly. Industrial development districts were unknown in 1982 but had spread to half of the states as of 2002. In the 1990s, special districts emerged to serve public welfare functions in 14 states.

One common misperception about special districts is that they exist primarily to finance the construction of infrastructure and public works. In fact, most special districts are direct service providers. As demonstrated in Table 2.3, 60 percent of districts directly provide services with their own employees and 30 percent provide services through contract with another public or private organization. At the same time, 22 percent of districts construct public facilities directly or indirectly, while 31 percent finance construction or issue debt. (Note that each district may engage in more than one of these activities, so the sum does not equal 100 percent.) In other words, while it is true that some districts are primarily

Table 2.4. *Elected Officials and Governments in the United States, 1992*

	Total	Members of Governing Boards	Other Elected Boards	Other Elected Officials	Number of Governments
Federal government	542	540[a]	—	2	1
State governments	18,828	7,461	1,331	10,036	50
All local governments	493,830	342,812	40,922	110,096	85,955
General-purpose					
County	58,818	17,274	10,835	30,709	3,043
Subcounty					
Municipal	135,531	107,542	4,157	23,832	19,279
Town or township	126,958	51,770	25,930	49,258	16,656
Special-purpose					
School districts	88,434	83,596	—	4,838	14,422
Special districts	84,089	82,630	—	1,459	31,555
TOTAL	513,200	350,813	42,253	120,134	86,006

[a] Includes nonvoting members of Congress.
Source: Census of Governments, 1992, Vol. 1, No. 2, "Popularly Elected Officials."

vehicles for financing capital projects, many more are direct or indirect service providers.

2.3 HOW ARE SPECIAL DISTRICTS GOVERNED?

The political independence of special districts is enshrined in their governing boards. Unlike general-purpose governments, special function districts rarely have an elected chief executive, although the governing board may select a district manager in much the same way that a city council selects a city manager under the council-manager form of government. More commonly, though, districts are managed by the governing board, which typically consists of five members, who may be elected, appointed, or a combination of both. Table 2.4 shows the number of elected officials by level of government in 1992, the last year in which the COG's survey of popularly elected officials was conducted. There are over half a million elected officials in the United States, 96 percent of whom serve in local government. Single-function governments collectively account for more than 170,000 elected offices, of which special districts account for

Table 2.5. *Elected Officials of Special District Governments*

	1992	1987	1977	1967
Total Districts	31,555	29,531	25,962	21,264
Total elected officials	84,089	80,538	72,377	56,943
Total elected district board members	82,630	79,190	71,192	55,076
Total appointed district board members	74,913	67,995	53,639	42,632
Average membership of district board (incl. appointed)	5.0	5.0	4.8	4.6

Source: Census of Governments, Government Organization Historical Database.

roughly half. The number of elected officials in special district governments has grown apace with the number districts over time, as shown in Table 2.5.

In addition to those elected to serve on special district boards, thousands more are appointed. Table 2.5 shows that approximately 75,000 members were appointed to special district boards in 1992. That appointees constitute 48 percent of board members would appear to suggest that most districts are evenly split between elected and appointed officials, but this is not the case. The vast majority of boards are composed of either entirely elected or entirely appointed members: 52 percent are entirely elected, 43 percent are entirely appointed, and only 5 percent are mixed. The composition of a district's board generally depends upon its tax authority. As will be explained later, about two out of three special districts have the authority to levy a property tax. Most of these taxing districts have all-elected boards, while most nontaxing districts have all-appointed boards, as indicated in Table 2.6. Most boards have 3 or 5 members—5 is the mean, median, and modal number—although a few have 15 or more.

2.4 HOW ARE SPECIAL DISTRICTS FINANCED?

Much of the remainder of this book is focused on analyzing local fiscal policy, and I wish to offer only the broadest overview of local budgets at this point. With that in mind, Table 2.7 provides a summary of special district revenue sources. Like most other local governments, special districts draw revenue from a wide range of sources. The most common source is a districtwide property tax, which is used by 63 percent of districts. Half of the districts receive grants or other intergovernmental

Table 2.6. *Special District Board Composition by Tax Authority Status*

Governing Board Composition	With Property Tax Authority	No Property Tax Authority
Average number of elected members	3.4	1.9
Average number of appointed members	1.6	3.1
Percent districts with all-elected board	68	38
Percent districts with all-appointed board	29	58

Source: Author's calculations from Census of Governments, 1992, Vol. 1, No. 2, "Popularly Elected Officials."

Table 2.7. *Revenue Sources of Special Districts*

	1992	1987
Total Districts	31,555	29,532
Districtwide property taxes	14,951	12,853
Other taxes (sales, payroll, etc.) imposed by district	1,174	823
Special assessments	5,702	4,028
Service charges and sales	9,797	7,116
Grants, shared taxes, rentals, and reimbursements from other governments	12,072	8,976
Not reported	7,687	9,857
Percent of Valid Responses		
Districtwide property taxes	63%	65%
Other taxes (sales, payroll, etc.) imposed by district	5%	4%
Special assessments	24%	20%
Service charges and sales	41%	36%
Grants, shared taxes, rentals, and reimbursements from other governments	51%	46%

Note: A district may have one or more of the revenue sources listed.
Source: Author's calculations from the Census of Governments, Government Organization Historical Database.

revenues. Two in five districts rely on user charges or sales of goods and services, while one in four is able to levy special assessments. About 5 percent of districts have access to a nonproperty tax base, such as sales or payroll taxes.

The numerical superiority of special districts has not yet been translated into budgetary superiority. In 2002, cities accounted for 34 percent of all local government own-source revenue, school districts for

Table 2.8. *Local Government Revenue and Debt, 2002*

Type of Government	Own-Source Revenue		Long-Term Debt Outstanding	
	Million	Percent of Total	Million	Percent of Total
Counties	$158,036	26%	$201,146	20%
Cities	$200,431	34%	$392,021	38%
Townships	$25,892	4%	$19,741	2%
Special districts	$61,751	10%	$215,023	21%
School districts	$151,249	25%	$191,376	19%

Note: Figures are in millions of dollars.
Source: 2002 Census of Governments.

25 percent, and special districts for 10 percent. The remainder is accounted for by counties (26 percent) and townships (4 percent), as demonstrated in Table 2.8. School districts are clearly the most fiscally powerful single-function government. At the same time, the $62 billion collected annually by other types of special districts cannot be overlooked: For every one dollar of revenue raised by a city, special districts collect 30 cents. Special districts play an even larger role in financing debt, holding 20 percent of total long-term debt outstanding from local governments.

The *average* special district share of revenue and debt hides a tremendous amount of variation from place to place. For example, in the most district-reliant county, more than 80 percent of all local government revenue comes from special districts; in other counties, special districts collect no revenue at all. Figure 2.2 provides a map of special districts' share of own-source revenue by county in 2002. Darker shades indicate more special district revenue. It is evident that districts are used heavily in western states, although heavily district-reliant counties can be found throughout the country. In addition, it is obvious that the degree of district activity changes discontinuously across state borders. Such border effects can be seen, for example, when comparing Illinois and Wisconsin or New York and Pennsylvania. Clearly, state-level factors play an important role in determining the use of special districts at the local level. I will return to this issue later.

2.5   HOW ARE SPECIAL DISTRICTS CREATED?

The legal basis for the creation of a special district is found in state enabling legislation. In most states, at least a few districts have been formed by the legislature through special legislation, that is, specific statutes that

Special Districts' Share of Local Revenue

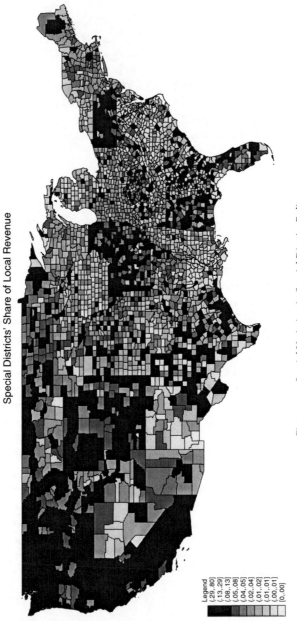

Legend
[.29,.80]
[.13,.29)
[.08,.13)
[.05,.08)
[.04,.05)
[.02,.04)
[.01,.02)
[.01,.01)
[.00,.01)
[0,.00)

Figure 2.2. Spatial Variation in Special District Reliance

establish just a single government. Most special districts, however, have been formed pursuant to general enabling legislation, which specifies a broad framework for creating districts, as well as the functions they may perform, their revenue- and debt-raising authority, and their form of governance. There are two common ways that districts can be created under general enabling statutes. First, one or more general-purpose governments may create a special district by resolution. Second, a citizen or group of citizens may initiate special districts by petition, subject to the provisions of the enabling legislation.

The procedure for establishing a park district in Illinois is a fairly typical example of how special districts are formed.[5] A district proposal is initiated with a petition signed by at least 100 voters. The petition is filed with the county circuit court, and if the signatures are deemed valid, the proposal will be put to a referendum. If the referendum receives a majority vote among those within the boundaries of the proposed district, the government is created. The referenda are typically held in April of odd-numbered years when no major state or national races are on the ballot. As a result, turnout is notoriously low.[6] Overall, then, the obstacles to creating districts are relatively low in most states.[7]

2.6 HOW BIG ARE SPECIAL DISTRICTS?

Another common misconception about special districts is that they are territorially expansive governments that tackle metropolitan or regional issues that cross the boundaries of many local governments. While some districts are indeed regional—a special district might run a metropolitan transit system that connects cities and suburbs, or it might govern regional environmental and natural resources issues—this is hardly the norm. Table 2.9 shows the distribution of special districts based on their area characteristics in 1992 (the last year in which this information was collected in the COG). Only about 10 percent of special districts cross the boundaries of two or more counties. It is far more common for districts to be smaller than, or coterminous with, existing jurisdictions. In other words, for the most part, special districts are not fulfilling roles that existing governments are too geographically limited to fill. Between 1967 and

---

5 See Illinois Commission on Intergovernmental Cooperation (2003). See Galvan (2007) for a discussion of the rules pertaining to the creation of municipal utility districts in Texas.

6 I discuss turnout in more detail in the next chapter.

7 An exception is California, where since the 1970s Local Agency Formation Commissions (LAFCOs) have attempt to check the proliferation of governments (Little Hoover Commission 2000; Martin and Wagner 1978).

Table 2.9. *Special Districts by Geographic Area Served*

	1992	1967
Total Number of Districts	31,555	21,264
Coterminous with another local government	10,799	5,263
Not coterminous, contained entirely within one county	13,221	13,679
Not coterminous, crosses two or more counties	2,763	2,322
Not reported	4,772	—
Percent of Valid Responses		
Coterminous with another local government	40%	25%
Not coterminous, contained entirely within one county	49%	64%
Not coterminous, crosses two or more counties	10%	11%

Source: Author's calculations from the Census of Governments, Government Organization Historical Database.

1992, in fact, the fastest-growing type of special district was one that shares exactly the same boundaries as an existing city or county. The multiplication of coterminous districts obviously cannot be explained be their greater territorial flexibility or the need for regional governance. Thus, while regional scope may be the rationale for some districts, it cannot be considered a general explanation for the growth in special districts.

2.7 HOW DO SPECIAL DISTRICTS CONTRIBUTE TO JURISDICTIONAL OVERLAP?

By *jurisdictional overlap*, I mean the situation in which the same territory is governed by multiple independent governments. I am especially interested in situations in which jurisdictional overlap results in *concurrent taxation*, meaning that the overlapping governments independently levy taxes on their shared tax base. The proliferation of special-function jurisdictions has pushed jurisdictional overlap to new heights and multiplied the problems of concurrent taxation. It is important to note, however, that jurisdictional overlap and concurrent taxation are general problems that exist even apart from special-function government. At the most basic level, every federal system is a system of jurisdictional overlap, and nearly every federation involves some degree of concurrent taxation. In the United States, for example, all citizens are under the jurisdiction of a state and a federal government and pay taxes to both.

In American local government, jurisdictional overlap is commonplace even among general-purpose governments. There are three types of general-purpose local governments: counties, municipalities, and towns or townships. Counties are administrative subdivisions of state governments and cover virtually the entire territory of the United States.[8] Municipal governments, including cities, towns, boroughs, and villages, are incorporated political subdivisions created to provide additional services beyond those received from the county. About two-thirds of the U.S. population live in areas with municipal governments. Township governments present a special case. First, they exist in only 20 states. Second, in some of these states they have the character of municipalities, and cannot overlap the territory of other municipal governments, while in others they operate more like special districts and can overlap municipalities.[9]

With three different types of general-purpose governments that are not territorially exclusive, jurisdictional overlap is the norm rather than the exception. Refer again to the tax bill shown in Figure 1.2: Taxes are being levied by a city, a town, and a county government, in addition to numerous special-purpose jurisdictions. Almost every incorporated municipality will share authority with an overlapping county government.[10] In states where townships are allowed to overlap municipalities, they compose a third layer of government. As Table 2.10 shows, 62 percent of the U.S. population live in an area with two layers of general-purpose local government, and an additional 5 percent live under three layers. Accounting for state and federal government, most U.S. citizens are subject to at least four layers of government even before special districts are added to the mix.

When general-purpose governments overlap, they effectively take on the character of special-function jurisdictions in that each provides only a subset of the services received by their citizens. The assignment of responsibilities across layers of general-purpose government varies greatly from place to place. Commonly, however, counties serve judicial and tax assessment functions, as well as general governmental functions for unincorporated areas, townships provide road maintenance and garbage

---

8 Only Connecticut, Rhode Island, and the District of Columbia lack county governments. In Louisiana, counties are known as *parishes*. In Alaska, *boroughs* function like counties, although they do not cover the entire state.

9 Specifically, towns may overlap the territory of municipalities in 11 states (Connecticut, Illinois, Indiana, Kansas, Michigan, Minnesota, Missouri, Nebraska, New York, Ohio, and Vermont). In the nine remaining states, towns are territorially separate from municipalities, with no overlap between the two kinds of units (Maine, Massachusetts, New Hampshire, New Jersey, North Dakota, Pennsylvania, Rhode Island, South Dakota, and Wisconsin). For details, see Bureau of the Census (1994).

10 City-county consolidations, where the two layers of government are consolidated into one, are an exception. However, there are only 38 consolidated city-county governments presently in existence.

Table 2.10. *Layering of General-Purpose Governments*

State	Population (2000 Census)	Percent Population by Layers of General-Purpose Local Government		
		One Layer	Two Layers	Three Layers
Alabama	4,447,100	41.6	58.4	
Alaska	626,932	81.4	15.3	
Arizona	5,130,632	21.2	78.9	
Arkansas	2,673,400	38.5	61.5	
California	33,871,648	21.1	78.9	
Colorado	4,301,261	42.6	57.4	
Connecticut	3,405,565	99.3	0.7	
Delaware	783,600	72.6	27.4	
Florida	15,982,378	55.4	44.6	
Georgia	8,186,453	67.1	32.9	
Hawaii	1,211,537	100		
Idaho	1,293,953	34.4	65.6	
Illinois	12,419,293	0.9	38.1	61
Indiana	6,080,485	12.9	37.4	49.7
Iowa	2,926,324	22.6	77.4	
Kansas	2,688,418	6.6	82.5	10.9
Kentucky	4,041,769	59.7	40.3	
Louisiana	4,468,976	61.6	38.4	
Maine	1,274,923	0.8	99.3	
Maryland	5,296,486	85.4	14.6	
Massachusetts	6,349,097	53.1	46.9	
Michigan	9,938,444	0	97.1	2.9
Minnesota	4,919,479	0.8	98.9	0.3
Mississippi	2,844,658	49.4	50.6	
Missouri	5,595,211	38.4	58.4	3.2
Montana	902,195	51.2	48.8	
Nebraska	1,711,263	16.2	79.5	4.4
Nevada	1,998,257	45.4	54.6	
New Hampshire	1,235,786	0	100	
New Jersey	8,414,350	0	100	
New Mexico	1,819,046	38.1	61.9	
New York	18,976,457	42.3	48.1	9.7
North Carolina	8,049,313	49.6	50.4	
North Dakota	642,200	7.6	92.4	
Ohio	11,353,140	0	85.8	14.2
Oklahoma	3,450,654	24.3	75.7	

State	Population (2000 Census)	Percent Population by Layers of General-Purpose Local Government		
		One Layer	Two Layers	Three Layers
Oregon	3,421,399	33.4	66.6	
Pennsylvania	12,281,054	12.4	87.6	
Rhode Island	1,048,319	100		
South Carolina	4,012,012	64.8	35.2	
South Dakota	754,844	15.4	84.6	
Tennessee	5,689,283	51.9	48.1	
Texas	20,851,820	24.5	75.5	
Utah	2,233,169	16.5	83.5	
Vermont	608,827	0	93.1	6.9
Virginia	7,078,515	93.9	6.2	
Washington	5,894,121	40.4	59.6	
West Virginia	1,808,344	64.4	35.6	
Wisconsin	5,363,675	0	100	
Wyoming	493,782	32.1	67.9	
U.S. Total	**280,849,847**	**32.9**	**61.8**	**5.3**

Source: Boyd (2008, p. 5).

collection, and municipalities control all residual services not provided by overlapping counties, townships, or special districts.

Clearly, then, jurisdictional overlap is not a problem born from special districts exclusively. However, whereas jurisdictional overlap is largely coincidental for general-purpose governments, it is the very essence of single-function governments. Specialized governments by their nature exist in groups, each relying on others, as well as on general-purpose jurisdictions, to provide other essential services. By design, therefore, special-purpose governments can overlap the territory of any other type of government, including other special-purpose governments performing different functions. John Bollens was among the first to discuss this important feature of special districts:

They can usually overlap one another, a permission not granted to other classes of governments, and they overlie other units to an extensive degree. They often initially contain and subsequently add territory without regard to other existing boundaries covering part or all of the same land. They usually have exceptional latitude as to locale and areal extent. Most of the pyramiding of governments at a specific location is caused by special districts. ... Many are coterminous with a general or special district unit, a practice otherwise in use in only a few cities and counties which are consolidated. (1957, p. 248)

With the widespread use of special-purpose governments, the vertical layering of jurisdictions in any local area is, in principle, limited only by the number of government services that are performed.

Figure 2.3 maps the number of functions performed by special districts in each county as of 2002. The average county had five functional layers of special districts, while the median county had four layers. Ninety-seven percent of counties had at least 1 type of special district in operation, while the most district-heavy counties had 10 or more types of special districts. Unsurprisingly, the geographic variation in the number of district functions resembles the map of jurisdictional overlap shown in Figure 1.3. While there are clear state boundary effects, there is also significant variation across counties within the same state. In Chapter 4, I discuss several alternative ways of measuring the extent of jurisdictional overlap.

2.8 EXISTING LITERATURE ON SPECIAL-PURPOSE LOCAL GOVERNMENTS

Given the numerical, fiscal, and political importance of special-function governments, the existing literature on these local institutions is surprisingly thin. And the literature that does exist has largely ignored the features that are, in my view, most essential, namely, jurisdictional overlap, concurrent taxation, and selective political participation. Before explaining why these three features are so important, which is the subject of the next chapter, I conclude the present summary of special-function governments by examining the major themes of the prior literature as well existing empirical evidence on related questions.

2.8.1   *Major Themes*

In the literature on local politics, there are two prominent schools of thought on special-function governments.[11] The reform tradition in public administration (e.g., ACIR 1964; Bollens 1957) contends that special districts are a source of wasteful duplication in the administration of public services, that special districts suffer from diseconomies of scale, and that their low visibility makes these jurisdictions politically unaccountable. Recently, the emergence of a "new regionalism" (e.g., Orfield, 1997) has refocused the debate on the proliferation of governmental units associated with urban sprawl. Proponents of the reform view argue

---

11 Foster (1997, chs. 2, 3) provides an insightful and extensive review of the literature on special-purpose governments.

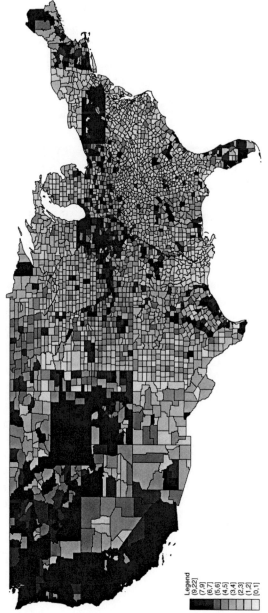

Figure 2.3. Number of Special District Functions, 2002

for metropolitan-wide multipurpose government and promote consolidation of existing jurisdictions (Downs 1994; Lyons and Lowery 1989;
Rusk 1993).

On the other hand, scholars of the public choice school and proponents of "polycentricity" (e.g., ACIR 1987; Oakerson 1999; Oakerson
and Parks 1989; Ostrom et al. 1988) argue that special district governments enhance desirable interjurisdictional competition, increase the
variety of public service bundles available to local citizens, and allow
jurisdictional boundaries to be tailored to the geographic scope of specific public problems.[12] Members of the public choice school prefer a
system of local government in which citizens are served by many overlapping jurisdictions performing different functions at different geographic
scales (Frey 2001; Tullock 1969).

Notice that both the public choice and municipal reform approaches
view special function jurisdictions more or less in the same way they view
general-purpose governments. That is, reformers disapprove of governmental fragmentation generally and tend to see special-function governments as representing just another example of undesirable fragmentation.
Meanwhile, public choice scholars see virtues in fragmentation and view
special-function government as another instance of desirable fragmentation. Neither approach makes a fundamental theoretical distinction
between horizontal and vertical fragmentation. Equally important, neither school of thought has produced anything approaching a theory of
the politics of special-function governments, taking into account the electoral motivations of the politicians that run them as well as the influence
of local voters and interest groups.

2.8.2   *Empirical Evidence*

The largest scholarly literature on local special-function governments is
devoted to the following question: Are special districts created to avoid
tax and expenditure limits (TELs) on general-purpose governments?[13]
Nelson (1990) finds a positive relationship between fiscal limits on municipalities and the number of special districts, while MacManus (1981),
Foster (1997), Burns (1994), Carr (2006), and Bowler and Donovan
(2004) find weak, inconsistent, or contingent effects of fiscal ceilings on
the creation of special districts. Heikkila and Ely (2003) argue that there

---

12 The contributions to McGinnis (1999) provide a useful sampling of the polycentricity literature.
13 As a general rule, special districts are exempt from the TELs imposed on
   municipalities.

is no connection between TELs and the formation of special districts. A limitation of most of these studies is that they are cross-sectional in nature and only show whether the number of districts is correlated with the number of TELs at a given point in time.[14] I will return to this issue again in Chapter 4.

A related body of research investigates the correlation between the number of special districts in a state or county and total government spending. Several studies find that spending is higher where there are more special districts (Eberts and Gronberg 1990; Foster 1997; Zax 1989), although others find that the relationship is insignificant or negative (Chicione and Walzer 1985; DiLorenzo 1981; MacManus 1981; Nelson 1987). As with the TEL studies, a major limitation of this literature is that most of the spending studies are cross-sectional, and thus show only whether the presence of special districts is contemporaneously correlated with overall spending.[15] Studies that do find a positive association between spending and the presence of special districts have tended to attribute it to geographic factors: Either special districts are too small to take advantage of economies of scale or special districts are tailored to the needs of small communities of interest that are willing to spend more. As I will show in Chapter 4, however, these arguments attributing higher spending to the size of districts are not supported by the data.

Nancy Burns (1994) provides a sustained inquiry into the creation of special districts. She emphasizes the role of business interests that seek private benefits from special-district activities. Most notably, Burns argues that real estate developers want the government to provide infrastructure investment to improve the value of their property, and that this is most easily attained by promoting the creation of a special district (also see Porter et al. 1992). Her evidence supporting this claim is that special districts are more likely to be formed in counties where there are more real estate developers. However, she finds that the relationship is significant only in the 1950s and 1960s, not in later decades.

Burns (1994) also suggests that race plays a role in the formation of special districts. Counties with more African Americans had more special district formations, although the relationship was significant only in the

---

14 When I run a simple panel regression of the number of special districts in a state on the number of TELs, using data from 1942 to 2002 and including state and year fixed effects, I find no significant relationship between the two variables. In other words, the number of special districts *within a state over time* does not appear to vary with the number of TELs. Details are provided in the Methodological Appendix, Section A.2.1.

15 MacManus (1981) and Foster (1997) are exceptions, although they reach opposite conclusions.

1950s. Burns presents some evidence that counties with more Latinos experienced more special district formations in the 1980s. Alesina, Baqir, and Hoxby (2004) reach somewhat different conclusions with respect to race and special districts. These authors posit a theory that more heterogeneous areas will desire more political districts to provide a greater variety of service combinations. They find, however, that while their theory can explain changes in the number of municipalities and school districts in a county over time, there is no significant relationship between population heterogeneity, including racial heterogeneity, and the number of special districts. They conclude that "arrangements for special districts are idiosyncratic" (Alesina et al. 2004, p. 391).

One of the few points on which the field is close to a consensus is the proposition that state laws substantially influence the formation of special districts (Burns 1994; Foster 1997; Heikkila and Ely 2003). Two types of laws appear to matter. First are laws enabling the creation of special districts themselves. Different states authorize different types of districts, and as Foster (1997, p. 142) concludes, "Put simply, states that permit more kinds of special districts have more special districts." Somewhat more interesting is the finding that state laws governing municipal incorporation and annexation influence the formation of special districts. Where it is more difficult to create or expand municipalities, special districts are more likely to form.[16]

In summary, neither the theoretical nor the empirical literature on special-purpose local government is large relative to the political and fiscal importance of the subject matter. Inroads have been made, but controversies linger over fundamental issues. Having established some baseline facts in this chapter about what special districts are, what they do, and how they do it, the remainder of the book is devoted to filling some of the most important gaps in the understanding of jurisdictional multiplicity generally and specialized local government specifically. I begin by proposing the first formal theory of the politics of overlapping special-function governments.

---

16 According to Foster (1997 ch. 5), it is the simultaneous presence of annexation *and* incorporation limits that spurs formation of special districts.

3

A Political Theory of Special-Purpose Government

Despite being the most common form of local government in the United States, spending more than all city governments combined, and having more civilian employees than the federal government, special-purpose governments have received precious little attention from scholars. Perhaps most surprisingly, no one has ever produced a theory of the *politics* of local special-purpose government. Fortunately, such a theory need not be constructed from whole cloth, for these local institutions bear a family resemblance to other, more familiar institutions of specialized jurisdiction, such as congressional committees and parliamentary ministries. In this chapter, I build a model of special-purpose government that is grounded in modern theories of political economy. I begin with a basic model of interest group competition with probabilistic voting (e.g., Hettich and Winer 1999; Persson and Tabellini 2000, ch. 7). I introduce two novel elements to the model: First, I allow for the existence of multiple independently elected governments, each providing a different public good; second, I allow for selective participation by the interest groups in the election of each government. Throughout, my emphasis is on understanding how outcomes differ when policy is made by one general-purpose government compared to multiple overlapping single-function governments.

The central intuition of my theory is that removing a policy issue from the purview of a general-purpose government and placing it under the jurisdiction of a single-function district enables the interest groups concerned with the issue to increase their influence over it. Because political participation is costly, when an election is concerned with only a single issue, those with a disproportionately large stake in the resolution of that issue will be the most likely to turn out. Thus, while a general-purpose government must balance the demands of many competing groups and make trade-offs when deciding policy priorities, a single-function jurisdiction will often confront one dominant interest group that has strong preferences with respect to the policy under consideration. As a result, the policies enacted by single-function governments are likely to reflect more closely the preferences of policy-relevant interest groups than when the same policy is one among many decided by a general-purpose government.

When it comes to fiscal policy, if spending on a particular function disproportionately benefits one group but taxes are spread among all groups, governance by single-function jurisdictions leads to a common-pool problem. Because each group fully values increased spending on its favorite service but pays only a fraction of the costs, each group demands more spending than is socially desirable. Single-function governments are more likely to try to satisfy such excess demands for spending than a general-purpose government would be. When there are many overlapping single-function jurisdictions, however, even the interest groups that benefit from increased spending on their own preferred services are ultimately worse off because of the taxes they must pay to finance increased spending by all the other jurisdictions. The most important comparative static derived from this analysis, which provides the motivation for the empirical analysis in subsequent chapters, is that aggregate taxes and spending in a community increase as the number of services provided by single-function governments increases.

While I will present my argument in terms of formal theory, its basic contours would not be unfamiliar to those professionally involved in single-function jurisdictions. Summarizing their interview with one special district officer, Flickinger and Murphy write approvingly that "Special district status is important, Naperville park director Glen Ekey believes. Historically, park and recreation departments within city or county government tended to take a back seat to streets, police, fire, utilities, and other 'mandatory' services when time came to set or cut budgets and hire qualified personnel. 'The advantage of the park district form of government,' says Ekey, 'is that we can concentrate on our major objectives without having to compete with other city or county departments" (1990, p. 153).

The reader who is not interested in the formal development of my model may skip ahead to Section 3.3 and find a nontechnical summary of the theory, ideally stopping along the way to read at least Section 3.1.4, which discusses evidence on the question of selective participation.

3.1 A THEORY OF SPECIALIZED GOVERNMENT

I begin with a basic model of interest group competition.[1] Consider a community with J distinct groups of identical individuals. Each individual is a member of one and only one group. The size of group $j = 1, \ldots, J$

---

[1] The foundations of this model, with only one government, can be seen in Persson and Tabellini (2000, ch. 7).

is denoted N_j and the size of the entire community is N. Assume that no single group is larger than $(N - 1)/2$; that is, no group alone constitutes a majority. There are J publicly provided goods in this community, and each good benefits only one group.[2] Let x_j be the per capita supply of a good that benefits group j only but must be provided in an equal amount per capita. Let $B(x_j)$ be the benefit received by a member of group j, and let $C(x_j)$ be the total cost of providing the good. Assume that benefits are increasing and concave and costs are increasing and convex as a function of the amount of spending: $B' > 0$ and $B'' \leq 0$; $C' > 0$ and $C'' > 0$.

The costs of providing the group-specific goods are financed through a per capita lump-sum tax, t, which is spread over all the groups. Assume that a balanced budget requirement equates total taxes with total spending, so that $Nt = \sum_j C(x_j) = T$, where T denotes aggregate taxation and, by definition, spending. Because of the balanced budget requirement, government policy consists of the vector $\mathbf{x}$ of group-specific public goods, with the tax rate residually determined.[3] The welfare of a member of group j is therefore

$$U_j(\mathbf{x}) = y + B(x_j) - t = y + B(x_j) - \frac{C(x_j)}{N} - \sum_{i \neq j} \frac{C(x_i)}{N}, \qquad (1)$$

where y denotes individual income, which is assumed to be equal across all groups and exogenously given, and $i \neq j$ indexes all groups other than group j. In other words, an individual has utility defined over the benefits of her group-specific good, her share of the cost of providing her group-specific good, and her share of the cost of providing goods for other groups.

As a point of reference, it is useful to begin by defining a socially optimal level of spending for the group-specific goods. First, note that for a member of group j, the change in utility from increased spending on her own favored good is simply

$$\frac{\partial U_j}{\partial x_j} = B'(x_j) - \frac{C'(x_j)}{N}. \qquad (2)$$

---

2 In classical distributive politics models, the groups often represent J districts in a national legislature. As will be clear, I depart from this by defining groups as members of the same community who desire different publicly provided goods. In other words, my groups are territorially overlapping interest groups rather than geographically distinct districts.

3 While I have portrayed a community that only provides group-specific goods, it is simple to imagine that there are also general-interest goods that benefit all groups. Assuming all groups agree on the provision of such general-purpose goods, they will be provided uncontroversially and the model could be extended to include them without altering any of the conclusions derived later.

For a member of a different group, i, the change in utility from increased spending on group j's favored good is

$$\frac{\partial U_{i \neq j}}{\partial x_j} = -\frac{C'(x_j)}{N}.$$

(3)

That is, a member of another group, i, receives no benefits from the provision of good j but pays a share of the cost. Putting (2) and (3) together, we see that the change in aggregate (Benthamite) welfare, $U = \sum_j N_j U_j$, associated with a change in one group's favored good can be written as

$$\begin{aligned}
\frac{\partial U}{\partial x_j} &= N_j \frac{\partial U_j}{\partial x_j} + \sum_{i \neq j} N_i \frac{\partial U_i}{\partial x_j} \\
&= N_j B'(x_j) - \frac{N_j C'(x_j)}{N} - \sum_{i \neq j} \frac{N_i C'(x_j)}{N} \\
&= N_j B'(x_j) - C'(x_j).
\end{aligned}$$

(4)

Thus, the first-order condition for maximizing the aggregate welfare function is

$$N_j B'(x_j) - C'(x_j) = 0 \quad \forall j$$

(4')

Note that this is the Samuelsonian optimum in which the sum of the marginal benefits equals the marginal cost (Samuelson 1954). In other words, social welfare is maximized when the sum of the marginal benefits to group j is equated with the total marginal costs imposed on all members of the community. As a normative benchmark, denote the optimal level of spending on each good as x^*_{Wj}, and the optimal policy vector as $\mathbf{x}^*_W$, and let aggregate spending associated with this welfare-maximizing policy vector be denoted T^*_W.

While defining an optimal level of aggregate spending is straightforward, the *actual* government policy enacted in any community will depend upon the political institutions in place. Next, I compare the outcomes under three different institutional regimes: general-purpose government, single-function government with full participation, and single-function government with selective participation. In every case, I assume that political decisions are made in the following manner. Two candidates, A and B, whose sole desire is to win the election, compete for office by proposing policy platforms, which are $\mathbf{x}$ vectors. Voters vote for the candidate whose platform yields them the highest welfare. If two or more platforms are equally desirable, the voters choose at random. The candidate who wins the most votes takes office and enacts the promised platform. The key distinction between the institutional regimes to be explored is whether policy is set by one general-purpose government or by J different single-function governments.

3.1.1 General-Purpose Government

Consider first a setting in which all policies are under the control of one general-purpose government. Voters elect one candidate, who then sets all policies. Define π_{Ai} as the probability that a member of group i will vote for candidate A if the individual votes in the election. Let π_{Ai} depend upon the differences in the utilities delivered by the two candidates' platforms: $\pi_{Ai} = f_i(U_{Ai} - U_{Bi})$, where $f_i(\cdot)$ is an increasing, continuous, and concave function. Further, assume that $\pi_{Bi} = 1 - \pi_{Ai}$ is the probability that an individual from group i will vote for candidate B if the individual votes. When candidates offer equivalent platforms, the voter flips a coin to decide her vote. This formulation says simply that an individual is more likely to vote for the candidate whose policies benefit her more, and that the probability of voting for the preferred candidate is increasing in the difference in the two platforms.

A candidate vying for the general-purpose office will set her policy platform so as to maximize her expected vote in the election.[4] The expected vote for candidate A can be written $EV_A = \sum_{i=1}^{J} v_i N_i \pi_{A_i}$, where v_i $(|U_{Ai} - U_{Bi}|, c) \in [0,1]$ is the probability that a member of group i votes in the election, which is increasing in the difference in the utilities promised by the two candidates' platforms, and decreasing in the costs, c, of electoral participation. *Taking candidate B's platform as given*, candidate A will therefore select an equilibrium policy vector (i.e., platform) such that spending on every good, x_j, satisfies the following first-order condition:

$$\frac{\partial EV_A}{\partial x_j} = \sum_{i=1}^{J} N_i \frac{\partial U_{Ai}}{\partial x_j} \left(\frac{\partial f_i}{\partial U_{Ai}} v_i + \frac{\partial v_i}{\partial U_{Ai}} f_i \right) = 0 \qquad (5)$$

Candidate B's problem is symmetric and, because the functions $v_i(\cdot), f_i(\cdot)$, and $U_i(\cdot)$ are continuous and concave, there is a Nash equilibrium in which both candidates announce the same platforms: $\mathbf{x}_B = \mathbf{x}_A$.[5] Under this common platform, marginal changes in electoral support are equalized across groups and policy areas.

Note that in formulating their vote-maximizing policies, both candidates are maximizing a weighted sum of voter marginal utilities, where the weights depend on two factors. The first factor is the probability that the voter actually votes. Let $\phi_i = \partial v_i / \partial (U_{Ai} - U_{Bi})$ be known as a group's *turnout propensity*. Groups with a lower propensity to turn out on election day receive less weight in the candidates' policy platforms. Second,

---

4 For a discussion of the connection between maximizing votes and maximizing the probability of winning an election in probabilistic voting models, see Patty (2002).
5 A proof of platform convergence in a similar probabilistic voting framework is provided by Enelow and Hinich (1989).

voters with higher $\theta_i = \partial f_i / \partial(U_{Ai} - U_{Bi})$ at the equilibrium are more likely to change their vote choice in response to differences in the candidates' policies. Thus, let θ_i be called group i's *responsiveness* to policy changes at the equilibrium, and more responsive groups receive more weight when the candidates formulate their platforms.

An important implication of this model is that when all voters are equally likely to turn out and equally responsive to policy differences— that is, when $\phi_j = \phi_i$ and $\theta_j = \theta_i$ for all i and j—then equation (5) simplifies to (4'). In other words, with equal voter turnout and policy responsiveness, the conditions for expected vote maximization are the same as those for maximizing the Benthamite social welfare function. To see this, note that when all voters are equally responsive and equally likely to turn out, the term in parentheses in equation (5) is a constant. Then, compare (5) to (4) and see that both are sums of voter marginal utilities, and when the term in parentheses in (5) is a constant, it is simply an equally weighted sum of voter utilities, which is equivalent to the unweighted sum in (4).

The important point is that political competition drives candidates to propose socially efficient policy platforms. The intuition behind this result is as follows. Suppose that candidate A proposes the socially efficient policy vector, which satisfies (5). If candidate B proposes reallocating spending among the groups, holding the total budget constant, he will receive fewer votes (in expectation) because the recipients of the increases will value the new spending less than the losing groups value the reductions. If candidate B proposes increasing the overall level of spending, he will also be worse off because at the margin all groups value a dollar of private consumption more than another dollar of spending on their group's good. Finally, if candidate B proposes reductions in spending, he will again be worse off because the groups prefer a dollar spent on their good to an equivalent reduction in taxes. Thus, the unique Nash equilibrium under general-purpose government is for both candidates to propose platforms that maximize the (weighted) social welfare function.[6]

Denote the optimal level of spending on each good under general-purpose government as $x^*_{Gj} = x^*_{Wj}$, and the optimal policy vector as $\mathbf{x}^*_G = \mathbf{x}^*_W$, and let aggregate spending associated with this welfare-maximizing policy vector be denoted $T^*_G = T^*_W$.

---

6 Proofs of this result are due to Coughlin and Nitzan (1981) and Ledyard (1984). The proofs require the additional condition that the policy space is compact and convex, which I assume to be satisfied here. Coughlin and Nitzan (1981) show that if $\pi_{Ai} = f_i(U_{Ai}/U_{Bi})$, then expected vote maximization leads to maximization of the Nash rather than the Benthamite social welfare function. Reviews are provided in Mueller (2003, ch. 12) and Persson and Tabellini (2000, ch. 2). Coughlin (1992) provides a comprehensive, although inscrutable, treatment of probabilistic voting.

3.1.2 Single-Function Government: Full versus Selective Participation

Up to this point, the model has been a familiar one (see Hettich and Winer 1999; Persson and Tabellini 2000). Now I will depart from the familiar by allowing there to be multiple independently elected governments and selective participation on the part of voters in each of the elections. The alternative institutional context I consider is single-function government. In this scenario, assume that there are J different specialized governments, each with jurisdiction over one of the J group-specific goods. The basic aspects of the political process are the same as under general-purpose government: Candidates announce platforms, voters select candidates, and the winning candidate enacts her promised policy. Now, however, there are J separate elections, and in each case a candidate's platform is one-dimensional: a spending proposal on the single good controlled by the jurisdiction in question.

First, suppose that voter participation and policy responsiveness are unaffected by the change from general-purpose to single-function government. Let $\phi_j^S = \phi_j^G$ and $\theta_j^S = \theta_j^G$, where the superscript S denotes single-function elections and G denotes elections for a general-purpose government. In this scenario, it is easy to see that policy outcomes under single-function government are exactly the same as under general-purpose government. The reason is that under general-purpose government, the candidates choose the vote-maximizing level of spending, defined in (5), *dimension by dimension.* That is, the candidate for general-purpose office sets x_j at the level where the increase in expected votes from group j from the last dollar of spending exactly offsets the expected loss in votes from the other groups. A candidate for the single-function office j can do no better. Thus, separating the policy space into J single-function districts does not affect policy outcomes if voter participation and responsiveness are identical under both regimes.

The assumption that voter turnout and responsiveness are unchanged in single-function elections is, however, a strong one. Suppose, for example, that participating in elections is costly to voters and that the costs are increasing in the number of elections. The voters who are willing to bear the costs of voting in any particular single-function election are likely to be those with the most at stake, namely, members of the group whose good is under consideration. I conceive the costs of electoral participation as having two components: first, the costs of going to the polls on election day to cast a vote; second, the costs of acquiring the information required to cast an informed vote. Costs of going to the polls will affect ϕ_j, while costs of becoming informed will affect θ_j. The nature of participation in single-function elections may differ from that of general-purpose elections either because some voters are less likely to go to the polls or because some voters are less likely to have sufficient information to cast an informed vote even if they go to the polls, or both.

Denote the turnout propensity of an individual from group i in a single-function election for policy j as ϕ_i^j, and denote i's responsiveness in election j as θ_i^j. The important determinant of policy platforms in a single-function election is not the absolute level of participation or responsiveness compared to that in a general-purpose election, but rather the relative levels. When group j voters have a higher turnout propensity in the single-function election j than in the general-purpose election, their preferences will receive greater weight. Similarly, when group j voters are more responsive to policy changes on issue j, they will receive greater weight. Define *selective participation* as the situation where at least one of the following inequalities holds: $(\phi_i^j/\phi_i^G) < (\phi_j^j/\phi_j^G)$ or $(\theta_i^j/\theta_i^G) < (\theta_j^j/\theta_j^G)$.[7] When there is selective participation, the policy outcomes under single-function elections will not match those under general-purpose government. Rather, each interest group will receive increased weight in the candidates' policy decisions in the group's own policy domain. Later, I will present empirical evidence that such selective participation does indeed occur with jurisdictional specialization. At this point, however, I will simply explore the implications of selective electoral participation without stipulating specifically its causes.

To see the implications of selective participation, begin by considering the extreme case in which each group votes only in the election related to its own policy, $v_i^j = 0$ and $v_j^j > 0$.[8] If members of group j are the only voters in the election, vote-maximizing candidates will propose platforms that maximize the group's collective welfare, $N_j U_j$, where U_j is as defined in equation (1) with respect to x_j. The optimal platform in this one-dimensional policy space is simply to set spending at the level where the marginal benefits equal the marginal costs to members of group j, or

$$N_j B'(x_j) - \frac{N_j}{N} C'(x_j) = B'(x_j) - \frac{1}{N} C'(x_j) = 0 \qquad (6)$$

Note that the candidate now equates the benefits received by group j with the costs paid by group j rather than the total social costs. So, spending will be higher under single-function government with selective

---

7 I will assume that it is never the case that group i has a higher turnout propensity or is more responsive in another group's election than in its own.
8 The implications of differential voter responsiveness are the same.

participation, and the differential will be greater the smaller is group j.[9] Let the level of spending that satisfies (6) be denoted x^*_{jj}. If one candidate is running on such a platform in a single-function election where only group j votes, any other candidate who proposes more spending will be defeated because the marginal costs exceed the marginal benefits to voters. Any candidate proposing less spending will be defeated for the opposite reason. Thus, electoral competition will involve both candidates proposing spending that maximizes group j's welfare, and indifferent voters from group j will chose between the candidates at random.

It is now possible to put bounds on the range of possible policy differentials between single-function and general-purpose government. At one extreme, if voter participation and responsiveness are the same under both institutional regimes, then the policy outcomes will also be the same. At the other extreme, if under single-function government each group participates only in the election for its own good, then candidates will set policy at the group's ideal point. That is, $x^*_{Wj} = x^*_{Gj} \leq x^*_{Sj} \leq x^*_{jj}$, where x^*_{Sj} denotes equilibrium spending on x_j under single-function government.

The situation is depicted in Figure 3.1, where the horizontal axis measures spending on x_j and the vertical axis measures the marginal political benefit (MPB) or cost (MPC) to candidate A of spending, taking candidate B's platform as given.[10] Let EV_{Aj} denote the number of votes that candidate A can expect to receive from group j. The downward-sloping curve, $MPB = \partial EV_{Aj}/\partial x_j$, reflects the marginal increase in votes from group j that candidate A receives from increasing proposed spending on x_j. The upward- sloping curves, $MPC = \Sigma_{i \neq j} \partial EV_{Ai}/\partial x_j$, indicate the loss in votes from groups other than j as spending on x_j is increased. MPC^G represents the MPC under general-purpose government and MPC^S the MPC under single-function government. With selective participation in single-function elections, the MPC curve is shifted downward, so that $MPC^S < MPC^G$ at all points.

The candidate's optimal policy is to set x_j where the MPB and MPC curves intersect. Under general-purpose government, this point lies at x^*_{Gj}. Under single-function government with selective participation, the MPC curve is shifted downward, so it intersects the MPB curve at a higher point of spending, x^*_{Sj}. Finally, in the most extreme form of selective

---

9 Note that this result is an incarnation of the familiar "law of $1/N$" associated with Weingast, Shepsle, and Johnsen (1981). The law is so named because if there are N groups of equal size and spending is financed from a common-pool tax base, then each group internalizes only $1/N$ of the costs of providing a good that benefits its members.

10 The terms MPB and MPC are borrowed from Hettich and Winer (1999), an excellent treatment of tax policy in a probabilistic voting framework.

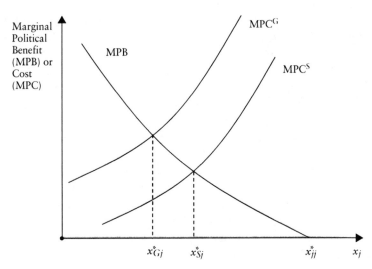

Figure 3.1. Vote-Maximizing Platform

The horizontal axis represents spending on good x_j, which benefits group j. The marginal political benefit curve (MPB) represents the change in votes from group j. The MPC curves represent the loss in votes from other groups. The MPC^G curve denotes general-purpose government with full participation. The MPC^S curve represents special-purpose government with selective participation. The vote-maximizing level of x_j is found where the MPC and MPB curves intersect.

participation, when groups other than j do not participate at all in the election for x_j, the MPC curve lies always at zero. Therefore, candidates set x_j where the marginal political benefits from increased spending are exhausted, namely, where $MBP = 0$, which is at group j's ideal point, x^*_{jj}. Spending beyond x^*_{jj} leads to vote losses even when no other groups participate in the election. Thus, Figure 3.1 demonstrates the main features of my argument: Spending on x_j is higher when it is provided by a single-function government to the extent that political participation is selective. But overspending by single-function government j is swayed by the electoral reaction of the general public (i.e., groups other than j), and in any case will never exceed the level preferred by the interest group that dominates issue j.

It is also worthwhile to mention a possible indirect effect of selective participation. Suppose that members of group j, after their single-function district is formed, reduce their involvement in the remaining activities of the general-purpose government. Then their preferences will receive less weight from candidates running for the general-function office, which will result in increased spending on the goods for the other groups. This idea is seen easily by imagining a general-purpose government that provides only two services, j and k. If good j is spun off into a single-function jurisdiction, then the erstwhile general-purpose government becomes actually a single-function jurisdiction for k. If selective participation operates as just outlined, then group j will participate less in the election concerned with good k than it did before the split. As a result, spending increases on both j and k. With many policies under the control of a general-purpose government, the spinning off of any one may have a small effect, but with a large number of single-function jurisdictions, the possible "siphoning off" of interest groups may be consequential. The existence of such indirect effects suggests that spending by general-purpose governments may also increase when single-function jurisdictions are created.

3.1.3   Comparison of Policy Outcomes

Having established the policy equilibrium under each of these alternative institutional arrangements, it is now possible to compare the outcomes. Clearly, single-function government with selective participation results in overspending compared to the social optimum, in that the sum of the marginal benefits from spending is less than the social marginal cost. However, any individual group may be better off in the scenario in which its good is provided by a single-function government in an environment of selective participation. The reason is that, starting from the socially efficient level of spending, $x^*_{W_j}$, each group would be unwilling to pay an additional dollar in taxes in exchange for an additional dollar in spending on its own good. But when spending on x_j is increased, group j only pays a fraction, N_j/N, of the additional costs. Thus, when its own good is provided by a single-function government, a member of group j will vote for a candidate promising to set spending at the level where the marginal benefit equals N_j/N of the marginal cost, as shown in (6). However, if every group does the same, then group j will be worse off than under general-purpose government—worse off because they must also pay the higher costs of taxation required to finance the increased spending for the other groups.

The change in welfare for a member of group j under single-function government versus general-purpose government is shown in (7), where $U^*_{S_j}$ represents the equilibrium level of utility for a member of group j under single-function government with selective participation and $U^*_{G_j}$ represents equilibrium utility for a member of j under general-purpose government. If no other group's good is provided under single-function government, then the last term on the right-hand side of (7) evaluates to zero. In this case, a member of group j is better off because $B(x^*_{S_j} - x^*_{G_j}) > C(x^*_{S_j} - x^*_{G_j})/N$. But if all the other groups follow the same policy, the final term is positive and $U^*_{S_j} - U^*_{G_j} < 0$. To see why, note that when every other group also raises its spending by a dollar, a member of group j pays an additional $N_j/N + \sum_{i \neq j} N_i/N = N/N = 1$ dollar in costs. But I have already established that a member of group j would be unwilling to pay an additional dollar in costs in exchange for an additional dollar of spending on x_j. Therefore, all groups are worse off under a system in which all goods are provided by single-function governments with selective participation than under a general-purpose government.

$$U^*_{S_j} - U^*_{G_j} = y + B(x^*_{S_j} - x^*_{G_j}) - \frac{C(x^*_{S_j} - x^*_{G_j})}{N} - \sum_{i \neq j} \frac{C(x^*_{S_i} - x^*_{G_i})}{N} \qquad (7)$$

The heart of the problem is that each group fully values spending on its own good but ignores the costs imposed on the other groups. If each group controls spending on its own good and is able to levy a general tax, then it will overspend compared to the social optimum; and when all groups do the same, total taxes exceed the benefits of spending for every group. In other words, the competing interest groups are involved in a J-player prisoners' dilemma: Each group's dominant strategy is to overspend, but when all follow this strategy, all are worse off. The prisoners' dilemma in this particular case takes the form of a *fiscal common-pool problem*, and the resulting overspending is analytically similar to the "overfishing" problem seen in environmental economics (e.g., Benhabib and Radner 1992).

A simple example will illustrate my argument that single-function government with selective participation represents a form of the prisoners' dilemma. Suppose there are only two groups in the community, one devoted to parks and another devoted to public transit. Each service is provided by a single-function government. Suppose that two candidates run for office in each jurisdiction: One candidate promises to provide spending on parks (transit) at the socially efficient level; the other promises the parks (transit) group's ideal point on spending, which is higher than the socially optimal level. Denote the socially efficient level of spending as L and the group's preferred spending on its own good as H. Each group prefers that its own good is provided at H and the other group's good at L. However, for the reasons outlined previously, each group prefers having both services provided at L over both at H. The strategic form of the game is shown in Figure 3.2.

In each cell, the payoff to the parks group is listed first, followed by the payoff to the transit group. Higher numbers indicate more preferred outcomes. Suppose that only the parks group votes in the parks election

Public Transit

		L	H
Parks	L	3,3	1,4
	H	4,1	2,2

Figure 3.2. Single-Function Government as a Prisoners' Dilemma
Higher numbers indicate more preferred outcomes.

and only the transit group votes in the transit election. If the transit group elects the candidate proposing high spending, the best response for the parks group is to elect the candidate proposing high spending too; otherwise, the parks group would end up simply paying higher taxes for transit spending. But note that if the transit group elects the candidate proposing L, then the parks group's best response is still to elect the candidate proposing H; then the parks group gets extra spending on parks without paying additional taxes for transit. The position of the transit group is symmetric, and thus its best strategy is also to vote for the H candidate regardless of what the parks group does.[11] The result is the groups end up in the HH cell, even though both would prefer to be in the LL cell. Both prefer a different outcome, yet neither has an incentive to deviate unilaterally. Finally, note that while I have used only two groups in this example, the logic generalizes naturally to a J-player prisoners' dilemma game.

3.1.4 Full Participation versus Selective Participation: Evidence

My argument is that the effect of single-function government on policy outcomes depends crucially on the nature of political participation. If all voters who would have participated in a general-purpose election also turn out for every single-function election, the resulting policy outcomes will be the same, as candidates in either setting seek to maximize votes dimension by dimension. On the other hand, when voters selectively participate in those single-function elections related to spending items that benefit them most, the outcome is higher spending on each function, which maximizes a candidate's votes among those *who turn out*. Which outcome is more likely: full or selective participation? In this section, I review the evidence on local political participation, which provides strong

11 With both groups having a dominant strategy to vote H, no candidate should actually run proposing L, but I ignore that for the purposes of this illustration.

reasons to believe that selective turnout is more common in practice than full participation. I first review evidence on the overall level of turnout in single-function elections, and then I examine the representativeness of single-function voters.

Is Turnout Lower in Special District Elections? It is widely known that turnout in local elections is significantly lower than in national elections in the United States (Hajnal, Lewis, and Louch 2002; Karnig and Walter 1983). However, the question at issue here is whether turnout in special-function local elections is higher or lower than in general-function local elections. While I am aware of no national data on turnout in local single-function elections, one of the major themes in the extant literature on special district governments is that their low visibility and multiplicity hinder voter participation and undermine accountability (e.g., Bollens 1957; Foster 1997). Indeed, the relative obscurity of special-function governments to citizens has led some observers to label them "shadow governments" or "ad-hoc governments," monikers that are repeated throughout the literature (Axelrod 1992; Smith 1974). As to the specific question of participation in special-function versus general-purpose elections, scholars who have examined the issue appear to concur in the conclusion that voter turnout in special district elections is usually much lower (e.g., Burns, 1994; Stetzer 2004).

Additional evidence can be obtained from studies of particular local areas. Among these, the most comprehensive analysis of local special district elections of which I am aware was conducted recently by the Nassau County Executive (Suozzi 2007). The study found that special district elections in Nassau County, New York, were held on 24 different days of the year and that there was at least one special district election in 11 of the 12 months of the year. *None* of these special district elections, however, was held on the same day as the general election in November. Some districts changed their election dates from one year to the next. Unsurprisingly, therefore, turnout in special district elections was low. According to the county comptroller, while turnout in the 2002 gubernatorial election was 44 percent in Nassau County, turnout in the succeeding special district elections ranged from only 2 to 14 percent (Weitzman 2005). The report concludes that "The scattered nature of the special district elections, and the extreme difficulty involved in obtaining some of their election dates, place an undue burden on voters. Even the most conscientious of Nassau residents would find it difficult to vote in all of the elections that concern them" (Suozzi 2007, p. 3). Meanwhile, Nassau County special districts, *not including school districts*, levied more than $489 million in taxes in 2007.

Studies of special district elections in other regions, though less comprehensive, tend to comport with the conclusions of the Nassau County report. An analysis of voting in Michigan school board elections in 2000 showed that turnout among *registered* voters averaged 7.8 percent, and three-quarters of districts had turnout of less than 10 percent (Weimer 2001). Almost all Michigan school board elections take place in June. Canon reports on a case in which a $14 million bond issue for a Texas utility district was approved with turnout from 32 voters (see Galvan 2007).

California's Little Hoover Commission (2000) found that the turnout in special district elections was significantly lower than the turnout for other types of local governments throughout the state. The report notes that Sacramento County was able to increase the turnout in its special district elections from 17 percent to 45 percent of registered voters by switching from odd- to even-year elections. Even after the change, however, special district elections still fell well below the comparable level of participation for city council elections (see Little Hoover Commission 2000, pp. 18–22). Townley, Sweeney, and Schmieder (1994) find similar patterns in a study of school districts in Riverside County, California, that changed their election dates from odd to even years.

My own analysis of elections in Cook County, Illinois, suggests that turnout in special district elections is almost universally lower than in general-purpose elections. In Cook County, elections for county offices are held in November of even-numbered years, while most special district elections are held in April of odd-numbered years. Nearly half of registered voters cast a ballot for the county executive in the November 2004 election. The following April, elections were held in 386 races for school, library, parks, fire, and community college districts. Turnout in these special district races was 21 percent on average. In all but four races, turnout was lower than for the county executive race in November. I estimate that a typical resident of Cook County is represented by 70 different elected officials and would have to go to the polls on six different dates to vote for all of them.

Are Special District Voters Representative? Even a conservative reading of the evidence leaves little doubt that participation in single-function elections is typically lower than in general-purpose elections. The more important question is whether special district voters are representative of general-purpose voters. If they are, then outcomes under the two institutions may not diverge. In terms of the model presented earlier, if all the v_j and f_j differ proportionally between single-function and general-purpose elections, then the resulting policy vectors will not change. Although only about half of eligible voters participate in national elections, for example, some have argued that the preferences of voters are fairly representative of those of the general public, and so electoral outcomes would not change if everyone turned out (e.g., Ellcessor and Leighley 2001; Highton and Wolfinger 2001; Verba, Schlozman, and Brady 1995, p. 512). However, Hajnal and Trounstine (2005) argue that voters are not representative of nonvoters at the local level. They present evidence that lower turnout leads to less minority representation on city councils and suggest that full participation would lead to different outcomes in mayoral elections.

Is it plausible that the small minority of voters who participate in single-function elections are representative of the preferences of the general public? The most important study on this question is by Terry Moe (2006), who examined 14 school district elections held in California in 1997 and 1999. Moe gathered data on the names and zip codes of school district employees and matched these names to county voter files to get each employee's voting history. He found that teachers were two to seven times more likely to vote in district elections than the average registered voter. But, of course, teachers differ from other citizens in observable and unobservable ways. Might not the higher turnout among teachers simply reflect differences in social class or overall public spiritedness? Moe used an ingenious design to disentangle these factors. He found that many teachers live in one district but work in another. If increased turnout among teachers were purely a function of social class or a commitment to education, they should be just as likely to vote in districts where they live but do not have an occupational stake in the outcome. In fact, Moe found huge differences in turnout between teachers who lived in the district where they worked and those who lived in another district.

According to Moe's results, median participation by registered voters in the school board elections he studied was 9 percent. For teachers living in one district but working in another, turnout was twice as high, 18 percent. But among teachers who lived and worked in the same district, turnout was an astounding 46 percent. Among other district employees, the pattern was similar: 14 percent of district employees who lived in one district but worked in another voted in their school board election; 35 percent of employees who lived and worked in the same district voted. These results strongly suggest that occupational self-interest played an important role in turnout for district employees. More to the point, in light of these findings, it is difficult to sustain the claim that voters in single-function elections are representative of the preferences of the general public. Rather, the pattern resembles selective participation by voters with a high stake in the single-function policy domain.

The timing of elections is a particularly important determinant of selective participation. When multiple elections are held on the same day, the marginal cost of voting in an additional election, given that one has already come to the polling place, is simply the cost of gathering the necessary information to cast an informed vote. When elections are held on separate days, by contrast, the marginal cost of participating is essentially the full cost, that is, the cost of going to the polls plus the cost of becoming informed. Holding elections on different days raises the costs of voting in each election and therefore is most likely to discourage participation by those voters who are least concerned with the policy issue under consideration in any given election. In other words, when elections take place on separate days, voters who were just on the margin of indifference about turning out will find that the additional costs lead them to stay home. In the terminology of my model, voters in other groups are relatively less likely to turn out when group j's election is held on a separate day.

Dunne, Reed, and Wilbanks (1997) present further evidence that not only is participation in single-function elections influenced by timing, but politicians are aware of the issue and use it to their advantage. They summarize their argument succinctly:

Voters will generally show up at the polls in the proportion to which a particular electoral decision is likely to affect them. If the benefits from a particular public choice are concentrated among voters, and the costs are dispersed, then voter self-selection will result in a disproportionate number of "yes" voters casting votes on election day. Politicians can encourage this self-selection by choosing voting dates and places that discourage "no" voters from voting. In this sense, politicians can be thought of as "choosing" the median voter. (p. 100)

Empirically, Dunne et al. find that school district officials systematically avoid holding bond elections at the same time as the general election in November, and that bond referenda are more likely to be approved the lower the turnout in the election. The authors also discuss the role of private sector consultants who advise school districts on how to win bond elections, in part by manipulating election timing.

In addition to manipulating the timing of elections, special-purpose governments often have leeway over the location of polling places. For instance, an editorial in the *Rocky Mountain News* decried the practice among Colorado special districts of locating polling places in their own facilities (Blake 2006). One fire district scheduled a referendum on a $43 million bond issue and an accompanying tax increase for a May date and offered 16 polling locations for its 300,000 constituents. All 16 were fire stations. Another fire district proposed a $26 million bond issue and an accompanying tax increase with four polling places for its 90,000 constituents, all fire stations. The author of the editorial mused that "If you're opposed, all you need is the courage to show up at any given station and ask a burly fireman where you go to vote against the tax increase." Similar examples abound for other types of districts, although the burliness of their employees varies.

Strategic manipulation of the timing and location of special-purpose elections is certainly consistent with my argument, although it is not essential. If politicians attempt to "choose the median voter," as Dunne et al. suggest, selective participation will only be strengthened.

A natural empirical application of my model would be to examine how turnout and government policy are affected by the timing of elections. In particular, the policies enacted by special-purpose jurisdictions whose elections are held separately should cater more to special interest groups than those enacted by special-purpose jurisdictions whose elections are coincident with major state and national races. My initial research on the topic supports this hypothesis. In a working paper written with Jacob Gersen, I find that California school districts whose elections are held in odd-numbered years negotiate significantly more generous contracts with teachers than do districts whose boards are elected in even-numbered years, coincident with major state and national elections (Berry and Gersen 2009). Comparing teachers at an equal salary "step," Gersen and I find that those working in districts with odd-year elections earn roughly $2,000 (or about 4 percent) more than those working in districts with even-year elections. Moreover, we find evidence that turnout goes up and salaries go down within a district when its election date is changed from odd to even years. Of course, these results are only for one state and one type of special-function government, so much work remains to be done. Unfortunately, data on the timing of local special-function elections are not systematically available. While I will therefore not specifically investigate election timing in this book, it remains an obvious and important topic for future research building on the selective participation model set forth here.

Finally, note that while I have cast the argument in terms of differential voter participation, the ϕ in the model, differential voter responsiveness, the θ, will have a similar effect. In fact, the familiar notion of *fiscal illusion* on the part of voters (e.g., Buchanan 1967, ch. 10) is essentially a theory of θ. That is, voters may not perceive the full costs of taxation when taxes are levied in smaller amounts by a larger number of less prominent governments. Thus, voters may be less responsive to a series of small tax increases imposed by several governments than to an increase of an equivalent sum by a single government. The possibility of differential voter responsiveness has been appreciated by members of single-function governments. For example, Stetzer writes that "Frequently, the need for referendum approval of a new tax levy is the death knell of a critical service. Special district development has been something of a soporific in that a rejected levy for city park purposes creates no excitement when it appears on the tax bill as a rate for park district purposes" (1975, p. 116). However, differential responsiveness is harder to measure than differential participation, and I have no direct evidence one way or another.

3.2 EXTENSIONS

The basic probabilistic voting model developed in the preceding section could be extended in any number of directions. It is straightforward to show that the same problems of selective participation that characterize the election of politicians to govern special-purpose jurisdictions also characterize referenda on the creation of the districts, as well as bond and budgetary referenda for the districts. In each case, those with a disproportionately high stake in the policy under consideration have a disproportionate incentive to turn out—that is, to reap concentrated benefits with diffuse costs. So the same common-pool, selective participation model can explain the formation of districts as well as their ability to overspend even when their budgets must be approved by a voter referendum. The same basic model applies more or less directly to these other types of elections related to special-purpose governments.

More interestingly, the model could be reformulated to include lobbying activities by special interest groups, ideological predispositions of voters, candidate valence on nonpolicy dimensions, spillovers among the services benefiting different groups, or the existence of individuals who are not members of any group.[12] The model could be extended to allow multiple layers of government to provide the same service, as in Volden (2005), which would create a second source of vertical externalities due to competitive credit-claiming.

While interesting, such extensions would complicate the analysis without altering the direction of the most important comparative static result of the model, namely, the positive relationship between single-function jurisdictions and spending. In this section, I focus on three extensions of the theory that are potentially more consequential for my main predictions about the fiscal effects of single-function government. First, I consider policymaking within a general-purpose legislature; then

---

12 Persson and Tabellini (2000, ch. 7) demonstrate extensions of the probabilistic voting model in several such ways.

I discuss the role of repeated interactions; and finally, I examine the impact of Tiebout competition.

3.2.1 Special Districts Are Not So Special

Up to this point, I have assumed that policymaking is determined entirely by the electoral process. Candidates announce platforms, voters choose candidates, and platforms are implemented. In this section, I consider policymaking *within* a general-purpose government, say a city council. I have two goals in doing so. First, some aspects of the problem of specialized government will be revealed that were not present in the purely electoral model. Second, the analogy to congressional institutions, to which I alluded in Chapter 1, will be made more explicit when I employ a modeling framework from that literature.

Consider a version of a canonical congressional distributive politics model in which legislators' constituencies are defined not by a geographic district, but by a policy interest.[13] Suppose that a community has three distinct groups: One group cares about schools, another about parks, and the third about public transit. Suppose further that one representative from each group has been elected to a three-person city council.

Simplify the policy space by assuming that each service can be provided at one of two levels: high (H) or low (L). For simplicity, normalize the benefit received by a member of group j when good j is provided at L to zero, and let $b_j > 0$ denote the incremental benefit received by a member of group j when good j is provided at H. Similarly, normalize the cost of providing good j at L to zero, and let $c_j > 0$ denote the incremental cost of providing good j at H.

The costs of providing the goods are paid through taxes, which are levied in an equal amount across all groups. The balanced budget requirement means that $T = C = \sum_{j \in H} c_j$ represents the incremental taxes necessary if any goods are provided at the high level. Because taxation is spread equally over all groups, the cost to group k when good j is provided at the high level is $c_j/3$. Each group therefore prefers that its own good is provided at the high level and the other groups' goods are provided at the low level.

Government policy consists of a vector of public good levels, **x**, defining whether parks, schools, and public transit are provided at H or L.[14]

---

13 The canonical model I have in mind is of the Shepsle–Weingast variety (e.g., Shepsle 1979; Shepsle and Weingast 1981; Weingast 1979; Weingast, Shepsle, and Johnsen 1981). See Persson and Tabellini (2000, chs. 6 and 7) for a review of related literature and models.

14 Because of the balanced budget requirement, the tax rate is residually determined.

Policy Vector			Net Payoff to Parks Group
Parks	Schools	Transit	
H	L	L	b – c/3
H	H	L	b – 2c/3
H	L	H	b – 2c/3
L	L	L	0
H	H	H	b – c
L	H	L	–c/3
L	L	H	–c/3
L	H	H	–2c/3

Figure 3.3. Government Policy and Group Payoffs

For instance, **x** = HHL indicates a policy of providing parks and schools at H and public transit at L. In this simple example with three groups and two possible levels of each public good, eight distinct government policies are possible, as shown in Figure 3.3. As just explained, the most preferred outcome for the parks group is that parks are provided at H and the other goods are provided at L. Second best for the parks group is that parks are provided at H and one other group's good is also provided at H (second best because now the parks group pays taxes on two H goods rather than just one). Meanwhile, the worst outcome for the parks group is when parks are funded at L and both schools and transit are provided at H. The parks group's second least preferred outcomes are those where parks are provided at L and only one of the other groups' goods is provided H.

Whether the group prefers LLL over HHH depends on whether the cost of providing each good at the high level exceeds the benefit. If so, then HHH is worse than LLL because paying taxes on three H goods exceeds the benefit the parks group receives from having parks funded at H. But if the benefits of each good exceed its costs, then HHH is preferred over LLL. The question of whether the benefits of group-specific public goods exceed the costs is an important one, to which I will return later.

Figure 3.4 presents the joint payoffs for each of the possible policy vectors. Under general-purpose government, policies on each dimension are decided by majority rule within the city council. A well-known result is that the equilibrium policy in this setting is unpredictable.[15] For example, suppose that the benefits of spending outweigh the costs, meaning that $b > c$. Then, starting from a position of LLL, HHH will win unanimously. But then a proposal to provide benefits to only two groups, HHL, will be preferred by those two groups over HHH (saving them the tax cost of providing H on the third policy). The losing group might, however,

15 See Mueller (2003, ch. 11) for a discussion.

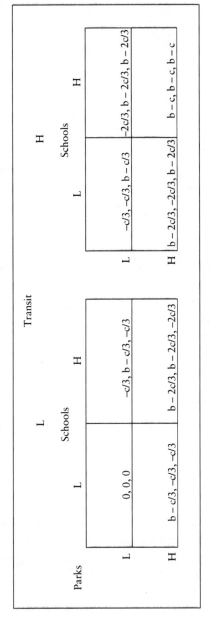

Figure 3.4. Group Payoffs in Normal Form

propose HLL, which would win a majority vote against HHL. But from HLL, a switch to LLL makes two of the groups better off and would therefore win a majority vote. However, LLL can be defeated by HHH, and the cycle is complete. Every policy vector can be defeated.

This situation has three undesirable properties from the perspective of the legislators. First, cycling implies policy instability, which may be socially disruptive. Second, a cost-effective policy that benefits a single group will nevertheless be defeated. In other words, even where $b > c$, meaning that the group would be willing to pay for the project itself, its project may be defeated when it must be financed jointly by all groups. Thus, some socially beneficial projects are not enacted. Third, each legislator fails to get her preferred policy some of the time. If cycling is random, for example, each legislator gets H only half of the time.

Now it becomes clear why the separation of the policy space into single-function jurisdictions might be desirable. Assume that each group had complete control over its own good. The resulting policy vector will be HHH. The outcome will be stable; each individual group has no reason to deviate from H on its own policy. Socially beneficial projects will always be approved, because the beneficiaries give the approval. And each group is guaranteed its preferred policy on its own good all of the time.

But would this switch to single-function jurisdictions be socially desirable? As mentioned previously and as indicated in Figure 3.4, the social desirability of HHH hinges on the question of whether $b - c$ is greater or less than zero, that is, whether the total benefits of high spending on each group's good exceed the costs. While I have left the values of b and c unspecified in this simple example, the model presented in Section 3.1.2 provides strong reasons to expect that $b > c$. The reason is that when a group dominates the jurisdiction providing its own preferred good, the group has both the opportunity and the incentive to ignore the costs imposed on other groups through generalized taxation. So with three equally sized groups, each would set its own spending at the level where $b' = (1/3)c'$. And if $b < c$, then each group would prefer LLL to HHH and the situation is once again a prisoners' dilemma game, which can be seen clearly in Figure 3.4. The problem is analogous to the problem of selective participation analyzed previously.

Two interesting points emerge from this example. First, the problem of forming special districts resembles the problem of forming congressional committees. Both have the advantages of bringing structure-induced equilibrium (Shepsle 1979) to an otherwise potentially chaotic policymaking process. Both serve to guarantee that all groups get something from government spending, smacking of universalism (Shepsle and Weingast 1981; Weingast 1979). And special-function jurisdictions, like congressional committees, may be dominated by "high demanders" of the relevant service or "preference outliers."[16] Even the idea of selective participation finds an analog in Congress, in light of the finding that interest groups devote more of their efforts to influencing congressional committees in their special policy domain (Loucks 1996; Munger 1989; Stratmann 1992).

The second important point is that special districts may serve a valuable function if they are used to finance socially desirable projects that would otherwise be opposed by a majority under general-purpose government (Wallis and Weingast 2005). When a particular service benefits only a minority of citizens, a special district can be a desirable way to provide it. But the problem is how to prevent that minority, having established control of a jurisdiction with powers of generalized taxation, from imposing excessive costs on the majority to finance its group-specific good.

3.2.2 Repeated Interactions

I have described the regime of concurrent taxation by overlapping single-function governments with selective participation as a prisoners' dilemma. But if the prisoners' dilemma is the most widely known element of game theory, surely the second most familiar must be the folk theorem. In this context, the folk theorem says, in essence, that when a prisoners' dilemma game is played repeatedly over an indefinite time horizon and the players' discount rates are sufficiently low, many different equilibria are possible, including stable, socially desirable equilibria. Assuming that local government resembles such a repeated game, in the sense that the same actors interact in an ongoing relationship with no clear end in sight, is it likely that the equilibrium outcome will still involve mutual overspending?

Two points are relevant in considering an answer. First, can voters be expected to use the sorts of complicated, history-dependent strategies that may be required to sustain an equilibrium in the repeated game that is different from the equilibrium in the static game?[17] Second, is a socially optimal equilibrium more likely than any other equilibrium with indefinitely repeated play? On the first point, I am dubious of the potential for a mass electorate to use complex strategies in a repeated game, although I am aware of no scholarship to address the issue specifically.[18]

---

16 There is a long-running debate among scholars of Congress as to whether committees are populated by preference outliers (e.g., Krehbiel 1990; Shepsle and Weingast 1987).

17 On the complexity of strategies in repeated games, see Osborne and Rubinstein (1994, ch. 9).

18 Suggestions along these lines would be most welcome.

The challenges are obvious. To give a simple example, suppose the groups use some sort of *trigger strategy*. If group j "defects" by electing a high-spending candidate, the others will "punish" that group by electing high-spending candidates in their own jurisdictions for some number of future rounds or by electing low-spending candidates in the domain favored by the defectors. How do the players, who are ordinary voters, know what strategy they are to use, for how many rounds to administer punishment, and so forth? If players cannot communicate with one another, they are less likely to be able to coordinate on the punishment mechanism they are using (Maskin and Tirole 2001). Moreover, punishment is costly, and each voter has an incentive to shirk on administering the punishment even when the strategy is known. In short, dynamic strategies in a mass electorate may be too difficult to learn and implement, and too likely to break down, to expect an equilibrium different from the static game. Moreover, and this is the second point, a huge number of dynamic equilibria are possible in a repeated prisoners' dilemma, and there is no particular reason to expect voters to achieve a socially desirable one (see Kreps 1990, pp. 95–128).

While I will stop short of making the strong claim that attaining a dynamic equilibrium different from the one-shot outcome is impossible among a mass electorate, I would like to make the weaker claim that such an equilibrium will be more likely with the aid of political elites. It is much easier to imagine that the individual politicians in control of each single-function government could reach a desirable repeat-play equilibrium among themselves than that the masses of voters who elected them could do the same. For instance, the heads of each jurisdiction might realize that the welfare of their constituents would be improved if they all coordinated on a socially efficient level of spending, and they might be able to sustain a low-spending equilibrium among themselves with repeated play. But note that there is a problem if the voters are not in on the strategy. Each group of voters still has a dominant strategy in the static game to oust the low-spending candidate at the next election and put a high spender in office instead. In other words, the situation is not improved if the politicians attempt to use a dynamic strategy while the voters continue to use their strategies from the static game. What is needed is an institution that links the strategies of voters and politicians. Here, the political party presents itself as a potential key to the attainment of a socially desirable dynamic equilibrium.

Political parties are the focus of Chapter 6, and I wish only to foreshadow the argument at this point. Let a political party be understood as a group of politicians who behave as though they were a unitary actor, in that each one fully internalizes the effects of her actions on the others in the party. The goal of the party is to maximize the number of local offices that it controls. Furthermore, assume that a party has a means of communicating information to voters. Then it is possible that the existence of a political party will make it easier to achieve a dynamic equilibrium that is Pareto superior to the static equilibrium. For example, suppose that a party were to run a slate of candidates—that is, one candidate for each office—all proposing to deliver the socially efficient level of spending on the good under their jurisdiction. This slate of candidates might defeat a slate proposing high spending on each good if voters realized the long-term benefits of the low-spending equilibrium, a realization that would be facilitated by the party's ability to communicate with the electorate. On the other hand, a party running a slate that promised high spending to a small majority of groups and socially efficient spending for the rest might defeat a slate promising efficient spending on all goods. Many other possibilities are imaginable, consistent with the recognition that many equilibria are possible in a repeated prisoners' dilemma.

Clearly, the existence of political parties is no guarantee that a community will find a socially desirable dynamic equilibrium. But I do suggest that the likelihood of obtaining a dynamic equilibrium that differs from the static equilibrium is greater with parties than without them. In this context, a political party can be thought of as an institution that repackages unbundled policy decisions. In a general-purpose election, the platform of a candidate is simply a multidimensional policy vector. With single-function jurisdictions, candidates instead propose policies dimension by dimension. I have already explained why these two regimes may produce different outcomes. But if a party is itself a sort of policy vector, constructed by linking politicians together across jurisdictions and offering a slate of candidates, then the choice of a party slate resembles the choice of a single candidate in a general-purpose election. Therefore, parties may make it possible for voters to obtain an outcome with single-function jurisdictions that resembles the outcome that would arise under general-purpose government. I return to this issue, and to an empirical examination of the effects of party organization on local government spending, in Chapter 6.

3.2.3 The Shadow of Tiebout

As explained in Chapter 1, the Tiebout (1956) model has been extremely influential in public choice scholarship on local government. Although the Tiebout model ignores the vertical dimension of intergovernmental competition and allows essentially no role for politics, it nevertheless captures fundamental insights that should be considered in any attempt to understand local public policy. The two fundamental and interrelated mechanisms at work in the Tiebout model are sorting and competition. In this section, I consider the implications of each for my analysis of single-function local government.

Sorting. One important implication of the Tiebout model is that if mobility costs are low enough, individuals will sort themselves into communities with completely homogeneous preferences with respect to public policy. With a sufficiently large number of communities available, each citizen can find a locality providing *exactly* her own preferred bundle of public policies. The citizen moves to her ideal community, along with others sharing the same preferences and income, and everyone then receives her ideal policy vector. If perfect sorting actually occurred in practice, my model would be meaningless. There would be no residual differences in preferences over publicly provided services and hence only one group in my model. Under this scenario, there would be complete unanimity on public good provision, dimension by dimension, and hence it would make no difference whether public goods were provided by a general-purpose government or a string of single-function governments.

Fortunately—for me, but not for Tiebout—there is little evidence that anything resembling complete sorting occurs in the real world. In the most persuasive study on Tiebout sorting, Rhode and Strumpf (2003) examine long-term trends in population heterogeneity across counties and municipalities in the United States from 1850 to 1990. They point out that an implication of the Tiebout model is that when mobility costs fall, sorting should increase, and therefore population heterogeneity across localities should also increase. But in fact, they find just the opposite to be true. They demonstrate that while mobility costs fell dramatically over their study period, population heterogeneity across localities, by almost any measure, actually *decreased* significantly. Rhode and Strumpf conclude that "Almost all of our empirical results stand in opposition to the Tiebout prediction of increasing heterogeneity across communities" (p. 1649). Aside from Rhode and Strumpf (2003), other studies of Tiebout sorting find at best mixed evidence.[19]

The important question in the context of my argument is not whether *any* population sorting occurs in practice—because surely it does—but rather whether the degree of sorting is sufficient to make local communities fairly homogeneous in their preferences for public goods. On the latter question, one does not need to study historical trends to see that the answer is *no*. Consider that the COG tracks spending on 37 different

19 See Ross and Yinger (1999, sect. 3.1.3) for a review of the evidence.

functional line items of spending by local governments. Assume that each function can be provided at only three levels: low, medium, or high. Then, in order to provide all the possible bundles of spending, such that a person with any combination of preferences could find a location with her preferred bundle, there would need to be 46,620 different jurisdictions available. If each good could be provided at just four levels, the number of jurisdictions required jumps to 1,585,080. Given that Tiebout sorting is generally thought to occur within metropolitan areas rather then between them, it is clear that there is no area in the United States where complete sorting by preferences is possible. Thus, I can build my theory on the mild claim that no matter how much or how little Tiebout sorting occurs in practice, there will *always* be residual variation in public preferences within a jurisdiction. My theory can therefore be thought of as an explanation of the politics of public spending decisions that happen after any plausible amount of sorting across jurisdictions has taken place.

Competition. The second important implication of the Tiebout model is that competition among jurisdictions enhances efficiency in the provision of public services. As long as residents and capital are mobile, and there are a large number of jurisdictions from which to choose, any jurisdiction that deviates from efficiency in its operations will suffer a loss of taxable assets through out-migration. In other words, if one government is behaving badly, taxpayers will "vote with their feet" by moving to a more desirable locality. Thus, the elasticity of the tax base provides automatic sanctions that promote governmental efficiency, or so the argument goes.

As many analysts have pointed out, relaxing some of the extreme assumptions of the Tiebout model reveals greater room for government discretion. In an influential paper, Epple and Zelenitz (1981) were among the first to recognize the implications of property taxation in a Tiebout setting. Their contribution is based on the recognition that while residents are mobile, land is not. That is, land cannot be relocated in response to a jurisdiction's tax-service package. Thus, jurisdictions compete for residents but not for land, so taxes on land are not competed away. As a result, governments have discretion in choosing their tax and service packages, or, as Epple and Zelenitz (1981, p. 1211) conclude, "the 'market' for local public goods does not force the government to act as a 'tax rate taker.'" But because taxes are capitalized into land prices, local governments must trade off higher tax rates against a diminishing tax base. Empirically, there is widespread evidence that changes in local taxes are indeed capitalized into property values—meaning that property values in a jurisdiction go down when taxes go up—although the matter is not without controversy.[20]

Incorporating residential mobility and housing markets into the model of local politics presented previously is no small challenge. Indeed, the field has yet to generate a workhorse model of local political economy that integrates sorting, voting, capitalization, and individual heterogeneity in preferences for publicly provided goods, although Dennis Epple has made important progress in this direction with a series of coauthors (Epple, Filimon, and Romer 1983, 1984, 1993; Epple and Platt 1998), as has Thomas Nechyba (1997). Recognizing that my comparative advantage does not lie in out-theorizing Epple and Nechyba, I have not attempted to formulate such a comprehensive model of the local public sector. However, I believe that the central insight of the Tiebout competition literature can be captured with a relatively simple extension of the model developed previously.

The central message of Tiebout competition is that inefficient local government policies, whether in the form of high taxes or poor service quality, will result in decrements to the local tax base. Governments that care about preserving their tax bases, therefore, should strive for efficiency.[21] In the present context, suppose that deviations from efficient policies negatively affect property values, and that this in turn reduces the well-being of voters. Then we can rewrite the voter's utility function, originally defined in (1), as follows:

$$U_j(\mathbf{x}) = y + B(x_j) - t * g\left(\sum_j |x_j - x^*_{Wj}|\right), \tag{8}$$

where $g(\sum_j |x_j - x^*_{Wj}|) > 1$ is a function of the differences between actual enacted policies and socially efficient policies on each dimension, x_j. Think of g as a "coefficient of capitalization," such that each increase in taxation has a direct cost as well as an indirect effect, or multiplier, that imposes additional costs on voters. The most natural way to think about this loss in utility is to assume that each voter is a property owner and that the value of this asset is diminished when the local government is inefficient. In other words, the voter, regardless of her own preferences with respect to x_j, suffers a loss in utility when x_j is provided above or below its socially efficient level.[22]

---

20 Ross and Yinger (1999) and Wilson (1999) provide useful reviews of the tax capitalization literature and its controversies.

21 The reasons why a government should care about the value of its tax base are not made explicit by Tiebout (1956). In my model, the mechanism is clear: Politicians maximize votes, and voters do not like policies that harm their property values.

22 The tax capitalization literature is primarily concerned with the possibility that property values are harmed when taxes are *too high*, not too low. Rewriting (8) in such a way would not alter the conclusions reached later.

The implications of allowing inefficient policies to harm voters are twofold. First, voters in groups other than j now have an additional reason to oppose excessive spending on x_j. Not only do they pay the direct costs of the additional taxes required to finance x_j, but they also suffer the indirect costs of a loss in their property values. At the same time, groups other than j now have a reason to support some spending on x_j because if it is provided at an inefficiently low level, their property values will suffer; higher taxes are offset by rising property values when spending on x_j is increased from a level that is inefficiently low. For voters in group j, the response is analogous. Group j voters now have a disincentive to demand spending on their own good that is too high; although they would receive more of their preferred service, their property values would suffer as a result of the departure from efficiency. Simultaneously, group j voters now have a double incentive to demand increases in x_j if it is being provided at a level that is too low; their property values increase and they get more of the service that benefits them. I believe these incentives are the crux of the Tiebout model.

The aggregate effects of adding a penalty for deviations from efficient service provision on the political equilibria under general-purpose and single-function government are depicted in Figure 3.5. First, remember that the socially efficient level of service provision on each x_j is unchanged; this is by design. What has changed is that the candidate now suffers lower marginal political costs (i.e., lost votes) and garners larger marginal political benefits when she proposes increasing spending from a level that was initially too low. On the other hand, the candidate now endures greater marginal political costs and receives smaller marginal political benefits when she proposes raising spending above the efficient level. In other words, the MPB and MPC curves both pivot on their axes, becoming steeper compared to the previous scenario when the voter's utility was defined by (1) rather than (8). In Figure 3.5, the thin curves represent MPB and MPC in the scenario without tax capitalization, and the thick curves represent MPB and MPC with capitalization.

The equilibrium policy under general-purpose government is unchanged, trivially, because the socially efficient policy is unchanged. Therefore, $x_{Gj}^{T*} = x_{Gj}^* = x_{Wj}^*$, where x_{Gj}^{T*} denotes equilibrium spending on good j under general-purpose government with capitalization (T is for Tiebout). Importantly, however, note that $x_{Sj}^{T*} < x_{Sj}^*$, where x_{Sj}^{T*} represents equilibrium spending under single-function government with capitalization. Capitalization decreases overspending under single-function governments because the j group's utility increases less, while the utility for groups other than j declines more, with each dollar of spending beyond the social optimum. Therefore, the vote-maximizing position involves

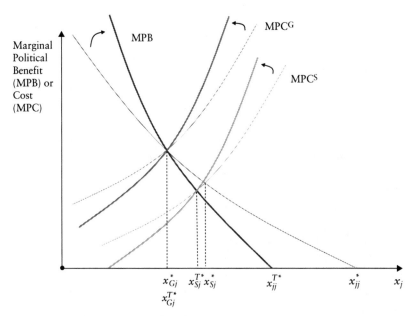

Figure 3.5. Vote Maximization with Tiebout Competition

Note: Thin lines indicate costs and benefits without tax capitalization; thick lines indicate costs and benefits with capitalization.

lower overall spending on x_j. In addition, $x_{jj}^{T*} < x_{jj}^*$. In other words, even when only group j votes, spending is lower with capitalization than in its absence. The point where *MPB* crosses the *X*-axis, denoted x_{jj}^{T*}, is where the marginal value of an additional dollar of spending on x_j, as perceived by a member of group j, is just equal to the marginal direct costs of taxation plus the marginal indirect costs associated with capitalization. Group j's ideal level of spending, $x_{jj}^{T*} < x_{jj}^*$, is lower by the implied value of capitalization

Clearly, capitalization works to constrain overspending in single-function governments by imposing a penalty for deviating from the socially optimal policy. An obvious question, then, is whether capitalization can ever be a sufficiently powerful force to completely constrain overspending and guarantee socially efficient policy under single-function government. The answer depends on the size of the interest groups. To understand why, let us suppose that, starting from the socially optimal level of spending, a member of group j seeks an increase in spending on x_j that satisfies the following first-order condition: $B'(x_j) - 1/NgC'(x_j) = 0$, where again g indicates the extent to which excess spending on x_j is translated into decreased property values. For example, a value of $g = 2$ would indicate that each dollar in excess spending results in a dollar of lost property value, effectively doubling the costs of providing x_j. How large would g have to be in order for a member of group j not to want to spend beyond the social optimum? We know from (4) that the socially optimal level of spending satisfies $B'(x_j) - C'(x_j)/N_j = 0$. Therefore, only if $g \geq N/N_j$ would a member of group j not want to spend beyond the social optimum. If group j composed half of the population, for example, g would need to be at least 2; if j were one-third of the total population, g would have to be at least 3, and so forth. The best empirical estimates available suggest that g is in the range of 1.15 to 1.60, and no credible study of which I am aware has ever produced an estimate of g greater than 2.[23] Therefore, capitalization might be a sufficient force to suppress attempts by a majority group to exploit a minority, but it will almost certainly never be sufficient to prevent a minority from exploiting the majority.

By way of illustration, let us take the previous case of selective participation in school board elections (Moe 2006a) to the extreme and assume that *only* district employees vote in the election. Presumably, district employees prefer higher salaries, more generous benefits, and easier working conditions for themselves than the average citizen not employed by the district might endorse. Vote-maximizing candidates know the electorate and cater to their desires. The question is, how high would district employees like to set spending if they had complete control over the decision? Assuming that no one else votes, there are only two countervailing forces working against the desire to increase spending. First, whatever benefits the employees receive from higher spending are at least partially offset by the additional taxes they must pay. Second, capitalization now means that the benefits of higher spending are also partially offset by decreases in their property values.

Suppose, in this completely stylized example, that district employees compose 10 percent of the population. In order to deliver $100 in additional benefits to themselves this year, therefore, they would only pay $10 in additional taxes, with nonemployees paying the remaining $90. At the same time, the $10 tax increase will be capitalized into the group's property values at some rate, g. Suppose that taxes were completely capitalized ($g = 2$), so that the additional taxes reduced property values for employees by $10. Effectively, it now costs the employees $20 to get $100 in benefits, and it now costs society $200. If the tax increase is expected to be permanent, then property values will actually decline by more than $10. Property values will decline by the present value of the entire future

---

23 In their review of the literature, Ross and Yinger (1999, p. 2032) state that most credible estimates indicate that taxes are capitalized into property values at a rate of 15 to 60 percent.

stream of additional tax payments. However, if the tax increase is expected to be permanent, then spending will also increase permanently, and the employees will expect to receive a continued stream of benefits into the future, which is greater than $100. As long as the discount rates for taxes and benefits are the same, and there is no reason that they should not be, the employee's calculation is unaffected.

The important point is that the employee's role as taxpayer and property owner weighs against her desire to spend more in the role of beneficiary of school spending. However, as long as the employees, as a group, compose a relatively small share of the population, the benefits of increased spending will tend to outweigh the costs (to them) of higher taxes and lower property values. The more significant constraint will be the threat of increased political participation by nonemployees unhappy with the increased taxes and lower property values that *they* incur to finance the burgeoning school district budget. When these nonemployees turn out in larger numbers, candidates will adjust their platforms accordingly, putting a cap on spending.

It should now be apparent that the reason tax capitalization does not fully suppress overspending by single-function governments is that capitalization is itself merely another instance of diffuse costs and concentrated benefits. That is, when property values suffer as a result of the actions of one group, all the overlapping groups share the adverse effects. The group that benefits from the increased provision of its good bears only a fraction of the costs associated with its overspending. In this respect, capitalization can be thought of as a second-order common-pool problem. That is, the same sorts of common-pool problems that provide the incentives for individual groups to overspend in the first place also dilute the effects of the competitive counterpressures that are thought to punish deviations from efficiency. The incentives for efficiency become weaker as more single-function governments share the same tax base.

While the analysis of capitalization I have just presented is admittedly oversimplified and fails to portray many of the complexities of the housing market, I believe it is true to the heart of the Tiebout model and captures the fundamental mechanism at work therein. The primary incentive for government efficiency in the Tiebout model is the elasticity of the tax base. But the common-pool problems associated with concurrent taxation weaken this incentive because any negative consequences arising from socially undesirable policies are also spread among the various groups sharing the tax base. As a result, Tiebout competition is likely to reduce, but never eliminate, the overspending bias in single-function governments.

3.3 NONTECHNICAL SUMMARY

At heart, my theory of special-purpose government is quite simple. Governments are run by politicians, whose main goal is to get elected. In order to win elections, the politicians propose policies that (they hope) will please voters. Specifically, the politicians choose how much to spend on several different public services. For each dollar they spend, they must raise a dollar in taxes to pay for it. Voters, for their part, like spending but dislike taxes. Moreover, voters are heterogeneous, and there are groups of them that like some public services more than others. For example, some voters want generous spending on schools, some want more money to go to transportation, and so on. I call a group of voters who care more than usual about a particular service an *interest group* for that service.

When there is only one government that controls all the public services, the politician must make trade-offs when deciding how much to spend on each service. Each dollar she spends on buses wins her some votes from the transportation interest group, but the taxes she must raise to pay for the buses cost her votes from other groups who do not use public transit. She keeps spending on buses right up to the point at which the votes she wins from the transportation group are equal to the votes she loses from everyone else. She repeats this calculation for every public service, and collectively these choices become her policy platform. At the end of this procedure, there is no way the politician could reallocate her budget that would win her more votes than it would cost her. In other words, she has found her vote-maximizing platform. Of course, under this final platform, the groups who are more likely to vote get more spending on their preferred services.

Now suppose the same politician is running for election to a government that controls only one service, say a transportation district. Would her platform be different? If the same people turn out to vote, no. Recall that she had already found the point at which the last dollar spent on transportation cost her just as many votes as it won her. So, if she proposed raising spending, she would lose more votes from the general public than she would win from the bus riders. If she proposed less spending, she would lose more votes from the bus riders than she would gain from the general taxpayers. Nothing has changed. So, the first important result is that if the voters are the same for general-purpose and special-purpose jurisdictions, then, for each service, the special-purpose jurisdiction will select the same policy as the general-purpose jurisdiction. The choice of institutions does not matter in this case.

But suppose different people vote in general-purpose versus special-purpose elections. In particular, suppose that the transportation interest group is more likely to turn out for the transportation district election, the library interest group for the library election, and so on. By the same token, the library voters are less likely to turn out for the transportation election and the transportation voters are less likely to turn out for the library election.[24] Now the politician's platform will be different. If the candidate proposes spending a little more on buses—relative to the optimal amount for a general-purpose government—she will gain more votes from the transportation group than she will lose from the other groups, since the other groups are less likely to turn out in the transportation election anyway. Of course, as the politician ratchets up spending on transportation—and, by necessity, the taxes needed to pay for it—the other groups will start to turn out in larger numbers. At some point, the additional votes from the transportation group from another dollar of spending will be just equal to the negative votes from the other taxpayers. And that point will be the politician's platform in the special-function election. So the second important result is that, when voting is selective, spending on any given function will be higher for a special-purpose government than for a general-purpose government.

The underlying reason that spending is higher for special-purpose jurisdictions is that the benefits of their spending are concentrated on a particular group, while the costs are spread across all tax payers. Suppose, for example, that bus riders constitute 10 percent of the population and get to charge taxes to subsidize bus fares. For every $10 in taxes, $1 of it comes from the bus riders themselves and $9 come from the other voters.[25] So, for each $1 they pay in taxes themselves, they get $10 in benefits. Obviously, they will be willing to raise a lot of taxes. Now suppose there is an election to decide whether to lower the taxes. If the tax is reset to $0, the bus riders lose $9 in value each (remember, they were paying $1 in taxes themselves), while the other voters gain $1 in value each. The average bus rider has nine times more reasons to turn out than the other voters.

The same situation is repeated for all the other services. Of course, in the context of some other election, say for libraries, the bus riders will be the ones paying taxes but receiving no benefits. If there are enough other specialized jurisdictions doing the same thing, the bus riders may actually be worse off than they would have been under a general-purpose government. For example, they may be paying $1 in taxes to each of

24 I use *turnout* loosely here to refer to casting a vote in the relevant race. Some individuals might not come to the polls at all. Others might come but fail to cast a vote for some offices. There are reasons to think that even if the elections were held on the same day, the bus riders would be more likely to vote in the bus election and the bookworms would be more likely to vote in the library election.

25 Assuming everyone has equal income and taxes are lump sum. This is just a toy example, so I am taking some liberties.

20 different jurisdictions. They get their $9 worth of value in bus subsidies but are still out $11. They would be better off if none of the jurisdictions engaged in this practice. But of course, the bus riders would not want to unilaterally lower bus subsidies. This is the sort of situation I have labeled a fiscal common-pool problem. There are other interesting details in the model, but a basic understanding of the fiscal common-pool problem is all that is necessary to follow the remainder of the book.

3.4 WHY SO MANY GOVERNMENTS?

If jurisdictional overlap with concurrent taxation generates a fiscal common-pool problem, why are special-purpose jurisdictions the most numerous and fastest-growing type of local government? In other words, if special-purpose governments create such problems, who creates them and why? There are several possible answers that can be accommodated within the theoretical framework just proposed.

The answer that flows most naturally from the fiscal common-pool theory is that each interest group would rather have the service it cares about provided by a single-function jurisdiction than a general-purpose government.[26] Given that the barriers to creating districts are relatively low in most cases, it is in the interest of each group to seek the creation of a separate jurisdiction to control its preferred service.[27] And the same issues of selective participation in district elections, described previously, can be expected to plague the process of creating the districts themselves. In other words, each group has a disproportionate interest in turning out to vote in the referendum creating a separate jurisdiction for its service and less incentive to turn out to block the creation of districts for other services. These incentives for selective participation will be even greater when the formation referenda are held on separate days from other major elections, as is common. So, the simplest explanation for the proliferation of single-function jurisdictions is that the ex ante institutional choice process inherits the same prisoners' dilemma problem that characterizes the fiscal policy process ex post.[28] That is, even if every group recognized that a fiscal common-pool problem would be the

---

26 For a related argument on the question of confederation versus separatism, see Cremer and Palfrey (1999).

27 This argument is consonant with Burns (1994), who suggests that special districts are created to deliver public benefits for private purposes. She focuses on the role of real estate developers, while my theory applies more broadly to special interest groups of all kinds.

28 For a general discussion of the idea that the choice of institutions inherits the same conflicts that the institutions themselves are designed to solve, see Riker (1980).

end result, each would nevertheless have a dominant strategy to seek the creation of its own special-function policy jurisdiction.

If my interest group story is correct, then an obvious question is, why has some higher authority not stepped in to put a stop to the spread of special districts? The answer is that states are starting to do just that. In fact, by 1992, five western states had created commissions tasked with limiting the creation of special districts (California, Nevada, New Mexico, Oregon, and Washington) (Liebmann 2002). While there have been some notable successes in limiting the formation of new districts, eliminating existing districts has proved notoriously difficult (Little Hoover Commission 2000).

Two additional, more positive, explanations for the growth in special-function jurisdictions are derived from the hypothesis that general-purpose governments, for one reason or another, spend *too little*. One reason for underspending by general-purpose governments has already been suggested in Section 3.2.1. Namely, there may well be some projects or services that, although desirable in the sense that social benefits outweigh social costs, nevertheless would fail under majority voting in a general-purpose government because those benefits accrue to a minority.[29] A special district devoted to providing such a service—and insulated from competition with other services due to selective participation—may enhance social welfare by enabling the minority to receive its desired outcome.

A final possibility is that special-purpose districts are created as a response to undertaxation by general-purpose governments induced not by majority voting, but by interjurisdictional competition. While I have just presented a model in which political competition leads to efficient tax and service policies by general-purpose governments, there is a school of thought, associated with the influential work of Wallace Oates (e.g., 1972, 1999), holding that competition for mobile businesses leads general-purpose governments to provide less than efficient levels of services. The central idea is that local communities have to keep taxes low to compete for business investment, and in so doing, they may underprovide services to their residents.

The problem of competition-induced undertaxation could be incorporated into the model from this chapter by assuming that there is an additional group, call it "business," that pays taxes but does not benefit

---

29 As explained in Section 3.2.1, the finding that socially desirable projects fail under general-purpose government requires departing from the probabilistic voting model used throughout the rest of this chapter. In the probabilistic voting framework, all services are set at their socially desirable level (assuming equal turnout for all groups).

directly from the services that the other interest groups desire. When taxes are raised to provide such services, at least some fraction of the business group will relocate to a more tax-friendly jurisdiction, thus reducing the tax base of the original jurisdiction. Now the other interest groups will worry about driving out the business group, and its tax revenue, and therefore they will constrain their spending demands accordingly, possibly to a level below which marginal benefits equal marginal costs (Oates 1972, p. 143). In this situation, introducing a special-function jurisdiction, which provides a countervailing incentive for each group to overspend, may enhance social welfare by causing an increase in a tax rate that would otherwise be inefficiently low.

The latter two explanations suggest that special-function governments are created as a response to undertaxation—due either to majority voting or interjurisdictional competition—within general-purpose governments. Even when this is the case, however, the challenge remains to prevent the interest group, once having established control of a single-function government with powers of generalized taxation, from spending excessively on its group-specific service. That is, while establishing a specialized district may *solve* a problem of underprovision, it may at the same time *create* a new fiscal common-pool problem leading to overprovision. This situation recalls Madison's famous dilemma in *Federalist* No. 51: "In framing a government to be administered by men over men, the great difficulty lies in this: you must first enable the government to control the governed; and in the next place oblige it to control itself." Untangling the interrelated problems of underprovision and overprovision, jurisdictional overlap as solution and problem, is difficult both theoretically and empirically. I will return to these issues in the remaining chapters.

3.5 CONCLUSION

The theory of special-purpose government presented in this chapter leads to a simple comparative static: The size of the aggregate budget in a community increases as the number of special-purpose jurisdictions increases. As I suggested previously, this result is consistent with existing fiscal common-pool models developed in other contexts, which suggest that an overspending bias emerges when authority over fiscal policy is shared by multiple officials or jurisdictions serving different constituencies. In the next chapter, I test this hypothesis by studying the response of county area spending to changes in the number of overlapping jurisdictions over time.

4

Piling On: The Problem of Concurrent Taxation

The preceding chapters have set the stage for an empirical analysis of public finance under jurisdictional overlap. In Chapters 1 and 2, I argued that institutional changes over the past 50 years challenge Tiebout's (1956) vision of the local public sector as a competitive marketplace. The rise of special-purpose districts as the most common and fastest-growing institution of local government in the United States means that spatially overlapping jurisdictions, not the fragmented territorial monopolies envisioned by Tiebout and his followers, dominate the contemporary local government landscape. In Chapter 3, I presented a formal argument that this sort of jurisdictional overlap leads to higher tax rates and fiscal externalities among governments that share a common tax base. These problems arise because individual jurisdictions seek to provide benefits to special-interest constituencies while the costs are borne by all taxpayers. The present chapter is dedicated to providing empirical evidence of the existence and magnitude of this *overlap effect*.

4.1 MEASURING JURISDICTIONAL OVERLAP

The model developed in Chapter 3 yields a simple hypothesis: There will be more aggregate spending, and hence higher taxation, for a given bundle of services the greater the number of functionally specialized jurisdictions involved in its provision. To test this hypothesis, ideally, one would want a comprehensive data set of the boundaries of all governmental entities in some set of geographic units, say counties or metropolitan statistical areas (MSAs). In addition, one would want data on the tax rates charged by each jurisdiction and the ability to compute the sum of tax rates for each distinct overlapping combination of jurisdictions. Finally, one would want precise data on the type, quantity, and quality of services provided by each jurisdiction. Unfortunately, such data do not exist. The most significant data limitation is the absence of any comprehensive national data set on the boundaries of special districts. Although maps of individual districts can often be obtained on a case-by-case basis, even this is not always possible.[1] Even the COG, the most bountiful source of data on special districts, does not provide such basic facts as the total population or land area served by individual districts. Without knowing the boundaries of special districts, it is not possible to measure jurisdictional overlap directly as the number of layers of government that concurrently tax a given parcel of land.

The COG does, however, provide comprehensive data on the number of special districts and municipalities operating in each U.S. county, as well as their finances. As explained by Bollens (1957) in the passage cited in Chapter 2, Section 2.7, the potential for jurisdictional overlap is a function of the number of special districts relative to municipalities, all else equal. Therefore, various measures of jurisdictional overlap can be computed from the COG data. I will posit several different measures and explain their advantages and disadvantages before settling on the specific measure that is used in the remainder of this chapter. I emphasize at the outset, however, that nothing hinges on my choice of how to measure jurisdictional overlap. As demonstrated in the Methodological Appendix, Section 2.2, all the different measures of jurisdictional overlap yield roughly comparable results in any of the analyses to be presented.

Perhaps the simplest indication of jurisdictional overlap in a county is the *total number of overlapping districts* in the county.[2] A limitation of this measure is that large counties may be subdivided into several smaller communities, each with a smaller number of districts. For instance, one county might have 10 cities within it, each with one overlapping jurisdiction. Another county might have only one city with 10 districts overlapping it. A simple count of overlapping districts treats these two counties

---

1 Burns (1994, pp. 12–13) provides an entertaining account of her ultimately unsuccessful attempt to obtain information on the boundaries of all the special districts in just one county.

2 Town (also called *township*) governments present a special case. First, town governments exist in only 20 states. Second, in some of these states, towns have the character of municipalities, while in others they operate more like special districts. Specifically, towns may overlap the territory of municipalities in 11 states (Connecticut, Illinois, Indiana, Kansas, Michigan, Minnesota, Missouri, Nebraska, New York, Ohio, and Vermont). In the nine remaining states, towns are territorially separate from municipalities, with no overlap between the two kinds of units (Maine, Massachusetts, New Hampshire, New Jersey, North Dakota, Pennsylvania, Rhode Island, South Dakota, and Wisconsin). For details, see Bureau of the Census (1994). Thus, in the 11 overlap states I count towns as overlapping districts. In the nine territorially exclusive states, I count towns as municipalities. I compute the number of overlapping jurisdictions in a county as the sum of special districts, school districts, and, where appropriate, townships.

the same way, although my theory clearly predicts that the second county should have a more severe common-pool problem.

Counting the number of overlapping districts may not always provide an accurate picture of the role they play in the local public sector. For instance, one county may have a few districts that provide mosquito abatement in summer months, while another may have the same number of districts that provide major urban services such as fire protection, parks, or sanitation. An alternative is to compute the fraction of expenditures (or taxes) controlled by special districts, which should better reflect their importance in the local public sector. Conversely, the fraction of expenditures controlled by municipalities should reflect the extent to which services are controlled by general-purpose, nonoverlapping governments. The greater the share of taxation accounted for by one government, the more likely that government is to internalize the effects of its policies on the aggregate tax base. All such measures based on the actual taxes or expenditures of individual governments present potential endogeneity problems. For instance, counties where special districts overspend, for whatever reason, will have a higher fraction of expenditures controlled by special districts. Thus, a positive correlation may be observed between the fraction of expenditures controlled by special districts and aggregate taxation even in the absence of a common-pool problem.

None of the measures of jurisdictional overlap discussed thus far makes distinctions among the many different types of special districts that may exist from place to place. Such distinctions are important because the propensity for territorial overlap is highest among jurisdictions performing different functions. As discussed in Chapter 1, municipalities never overlap each other's territory, whereas special districts may overlap municipalities and each other. However, it is less common for special districts of the same type to overlap. School districts generally do not overlap other school districts, nor sanitation districts other sanitation districts, and so on.[3] So, 10 school districts in a county likely represent just one layer of government, whereas a county with 10 different functional types of districts may well have 10 layers of government. Counting the number of distinct functional types of districts in a county thus represents another measure of jurisdictional overlap. Indeed, if each district type covers the entire county, then the number of functional layers corresponds perfectly with the notion of jurisdictional overlap introduced in Chapter 1. To the extent that different functional layers cover

---

3 This is not to say that overlap of districts of the same type is impossible. A common situation in which jurisdictions of the same type overlap is when regional and local parks districts provide recreation facilities in the same service area.

only segments of the county, however, the number of layers will be a noisy measure of jurisdictional overlap. In addition, relating the number of functional layers of government in a county to total expenditures risks conflating jurisdictional overlap with the diversity of functional performance.

A better measure of jurisdictional overlap, I suggest, is the *number of overlapping districts per municipality*. This measure approximates the number of jurisdictions that overlap the average city within a county. An important advantage of this measure is that the denominator encapsulates horizontal fragmentation (the number of municipalities), while the numerator represents vertical layering (the number of single-function governments).[4] Therefore, adding a municipality will lower the overlap ratio, which captures the Tiebout-inspired notion that more municipalities instill greater competition in an area. By the same token, adding special districts increases the ratio, reflecting the notion that jurisdictional overlap rises as the number of districts overlapping a given territory is increased. The shortcoming of this metric is that it will overestimate the degree of overlap in cases where many small special districts overlap only a portion of the territory of a general-purpose government.

Each of these metrics is a plausible measure of jurisdictional overlap. The Methodological Appendix, Table A5, shows that all the measures are significantly correlated with one another. In other words, the various measures tap into a common underlying phenomenon, although they are hardly perfect substitutes for one another. If the choice of one measure of jurisdictional overlap over another made an important difference for the analysis to follow, further investigation into more subtle differences among the measures would clearly be warranted. As it stands, however, all of the measures produce similar statistical and substantive results, which can be seen in the Methodological Appendix, Table A6. Therefore, for the analysis presented here, I chose the measure that corresponds most closely to the theoretical model presented in Chapter 3, namely, the number of overlapping jurisdictions per municipality. To be precise, I define the overlapping jurisdictions (the numerator) as special districts, school districts, territorially overlapping townships, and the county. I define municipalities (the denominator) as cities and territorially exclusive towns. Because the ratio of overlapping jurisdictions per municipality has a long right tail—the median value is 3, while the 99th percentile value is 21—I take the natural log of the value as my measure

---

4 I note that similar results can be obtained by entering the two variables separately into the models. The commonality of the two approaches arises because $\ln(x/y) = \ln(x) - \ln(y)$.

of jurisdictional overlap. I shall hereafter refer to this variable generally as *jurisdictional overlap*.

My primary dependent variable is general own-source revenue per capita. In other words, the numerator is the sum of own-source revenue across all governments in a county and the denominator is county population.[5] Own-source revenue refers to all locally raised revenue and excludes intergovernmental transfers. It can be considered a rough representation of the aggregate tax burden in the county. Own-source revenue accounts for 58 percent of all local government general revenue during my study period, with the remainder coming from federal and state aid. My results are substantively unchanged if I use the natural log of own-source revenue per capita as the dependent variable rather than the dollar value.

4.2   ESTIMATION STRATEGY

When attempting to estimate the effects of institutions on fiscal outcomes, simultaneous causation is an obvious concern (see Persson and Tabellini 2003, ch. 5). In other words, it is possible that special districts are created from a desire to spend more, rather than, or in addition to, being a cause of increased spending via the common-pool mechanism described previously. If that is the case, then measures of jurisdictional overlap may be correlated with the errors in an ordinary least squares (OLS) regression, leading to biased estimates. To a large degree, concerns about reverse causation should be allayed by the fact that variation in the extent of jurisdictional overlap is determined largely by differences in long-standing state laws that make it easier or harder to create overlapping jurisdictions. For example, a set of state dummy variables explains about two-thirds of the variation in jurisdictional overlap across counties and over time.[6] Nevertheless, concerns about possible endogeneity can be addressed directly, and I do so in two ways. First, in analyses presented subsequently, I provide several empirical tests that substantively distinguish the common-pool explanation from other arguments based on reverse causation. Second, I address concerns about endogeneity econometrically through the use of fixed effects and instrumental variables analysis.

The panel structure of the data, with each county observed at five-year intervals from 1972 to 2002, allows me to employ fixed effects

---

5   In principle, the aggregate tax rate is an ideal dependent variable. However, due to variation in assessment practices across jurisdictions and complexity of tax codes, calculating the effective tax rate in a county is prohibitively difficult.

6   A regression of county-level jurisdictional overlap from 1972 to 2002 on a set of state dummy variables yields an adjusted R-squared of 0.63, with 21,198 observations.

estimation.[7] Fixed effects estimation is comparable to including dummy variables for all but one county or, equivalently, subtracting the county-level mean of each variable from each observation. The advantage of the fixed effects model is that identification comes from changes within counties over time. (For this reason, fixed effects is sometimes called the *within estimator*.) Thus, whereas a cross-sectional analysis effectively asks whether counties with more overlapping jurisdictions have higher taxes than other counties with fewer overlapping jurisdictions, the fixed effects analysis asks whether counties have higher taxes during those years in which jurisdictional overlap is higher than average. In other words, jurisdictional overlap will have explanatory power in the fixed effects model only if individual counties have spending above (below) their own mean during the years when jurisdictional overlap is above (below) its mean for those counties. The fixed effects effectively control for all observable *and unobservable* county-level attributes that do not change over time. Therefore, omitted variables such as state laws, local culture and institutions, geography, and so forth will not bias fixed effects estimates to the extent that they do not change significantly over time. In addition, the inclusion of time effects—that is, dummy variables for all but one year—controls for any secular changes that affect all counties, such as inflation and other broad economic forces.

Figure 4.1 shows the source of identification in the fixed-effects model. For each county, I computed the difference in jurisdictional overlap between 1972 and 2002. Because jurisdictional overlap is measured in log form, the difference is roughly equal to a percentage. With the fixed effects specification, I am essentially trying to explain changes in spending with these changes in jurisdictional overlap within counties over time, rather than trying to explain the level of spending with the level of jurisdictional overlap. The map demonstrates that changes in jurisdictional overlap occurred throughout the nation, so the results should not be driven by idiosyncratic regional or state trends.[8]

The FE estimator does not rule out serial correlation in the errors. Simply put, it is likely that the residuals for a given county are correlated over time. Therefore, it is not proper to treat multiple years of data from the same county as independent observations. To address serial correlation, I use robust standard errors clustered by county (Arellano 1987; White 1980). The resulting standard errors are robust to arbitrary forms

---

7 See Wooldridge (2002, ch. 10) for an explanation for fixed effects and other panel data models.

8 The map also raises the issue of spatial correlation in the data. I examine this issue in the Methodological Appendix, Section A.2.2, and demonstrate that the results are robust to methods that allow for spatial correlation in the errors.

Figure 4.1. Within-County Variation in Jurisdictional Overlap, 1972–2002

Note: The values in the map represent ln(Jurisdictional Overlap in 2002) – ln(Jurisdictional Overlap in 1972).

Legend
(.45,2.65]
(.29,.45]
(.19,.29]
(.13,.19]
(.08,.13]
(.03,.08]
(0,.03]
(-.07]
(-.22,-.07]
[-2.30,-.22]
No municipalities or missing data

of serial correlation within counties, as well as to arbitrary forms of heteroskedasticity.[9] While there are strong theoretical reasons to choose the FE model with clustered standard errors for this analysis (e.g., see Bertrand, Duflo, and Mullainathan 2004), I emphasize that the results do not depend on this particular econometric choice. The Methodological Appendix shows that similar results are obtained from several other plausible estimation strategies.

4.3   VARIABLES, DATA SOURCES, AND CASE SELECTION

The fixed effects account for all attributes of the counties that do not vary over the study period, which alleviates many concerns about omitted variable bias. However, it is important to control for those observable attributes of counties that do change over time and that may be associated with local taxation and the level of jurisdictional overlap. Therefore, I use a set of control variables with a strong foundation in the literature.

The first control is income per capita. Following Wagner's "law," the expectation is that demand for government services increases with income (Musgrave and Peacock 1958). Next, I control for several population characteristics that may reflect tastes for public goods (e.g., Cutler, Elmendorf, and Zeckhauser 1993). I include the proportion of the population under 18 years of age to control for demand for education, a large component of local spending. I also include the fraction of the population over 65, as it is often argued that the older population prefers lower spending on education (Poterba 1997). On the other hand, there may be additional costs associated with serving an elderly population.

It is also important to control for the racial and income heterogeneity of the population. Alesina, Baqir, and Easterly (1999) argue that population heterogeneity leads to increased pressure for group-specific spending programs but fewer nonexcludable public goods. While their theoretical model is ambiguous as to the net effects, their empirical results show a positive association between ethnic heterogeneity and total expenditures and taxes. The lack of comparable racial and ethnic data in

---

9 Proper estimation of standard errors in panel data models is a topic that has received increasing attention over the past few years. Wooldridge (2006) provides a useful review of the issue and of estimation techniques. Peterson (2007) provides extensive simulation results comparing different techniques, which favor the use of clustered standard errors for panel data. I have tried several different methods for calculating standard errors and found clustering generally to be the most conservative approach for my data (i.e., producing the largest standard errors). Details are provided in the Methodological Appendix, Section A.2.2.

the U.S. Census over time makes it impossible for me to compute the precise ethnic fragmentation measure used by Alesina and his coauthors (1999). As a proxy, I use the percentage of the county population that is nonwhite.[10]

I control for county population to account for possible economies of scale in the provision of public services. In other words, it may be cheaper, on a per capita basis, to provide public services to a large population than a small one, all else equal. At the same time, it may be that economies of scale enable counties with large populations to provide a wider variety of services than would be feasible in a sparsely populated area. In addition to the level of population, I also control for the population growth rate over the preceding five years. Rapidly developing areas may have new infrastructure needs that temporarily boost expenditure levels. However, prior research (e.g., Cutler et al. 1993) has also shown that there is a lag before per capita expenditures catch up with new population. Given the theoretical ambiguities in both cases, I do not have a priori expectations as to the sign of the coefficients for either of these population variables.

In addition to own-source revenue, the other major sources of revenue for local governments are state and federal aid. Presumably, increased receipts from these outside sources will dampen the need for local taxation. The extent to which intergovernmental aid offsets local taxation, however, is a matter of some dispute in the literature.[11] I control for state and federal aid per capita to account for these factors. Because it is likely that local revenue and outside aid are jointly determined—that is, the amount of outside aid is influenced in part by local revenue raised, and vice versa—I use five-year lags of state and federal aid rather than their contemporaneous values. While lagging these variables addresses endogeneity concerns, I note that the main results pertaining to jurisdictional overlap do not change importantly if I use contemporaneous values of intergovernmental aid, if I instrument current values with lagged values, or if I simply exclude intergovernmental aid from the analysis. Details are provided in the Methodological Appendix, Table A9.

Finally, I control for the functions performed by the governments in each county. Long-standing differences across states in the responsibilities assigned to local governments will be subsumed in the fixed effects, but it remains important to control for possible changes in functional

10 I am able to compute the Alesina, Baqir, and Easterly (1999) ethnic fragmentation measure using 1990 census data. In that year, the correlation between ethnic fragmentation and percent nonwhite at the county level is 0.85.

11 See Bailey and Connolly (1998) and Hines and Thaler (1995) for discussions of the flypaper effect.

performance over time. For instance, an obvious concern is that taxes increase when a new government is added in a county because it provides a new function. I want to distinguish such changes in functional performance from changes in taxation arising from increasing common-pool externalities. To do so, I use three approaches to control for functional performance (more on this later). First, I compute a functional performance index that represents the amount that would be spent by the median county providing the same bundle of services. Second, I include a full set of dummy variables for each function tracked in the COG. Third, I restrict the analysis to expenditures on a set of common functions performed in nearly all counties. Each of these approaches is discussed in greater detail in Section 4.4.

My main data sources are various editions of the COG and the *Census of Population and Housing* (CPH), both published by the U.S. Census Bureau.[12] Although the COG was conducted as early as 1942, comparable data with a full set of functional spending variables are available only from 1972 on. I exclude Alaska from the analysis because that state uniquely relies on boroughs rather than counties, and boroughs do not cover the entire land area of the state. In addition, a total of 110 observations from 18 counties did not contain data in both the COG and CPH and were therefore dropped from the analysis. Finally, I dropped 447 observations from 61 counties that had no incorporated municipalities in one or more years. Beginning with a total of 3,138 counties in the COG data set, I retain a total of 3,032 counties for the analysis after deleting Alaska and the other cases. The main analysis covers the period 1972 to 2002, during which each county is observed up to seven times at five-year intervals, yielding a total of 21,198 county-by-year observations. The Methodological Appendix, Section A.1.2, provides details of the case selection as well as summary statistics for all the variables used in this chapter.

4.4 RESULTS

The central prediction of the fiscal common-pool model—that aggregate taxes and spending should be higher where there are more overlapping jurisdictions—is tested in Table 4.1. As discussed previously, all the models include county and year fixed effects and use standard errors clustered by county. Model (1) regresses aggregate county own-source

---

12 I am grateful to Steve Ansolabehere and Jim Snyder for sharing their county CPH data with me. Values for CPH variables are linearly interpolated for years between the decennial censuses.

Table 4.1. *Jurisdictional Overlap and Own-Source Revenue*

	(1)	(2)
Jurisdictional overlap	148.07	140.67
	(37.12)***	(35.18)***
Per capita income		0.03
		(0.00)***
ln(population)		31.07
		(38.24)
Five-year change in population		−294.56
		(90.05)***
Percent nonwhite		181.60
		(158.91)
Percent age ≤18		611.41
		(481.68)
Percent age ≥65		424.14
		(524.25)
Federal aid, five-year lag		0.03
		(0.03)
State aid, five-year lag		−0.08
		(0.04)**
Constant	834.49	305.99
	(44.81)***	(418.79)
R-squared (within)	0.26	0.28
Observations	21,198	21.198
# of clusters	3,032	3.032

Notes: The dependent variable is general own-source revenue per capita. All dollar values are CPI-adjusted to year 2002 dollars. Standard errors, clustered by county, are reported in parentheses. All models include county and year fixed effects.
*significant at 10%, **significant at 5%, ***significant at 1%.

revenue against jurisdictional overlap, measured as the natural log of the number of overlapping jurisdictions per municipality, with no other controls except the county and year fixed effects. The coefficient is highly significant statistically and in the expected (positive) direction. Model (2) adds the full set of time-varying control variables described previously. Controlling for these additional county attributes does not notably affect the estimated effect of jurisdictional overlap on own-source revenue. Thus, it does not appear that jurisdictional overlap is simply standing in for some other attribute of the counties under study.

The estimated effect of jurisdictional overlap on own-source revenue is not only highly significant statistically but also substantively consequential. To illustrate the potential impact of jurisdictional overlap, consider the point estimate in model (2) of $141. The 25th percentile value of jurisdictional overlap is 0.69, and the 75th percentile value is 1.61, which is equivalent to two and five overlapping jurisdictions per municipality, respectively. Therefore, the coefficient indicates that increasing the extent of jurisdictional overlap in a county from the 25th to the 75th percentile—that is, increasing from two to five overlapping jurisdictions per municipality—results in a $130 increase in own-source revenue per capita.[13] To put this effect in context, consider that median own-source revenue in the sample is $1,150, so $130 represents an 11 percent increase. Moreover, compared to other possible measures of jurisdictional overlap, the one used here (log of overlapping jurisdictions per municipality) produces a fairly typical estimate of the common-pool effect on own-source revenue. The Methodological Appendix, Table A6, shows estimates of the common-pool effect based on each of the different measures of jurisdictional overlap described previously.

In addition to affirming the central prediction of my fiscal common-pool model, the results shown in Table 4.1 contain some evidence supportive of the Tiebout (1956) model of interjurisdictional competition. While the original Tiebout model makes no prediction as to the effect of competition on aggregate government spending, some (e.g., Brennan and Buchanan 1980, ch. 9) have interpreted the model as implying that spending will be lower where there are more competing general-purpose governments. The same prediction emerged from my model when I introduced tax capitalization resulting from interjurisdictional competition (see Section 3.2.3 in Chapter 3). The positive coefficient on the ratio of overlapping jurisdictions per municipality in Table 4.1 supports this prediction. That is, as the number of municipalities increases, the ratio declines, implying lower own-source revenue. Assuming that the level of horizontal (i.e., Tiebout) competition increases with the number of municipalities in a county, then these results support the basic prediction that interjurisdictional competition constrains spending. In sum, the positive coefficient on the ratio of overlapping jurisdictions per municipality can be interpreted as indicating that an increase in vertical overlap (the numerator) increases local taxation, while an increase in horizontal competition (the denominator) reduces local taxation. The existing literature has fixated on the horizontal dimension, while I seek to investigate the vertical dimension. But, as I demonstrated in Chapter 3, the two forces are not logically inconsistent or mutually exclusive.

---

13 That is, 1.61 − 0.69 = 0.92 × $141 = $130.

Several of the control variables in model (2) are highly significant and warrant explanation. Income per capita is highly positively correlated with county own-source revenue, meaning that more affluent counties spend more on public goods and services. Each dollar of increased per capita income results in about 2.7 cents of additional own-source revenue collected by local governments. The preceding five-year change in population is negatively related to own-source revenue per capita, suggesting that it may take time for aggregate spending to catch up with population growth (Cutler et al. 1993). Finally, when counties receive more intergovernmental revenue from the state, they raise less revenue from their own sources. The point estimate suggests each dollar of aid received from the state translates into 8 cents reduced from locally raised revenue.

The results presented in Table 4.1 provide support for the fiscal common-pool model: An increase in jurisdictional overlap is associated with a significant increase in local taxation. At the same time, however, these results may also be consistent with other theories of the local public sector. Three alternative explanations, in particular, may account for these findings. First, it may be that counties with more overlapping jurisdictions provide a greater range of public services, which accounts for higher spending. A second possibility is that special districts are created specifically to finance costly infrastructure construction, so that higher spending reflects greater capital investment rather than common-pool exploitation. Third, overlapping jurisdictions may be created as channels for spending increases when general-purpose governments face tax and expenditure limitations.

In the remainder of this chapter, I examine each of these alternative hypotheses in turn. I emphasize at the outset, however, that the various hypotheses are not inconsistent either with each other or with the fiscal common-pool model. Each explanation may account for an important aspect of local fiscal patterns. Thus, my objective is not to refute the alternative theories, but to demonstrate the robustness of the common-pool theory in accounting for the effects of jurisdictional overlap.

4.4.1 Functional Performance

One possible explanation for higher spending where there are more overlapping jurisdictions is that counties with more jurisdictions simply provide a broader array of government services. In other words, it is possible that the creation of a new special district represents the creation of a new service, rather than the transfer of authority over an existing service from a general-purpose to a special-function jurisdiction. It is unclear whether greater service variety is a challenge or a complement to the common-pool theory presented in Chapter 3. On the one hand, providing an increased array of services could produce increased spending quite apart from any common-pool effect. On the other hand, given the opportunity to deliver concentrated benefits with diffuse costs, an interest group desiring a new public service would have a strong incentive to seek the creation of a special district to provide it. In the latter case, an increasing array of services associated with jurisdictional overlap would comport with the common-pool model. In either case, it will be useful to disentangle the portion of the increase in the budget that is due to an increasing variety of services from the portion that is attributable to increased spending on a constant bundle of services.

As a first step, I compute a functional performance index (FPI), which sums nationwide median spending for each service provided in the county.[14] The FPI represents the amount a county area would spend if it spent the nationwide median amount on each service that is provided. The FPI is determined entirely by the mix of services provided in each county area: If the addition of a new layer of government coincides with the addition of a new service, the FPI will increase by the median amount spent on that service nationwide.

If jurisdictional overlap influences spending primarily by influencing functional performance, it should be strongly related to the FPI. To test this hypothesis, I regress jurisdictional overlap on the FPI, including county fixed effects and the usual set of control variables. Model (1) of Table 4.2 shows that the coefficient for jurisdictional overlap is both insignificant and substantively small when the FPI is the dependent variable. A one-unit increase in jurisdictional overlap results in only a (statistically insignificant) $7 increase in the FPI.

14 The FPI is defined as follows. For each functional spending category in the COG, I create a 0/1 variable for each county area indicating whether it registers positive spending for that function in a given year. Next, I compute median spending on each function in each year among those counties in which the function is provided. For each county area, I then sum nationwide median spending on each function it provides in each year. This summary index indicates the amount a county area would spend if it spent the nationwide median amount on each service it provides. Formally, the index is defined as

$$FPI_{jt} = \Sigma_{it} \alpha_{ijt} \mu_{it},$$

where i indexes functional spending categories, j indexes county areas, and t indexes years; α_{ijt} is 1 if county area j has positive spending on service i in year t and 0 if it does not; and μ_{it} represents nationwide median spending on service i in year t among all county areas where that service is provided. Thus, a county area's FPI will increase whenever it adds a new service and whenever nationwide median spending on its existing services increases. This is a variation on the method of Clark, Ferguson, and Shapiro (1982).

Table 4.2. *Overlap and Functional Performance*

	FPI	Number of Functions
	(1)	(2)
Jurisdictional overlap	7.55	0.11
	(8.49)	(0.09)
ln(population)	–3.75	0.50
	(11.25)	(0.11)***
Per capita Income	0.00	0.00
	(0.00)***	(0.00)***
Percent nonwhite	214.38	–1.26
	(55.47)***	(0.51)**
Five-year change in population	–13.39	–0.46
	(16.50)	(0.21)**
Percent age ≤18	481.41	–1.22
	(108.90)***	(1.26)
Percent age ≥65	398.00	0.96
	(131.45)***	(1.37)
Federal aid, five-year lag	0.02	0.00
	(0.01)*	(0.00)**
State aid, five-year lag	0.02	0.00
	(0.01)***	(0.00)*
Constant	2,124.13	16.74
	(129.06)***	(1.24)***
R-squared (within)	0.9	0.16
R-squared (overall)	0.75	0.35
Observations	21,198	21,198
# of clusters	3,032	3,032

Notes: The dependent variables are the FPI in model (1) and the number of functions performed in a county in model (2). All dollar values are CPI-adjusted to year 2002 dollars. Standard errors, clustered by county, are reported in parentheses. All models include county and year fixed effects (not reported).
*significant at 10%, **significant at 5%, ***significant at 1%.

Next, in model (2) of Table 4.2, I simply use the number of locally provided government functions as the dependent variable. Once again, jurisdictional overlap has a substantively small and statistically insignificant effect. In other words, jurisdictional overlap is not significantly related to either the number of local government functions or the FPI, but it is a robust predictor of actual taxes and spending. These results strongly suggest that the effect of jurisdictional overlap on local budgets is not simply an artifact of changes in local functional performance, but rather reflects increased spending on the same functions that would otherwise be provided by general-purpose governments.

Table 4.3 presents several models that attempt to recover the effect of jurisdictional overlap on own-source revenue purged of any effect on functional performance. Model (1) of Table 4.3 shows the results of adding the FPI as an additional control variable in the baseline model of own-source revenue per capita. The FPI should absorb changes in spending over time that are associated with changes in functional performance. That is, controlling for the FPI, any remaining increase in taxation resulting from an increase in jurisdictional overlap should be attributable to the common-pool effect rather than a change in functional performance. As shown in model (1), the estimated effect of jurisdictional overlap declines very slightly, relative to the baseline model (2) of Table 4.1, but remains highly statistically significant. Specifically, the coefficient on jurisdictional overlap declines from $141 to $134, suggesting that $7 of the effect of jurisdictional overlap is due to the addition of new functions, which is exactly (and unsurprisingly) the $7 recovered in model (1) of Table 4.2.

The FPI itself is, as expected, a powerful predictor of own-source revenue. Each dollar of increased functional performance results in 92 cents of additional own-source revenue. Note that local jurisdictions also receive revenue from federal and state transfers, so there is no reason that the FPI coefficient should be exactly 1.00. The FPI carries a t-statistic of 25 and improves both the R^2 within and between notably.

Model (2) of Table 4.3 presents a more elaborate specification that uses a full set of functional dummy variables rather than the FPI. In other words, a dummy variable is included for each of the 37 services tracked by the COG. The dummy is set equal to 1 if the county area has positive spending on the service, 0 otherwise. The idea behind using the functional dummies is similar to the FPI: If the addition of a new layer of government coincides with the addition of a new service, the dummy variable for that service is "turned on" to account for the change. Once again, we see that jurisdictional overlap remains highly significant and positively associated with own-source revenue per capita. The coefficient of $118 for jurisdictional overlap in the presence of the full set of functional dummies suggests that most of the effect of overlap on spending is not occurring through the addition of new functions. Functional performance alone cannot explain away the common-pool effect.

As a further check on the (un)importance of functional performance in explaining the correlation between jurisdictional overlap and government size, I employ the *common functions* approach commonly used

Table 4.3. *Controlling for Functional Performance*

	Revenue (1)	Revenue (2)	Common Spending (3)	Common Spending Less Education (4)
Jurisdictional overlap	133.73 (33.46)***	118.02 (33.55)***	126.60 (32.06)***	99.96 (26.49)***
FPI	0.92 (0.04)***		0.06 (0.03)*	0.04 (0.02)*
Per capita income	0.02 (0.00)***	0.03 (0.00)***	0.01 (0.00)***	0.01 (0.00)***
ln(population)	34.51 (37.63)	56.61 (37.57)	−52.44 (30.48)*	31.93 (24.30)
Five-year change in population	−282.26 (89.77)***	−294.14 (91.03)***	−233.65 (68.00)***	−198.71 (54.36)***
Percent nonwhite	−15.38 (150.66)	309.64 (155.46)**	169.07 (125.43)	16.45 (94.00)
Percent age ≤18	169.10 (463.29)	613.56 (471.73)	1,544.15 (389.17)***	−69.98 (317.31)
Percent age ≥65	58.47 (502.80)	285.46 (497.89)	388.05 (428.07)	1,014.35 (355.94)***
Federal aid, five-year lag	0.02 (0.03)	0.02 (0.03)	0.02 (0.02)	0.03 (0.02)
State aid, five-year lag	−0.11 (0.04)***	−0.08 (0.04)**	0.20 (0.04)***	0.08 (0.03)***
Constant	−1,645.65 (408.46)***	−567.04 −418.79	1,473.28 (357.34)***	−210.31 −278.61
R-squared (within)	0.33	0.32	0.45	0.17
Observations	21,198	21,198	21,198	21,198
# of clusters	3,032	3,032	3,032	3,032

Notes: The dependent variable is general own-source revenue per capita for models 1 and 2; common-function spending per capita for model 3; and common-function spending (minus education) per capita for model 4. All dollar values are CPI-adjusted to year 2002 dollars. Standard errors, clustered by county, are reported in parentheses. All models include county and year fixed effects (not reported). Model 2 also includes a full set of functional performance dummies (not reported).
*significant at 10%, **significant at 5%, ***significant at 1%.

in the local public finance literature.[15] First, I identify a set of common functions provided in nearly all counties. I define common functions as those services provided in at least 90 percent of the county-years in my sample.[16] Together, common functions account for 80 percent of direct general expenditures by local governments over my study period. Next, I test whether there is any relationship between jurisdictional overlap and spending devoted to common functions. If jurisdictional overlap simply expands the bundle of public goods without affecting core local services, we should expect to find little or no effect of overlap on common-function spending.

Model (3) of Table 4.3 uses jurisdictional overlap and the usual set of controls to predict common-function spending. The result is a direct apples-to-apples comparison that shows whether, for the same bundle of services, spending is higher when there are more overlapping jurisdictions. Indeed it is, and the overall magnitude and significance of the effect, $127, are comparable to what is shown in all the other models. Based on the accumulated results of Tables 4.2 and 4.3, it appears that only a small fraction of the effect of jurisdictional overlap on taxes and spending is attributable to more diversity in service provision.

Finally, model (4) addresses one lingering concern about functional performance. Because education constitutes the largest single functional expenditure in most counties, and because school districts are the most common type of special district, one might reasonably wonder whether the estimated effect of jurisdictional overlap on spending and taxation is somehow an artifact of school funding. The dependent variable in model (4) is common-function spending minus education spending; in other words, it represents spending on all other common functions. Looking only at noneducation common-function expenditures, the estimated effect of jurisdictional overlap is $100. Thus, the inflationary effect of jurisdictional overlap on spending is not specific to education but rather applies broadly to core local services. Moreover, the effect of jurisdictional overlap is proportionally larger for noneducation common-function spending: The $100 coefficient amounts to 17 percent of median spending ($582).

Results for a few of the control variables also warrant mention. First, note that the FPI is far more predictive of aggregate revenue than of

---

15 The common functions approach is widely used in local public finance to facilitate comparisons among cities and has a long history dating back at least to Brazer (1959).

16 As before, I use the sum of spending by all governments within the county, not just by the county government itself. A detailed breakdown of common and noncommon functions is provided in the Methodological Appendix, Section A.1.3.

common-function spending. This is reassuring, in that the purpose of analyzing common-function spending is to eliminate, to the greatest extent possible, variations in the functions performed in different localities. That the FPI is only weakly related to common-function spending suggests that this strategy was largely successful. Second, note that areas with more children have higher common-function spending, but not when education is removed (models (4) vs. (5)). The reverse pattern is true for counties with a higher population over 65, which spend more on common functions other than education. Both of these results are sensible, suggesting that areas with more children spend more on education, while areas with more older people spend less on education and more on other services. Finally, increasing state aid results in lower own-source revenue but higher spending, which simply indicates that localities substitute state aid for their own sources of revenue and that the aid translates into higher spending.

4.4.2 Sources of Revenue

Jurisdictional overlap leads to *spending* increases across a wide range of functions. Next, I ask whether the *revenue* increases associated with jurisdictional overlap are equally diversified. As noted in Chapter 2, special districts raise revenue from a variety of sources, most notably property taxes and user charges. In fact, while a larger number of districts use property taxes, a larger proportion of all special district revenue is due to user charges. User charges account for almost 60 percent of aggregate special district revenue, and hospital districts account for by far the largest share of all user charges. Hospital district user charges, totaling $16.6 billion in 2002, constitute nearly half of all district user charges and almost one-third of total special district revenue. Hospital districts tend to operate public hospitals that disproportionately serve the needy (Foster 1997).

Some have argued that user charges are efficient in the sense that those who use a service pay for its costs (Ostrom et al. 1988). In the context of the model put forth in Chapter 3, user charges might be an efficiency-enhancing device if they were used to finance a service that a minority is willing to pay for but that would be defeated in majority voting if financed through general taxation (see Section 3.2.1). That said, the efficiency of publicly operated hospitals is open to question, and cost shifting from insured patients to uninsured patients may undermine the principle that those who use the services pay for them (e.g., Dranove 1988). I do not wish to enter into the debate over the efficiency of user charges or of public hospitals. But it is important to know how much these factors contribute respectively to the overlap effect estimated in the preceding models.

To get at these issues, I decompose the overlap effect into its effects on the components of own-source revenue. Table 4.4 presents the results. Note that the coefficients for property taxes, user charges, and other revenue in Table 4.4 sum to the value of the coefficient for total own-source revenue in model (1) of Table 4.3, so I am showing the sources of revenue that make up the aggregate overlap effect. The largest effect of jurisdictional overlap is on property taxes. The coefficient of $60 suggests that increasing jurisdictional overlap from the 25th to the 75th percentile results in an increase equal to roughly 8 percent of average property taxes ($670). Meanwhile, for an equal change in jurisdictional overlap, the $45 coefficient for user charges represents an increase of about 12 percent for the average county ($339). Finally, repeating the exercise in model (3), the coefficient of $29 suggests an increase of about 9 percent of the average county's other revenue sources ($289), which are primarily nonproperty taxes and special assessments. I conclude from this analysis that jurisdictional overlap has a slightly disproportionate effect on user charges but a larger absolute effect on property taxes. That user charges constitute a larger share of special district revenue but a smaller share of the overlap effect suggests that the shared tax base, local property, is the resource being disproportionately exploited, which is entirely consistent with the common-pool model.

To address the concern that jurisdictional overlap may reflect a switch away from taxes and toward user charges, model (4) uses the *percentage* of revenue from user charges as the dependent variable. The coefficient suggests that a movement from the 25th to the 75th percentile of jurisdictional overlap results in a 1 percentage point increase in the share of revenue from user charges. User charges constitute 25 percent of revenue in the average county, so a 1 percentage point increase hardly represents a dramatic change in the revenue structure.

Next, I consider the issue of hospital districts. Any concern that hospital districts are driving my results should be allayed by the fact that the overlap effect holds up when I control for the functional performance index; include a hospital function dummy (one of the set of functional dummies used in model (2) of Table 4.3); or use only common-function spending as the dependent variable (public hospitals are not a common function). As a final robustness check, I exclude all counties with a hospital district in model (5) of Table 4.4. The jurisdictional overlap coefficient declines slightly but is in the same ballpark and remains highly significant.

The results from Table 4.4 provide no reason to believe that the overlap effect simply reflects a shift toward user charges or the presence of public hospitals. While reliance on user charges does increase where there

Table 4.4. *Overlap Effect by Revenue Source*

	Property Taxes	User Charges	Other Revenue	Percent Charges	Excl. Hospital Districts
	(1)	(2)	(3)	(4)	(5)
Jurisdictional overlap	59.74	44.67	29.33	0.01	90.71
	(20.19)***	(16.22)***	(14.57)**	(0.01)**	(35.80)**
FPI	0.06	0.80	0.06	0.00	0.89
	(0.02)***	(0.03)***	(0.01)***	(0.00)***	(0.04)***
Per capita income	0.01	0.01	0.01	0.00	0.02
	(0.00)***	(0.00)***	(0.00)***	(0.00)	(0.00)***
ln(population)	28.74	−79.46	85.23	−0.04	111.55
	(22.57)	(16.00)***	(18.79)***	(0.01)***	(45.48)**
Five-year change in population	−192.85	−49.17	−40.24	0.00	−245.79
	(35.36)***	(30.79)	(69.50)	(0.01)	(105.42)**
Percent nonwhite	−261.89	108.96	137.55	0.01	131.42
	(96.07)***	(79.49)	(80.43)*	(0.03)	(180.53)

(continued)

Table 4.4. *(continued)*

	Property Taxes	User Charges	Other Revenue	Percent Charges	Excl. Hospital Districts
	(1)	(2)	(3)	(4)	(5)
Percent age ≤18	321.03	342.37	-494.31	0.18	105.20
	(270.08)	(196.53)*	(219.33)**	(0.08)**	(504.57)
Percent age ≥65	-440.18	852.27	-353.63	0.42	338.96
	(312.66)	(219.79)***	(251.26)	(0.09)***	(546.26)
Federal aid, five-year lag	-0.02	0.04	0.00	0.00	0.00
	(0.01)	(0.03)	(0.01)	(0.00)	(0.02)
State aid, five-year lag	-0.18	0.06	0.01	0.00	-0.10
	(0.02)***	(0.01)***	(0.02)	(0.00)***	(0.04)**
Constant	132.04	-1,120.09	-657.6	-0.2	-1,753.29
	-229.25	(199.58)***	(206.94)***	(0.09)**	(477.76)***
R-squared (within)	0.14	0.37	0.12	0.25	0.29
Observations	21,198	21,198	21,198	21,198	17,100
# of clusters	3,032	3,032	3,032	3,032	2,713

Notes: The dependent variable is property taxes per capita for model 1; user charges per capita for model 2; other own-source revenue per capita for model 3; user charges (as a percentage of total own-source revenue) for model 4; and general own-source revenue per capita for model 5. Model 5 excludes counties with a hospital district. All dollar values are CPI-adjusted to year 2002 dollars. Standard errors, clustered by county, are reported in parentheses. All models include county and year fixed effects (not reported).
* significant at 10%, ** significant at 5%, *** significant at 1%.

are more overlapping jurisdictions, property taxes increase by a larger amount, as might be predicted from the common-pool model. Even if it were the case that user charges are entirely efficient—that is, pure *benefits taxes*, to use public finance jargon—charges constitute only about one-third of the overlap effect. Indeed, the fact that the overlap effect does not derive primarily from user charges or public hospitals, but from property and nonproperty taxes, can be seen as further support for the idea that concurrent taxation generates a common-pool problem among overlapping jurisdictions.

Among the remaining variables, note that the FPI has a much larger effect on user charges than on other revenue sources, which suggests that user charges are disproportionately used to fund new services. Larger counties appear to rely less on user charges and more on other sources of revenue, such as income and payroll taxes. Counties with more children or more people over 65 generate more revenue from user charges and less from other revenue sources. Finally, it appears that state aid is disproportionately used to reduce local property taxes.

4.4.3 Current versus Capital Expenditures

Some suggest that real estate developers promote the creation of special districts to raise capital for costly infrastructure improvements (e.g., Porter et al. 1992). If special districts are created to provide infrastructure, then their positive relationship to local taxation may reflect temporary capital needs for new developments, not overexploitation of the fiscal common pool. In order to test this hypothesis, I utilize data on current versus capital expenditures. If higher spending in counties where there are more overlapping jurisdictions is merely a reflection of capital expenditures, then we should not see a significant relationship between jurisdictional overlap and spending on current operations.

The results in Table 4.5 show that jurisdictional overlap indeed has a positive effect on spending for current operations. The coefficient, $121, remains highly significant and is of roughly the same magnitude as the effects on own-source revenue and common-function spending shown in Table 4.3. Note that county area median own-source revenue in the sample is $1,150, while the median current expenditure is $1,690 per capita. Expenditures exceed own-source revenue because local governments receive additional revenue from federal and state transfers. As a result, the overlap effect represents a smaller fraction of median expenditures (7 percent) than of median own-source revenue (9 to 11 percent).

It is also true that jurisdictional overlap has a positive effect on capital spending, as shown in model (2) of Table 4.5. The coefficient of $45

Table 4.5. *Current versus Capital Spending*

	Current Spending (1)	Capital Spending (2)
Jurisdictional overlap	121.27	44.61
	(24.51)***	(20.74)**
FPI	0.83	0.07
	(0.03)***	(0.02)***
Per capita income	0.01	0.01
	(0.00)***	(0.00)***
ln(population)	−266.62	86.18
	(27.34)***	(17.33)***
Five-year change in population	−469.02	199.29
	(49.08)***	(40.19)***
Percent nonwhite	517.53	−31.26
	(110.54)***	(74.41)
Percent age ≤18	1,676.81	−100.04
	(341.46)***	(193.63)
Percent age ≥65	1,344.44	−183.94
	(369.43)***	(223.57)
Federal aid, five-year lag	0.08	−0.02
	(0.04)**	(0.02)
State aid, five-year lag	0.27	0.03
	(0.03)***	(0.02)
Constant	1,755.48	−915.22
	(310.23)***	(211.06)***
R-squared (within)	0.69	0.06
Observations	21,198	21,198
# of clusters	3,032	3,032

Notes: The dependent variable is general expenditures for current operations per capita for model 1; general capital outlays per capita for model 2. All dollar values are CPI-adjusted to year 2002 dollars. Standard errors, clustered by county, are reported in parentheses. All models include county and year fixed effects (not reported). *significant at 10%, **significant at 5%, ***significant at 1%.

suggests that increasing jurisdictional overlap from the 25th to the 75th percentile results in $41 of increased capital expenditures. Median capital expenditures in the sample are $205 per capita, so the $41 represents an increase of roughly 20 percent. In other words, jurisdictional overlap has a much larger *absolute* effect on current spending but a larger *proportional* effect on capital spending.

Two points emerge from the results shown in Table 4.5. First, special districts do indeed appear to be connected to infrastructure investment. Of course, it is worth emphasizing that the same common-pool logic that leads governments to overexploit the shared tax base for current expenditures could also explain the jump in capital expenditures where jurisdictions overlap. Indeed, common-pool problems in public debt are quite familiar outside the United States (Poterba and von Hagen 1999; Rodden 2005). So it is entirely possible that, rather than being an exception to the common-pool model, the results showing greater capital spending actually constitute additional evidence in favor of the common-pool model. Unfortunately, I have no way of distinguishing the use of special districts for normal finance of capital investment from common-pool problems in public debt arising from the layering of jurisdictions on top of one another.

In any case, the second important point is that even if we take the conservative approach and attribute the entire overlap effect on capital spending to everyday infrastructure spending—that is, even if we say that the common-pool model does not explain these results at all—we are still left with the central finding that jurisdictional overlap causes significant increases in current spending. And current spending represents the more consequential category: Average current expenditures in the sample are $1,846 per capita, whereas average capital expenditures are $267 per capita. Thus, the question of whether the common-pool model *might* explain capital spending is substantively much less important than the finding that jurisdictional overlap *does* indeed cause increases in current spending.

Table 4.5 also shows that counties where population is growing faster have greater capital spending and less current spending, consistent with the ideas that a growing population requires expanded infrastructure and that overall spending is slow to catch up with population growth.

4.4.4 *Tax and Expenditure Limitations*

In states where municipalities are subject to debt, tax, or expenditure limitations, it may be the case that special districts, which are not commonly subject to such restrictions, are formed to evade the ceilings on municipal budgets. The few existing studies on this topic have yielded mixed results, as discussed in Chapter 2. Nevertheless, it is important to control for the possibility that fiscal restrictions on municipalities are behind the relationship between jurisdictional overlap and local government taxation. To begin, I note that the county fixed effects will absorb any fiscal restrictions that do not change over time. So, the only remaining concern is that *changes* in fiscal restrictions over time lead to *changes* in the degree of jurisdictional overlap over time. In Chapter 2, I suggested that changes in fiscal constraints are an unlikely explanation for changes in the number of overlapping jurisdictions. Nevertheless, to address this concern, I turn to the Advisory Commission on Intergovernment Relations (ACIR) (1995) tax and expenditure limitations (TEL) data, as updated by Mullins and Wallin (2004). Based on these data, I coded each state and each year as to whether any of the following TELs existed for municipalities, counties, or school districts: an overall property tax rate limit, a specific property tax rate limit, a property tax revenue limit, an assessment increase limit, a general revenue limit, a general expenditure limit, and a full disclosure requirement. With each of the seven types of TELs coded for each of the three types of local government, I have a total of 21 TEL indicator variables for each state in each year. As an overall measure of the fiscal restrictiveness of the state's laws on non–special district governments, I sum the 21 dummy variables. The resulting variable is the total number of local government TELs in effect in each state and each year, which ranges from 0 to 15, with a mean of 3.7. In the Methodological Appendix, Section A.2.2, I discuss alternative ways of measuring fiscal restrictiveness — including using the full set of 21 TEL indicator variables — and show that the results do not change notably from those to be presented here.

If the correlation between jurisdictional overlap and taxation is merely a by-product of changing fiscal constraints on general-purpose governments, then controlling for these constraints should cause the overlap variable to become insignificant. In Table 4.6, I add the total TEL variable and its interaction with jurisdictional overlap to the models of general own-source revenue estimated previously.[17] Model (1) shows the results of adding total TELs to the model. The variable is positive but the relationship does not even approach statistical significance, consistent with the results of past studies (see Mullins and Wallin 2004). With total TELs included in the model, the coefficient for jurisdictional overlap is virtually unchanged.

Next, I test the interaction between tax restrictions and jurisdictional overlap, as shown in model (2) of Table 4.6. If it is correct that special districts are created primarily to evade fiscal constraints on other types

17 Because the TEL measure is a statewide variable, I cluster the standard errors by state in these models to account for correlation between counties within the same state. Because clustering by state allows for arbitrary correlation of residuals for observations within the same state, this approach subsumes (i.e., is more general than) clustering by county. Clustering by state is a more conservative approach, however, yielding only 50 clusters, compared to over 3,000 in the models presented previously that cluster by county.

Table 4.6. *Tax and Expenditures Limitations*

	(1)	(2)
Jurisdictional overlap	135.85	160.14
	(56.78)**	(60.36)**
Total TELs	5.88	1.28
	(13.33)	(16.20)
Total TELs * jurisdictional overlap		21.28
		(19.21)
FPI	0.92	0.92
	(0.07)***	(0.07)***
Per capita income	0.02	0.02
	(0.01)***	(0.01)***
ln(population)	25.14	29.41
	(86.87)	(85.80)
Five-year change in population	−282.24	−286.30
	(133.00)**	(132.44)**
Percent nonwhite	−57.31	−32.67
	(352.10)	(332.95)
Percent age ≤18	160.20	230.24
	(899.49)	(885.85)
Percent age ≥65	53.93	100.55
	(791.00)	(784.66)
Federal aid, five-year lag	0.02	0.02
	(0.03)	(0.03)
State aid, five-year lag	−0.11	−0.11
	(0.06)*	(0.06)*
Constant	−1,571.32	−1,680.80
	(885.56)*	(859.83)*
R-squared (within)	0.33	0.33
Observations	21,198	21,198
# of clusters	49	49

Notes: The dependent variable is general own-source revenue per capita. All dollar values are CPI-adjusted to year 2002 dollars. Standard errors, clustered by state, are reported in parentheses. All models include county and year fixed effects (not reported).
*significant at 10%, **significant at 5%, ***significant at 1%.

of local governments, then jurisdictional overlap should exert a greater effect on taxation when TELs increase; that is, the interaction term should be positive. With the interaction term included, the main effect of jurisdictional overlap remains positive and highly significant. The positive sign on the interaction between fiscal constraints and jurisdictional overlap does suggest that overlap has a larger effect when there are stronger fiscal constraints on other types of governments, but the interaction is not statistically significant. The main effect of TELs also fails to attain statistical significance in model (2). Thus, there is no evidence that the positive relationship between jurisdictional overlap and government size can be attributed to the effects of fiscal constraints placed on other types of local governments.

4.4.5   Area Flexibility

As discussed previously, special-purpose jurisdictions have unusual territorial flexibility, and their boundaries do not necessarily correspond to those of underlying general-purpose governments. If districts' geographic flexibility allows public service provision to match more closely communities of interest, then residents may be willing to spend more on those services.[18] For example, if only a small area within an existing jurisdiction demands a particular service, a district can be formed to match local tastes. Residents might be willing to support additional spending that they would have opposed if services had to match the boundaries of existing general-purpose governments. These issues are difficult to analyze directly without additional information on local and regional variation in tastes for public goods. Nevertheless, a relatively simple test is possible.

The COG provides limited information about the geographic area of special-purpose jurisdictions. Although the precise boundaries or size of these jurisdictions is not available, the COG does identify those districts that are coterminous with a city or county, which constitute about 40 percent of all districts, as well as those that are contained entirely within a county but are not coterminous with a general-purpose government, which constitute about 50 percent of all districts.[19] Based on this categorization, I created two new jurisdictional overlap measures, one each for coterminous and within-county noncoterminous jurisdictions. Higher spending by coterminous districts obviously cannot be attributed to a greater capacity to match services to local tastes.

18 This hypothesis is associated with the economic historian John Wallis, although he apparently has never published a statement of it directly (see Oates 1985).

19 The remaining category is multicounty districts, which account for 10 percent of all districts. Because there are relatively few such districts, resulting in a large number of zeroes at the county level, I did not attempt to separately estimate their effects. See Chapter 1 for further discussion of the geographic scale of special-purpose districts.

Before turning to the results of this analysis, an important caution must be noted. The geographic area variable is not available in electronic form for most of the years of my study. I use data from 1992. With data for only one year, I cannot include county fixed effects in the analysis. Instead I use state fixed effects. More troubling, due to survey nonresponse, the variable has missing values for 15 percent of special districts and I have no evidence that these values are missing at random. The item was not asked for township governments. Therefore the geographic data are not ideal. However, finding that the results are similar for coterminous and noncoterminous districts should provide some reassurance that the association between jurisdictional overlap and taxation is not simply an artifact of geographic flexibility.

The results are shown in Table 4.7. First, note that the effect for coterminous districts is larger than that for noncoterminous districts, and the latter coefficient falls shy of statistical significance. This result is contrary to the idea that greater territorial flexibility is the root cause of the overlap effect. In any case, I cannot reject the hypothesis that the estimated effects for coterminous and noncoterminous overlapping jurisdictions are equal ($p = 0.16$). While the aforementioned data limitations preclude a certain answer, I find no evidence to support the argument that the relationship between jurisdictional overlap and taxation arises from the greater territorial flexibility of special districts relative to general-purpose governments.

4.4.6 *Instrumental Variables Estimation*

The preceding results establish that an increase in the number of overlapping jurisdictions leads to an increase in aggregate public sector taxes and spending. The fixed effects specification of all the models accounts for the influence of observable and unobservable time-invariant attributes of the counties under study. One lingering concern may be that there is some factor that is changing over time within counties that causes both an increase in jurisdictional overlap and an increase in taxes and spending. On this point, note that my theory does not imply that the formation of special-function jurisdictions is exogenous to demands for spending. In fact, my theory suggests that an interest group desiring additional spending on its preferred service would be wise to seek the creation of a single-function jurisdiction to provide it. Therefore, it remains to be demonstrated that the increase in spending associated with jurisdictional overlap is due to the institutions themselves and not merely to the unobserved influence of local interest groups.

Before turning to the empirics, note that endogeneity in this case could bias my coefficients in either direction. One possible story is that special

Table 4.7. *Geographic Scale, 1992*

Coterminous districts per municipality	157.90***
	(48.44)
Within-county districts per municipality	66.36
	(42.99)
FPI	1.34***
	(0.10)
Per capita income	0.08***
	(0.01)
ln(population)	−853.88***
	(186.30)
ln(population)^2	30.61***
	(8.46)
Five-year change in population	−1,172.88***
	(422.09)
Percent nonwhite	194.38
	(151.15)
Percent age ≤ 18	113.15
	(1,005.60)
Percent age ≥ 65	−2,017.67*
	(1,057.00)
Federal aid, five-year lag	0.36**
	(0.17)
State aid, five-year lag	−0.16
	(0.14)
Constant	3,068.17***
	(1,092.99)
Observations	3,028
R-squared	0.251
# of clusters	48

Notes: The dependent variable is general own-source revenue per capita. The model includes state fixed effects (not reported). Robust standard errors clustered by state are in parentheses.
***$p < 0.01$, **$p < 0.05$, *$p < 0.1$.

interest groups seek the creation of a special district for their pet service in situations when it would otherwise be provided at a relatively low level, that is, when the general-purpose government is fiscally conservative. If so, then we would be more likely to see special districts created at times when spending is otherwise prone to be relatively low. This would bias the coefficients in my models downward, meaning that I have *under-estimated* the effect of jurisdictional overlap.

An alternative story is that special-purpose governments are more likely to be formed when interest groups are strongest. In this case, the concern would be that it is interest group strength, not the districts themselves, that pump up spending. That is, when interest groups become more influential, they will obtain the increased spending they desire regardless of the institutions in place. This would bias my coefficients upward. But note that there is a hole in this account. If it is really the interest groups that matter and not the institutions—that is, if interest groups can just as easily fulfill their demands through a general-purpose government—then it is not at all clear who would bother forming special-function jurisdictions to begin with, given that formation is costly. In other words, if increases in jurisdictional overlap do not really cause increased spending but are merely correlated with it, then one must still explain the reason for the correlation. I find this form of the endogeneity argument dubious from the outset. Nevertheless, it is possible to dispense with this concern empirically.

My strategy is to locate a source of exogenous variation in the level of jurisdictional overlap. I rely on state enabling laws for the creation of special districts. Specifically, I tabulate the number of special district functional types allowed by law in each state for each year, based on information provided in the COG. This variable, called *functional breadth*, ranges from 1 in Hawaii to 34 in Illinois in 2002.[20] I then use functional breadth to instrument for the actual value of jurisdictional overlap. By *instrument for*, I mean running a two-stage least squares model (2SLS) where the count of permitted district types is used as an instrumental variable (IV) for the level of overlap.[21] In the first stage, I regress the contemporary value of jurisdictional overlap against functional breadth lagged by five years. From this first-stage regression, I recover the *predicted* contemporary value of jurisdictional value. This predicted value replaces the actual value of overlap as a regressor in the second-stage model, where the dependent variables is total own-source revenue. The full set of control variables introduced previously appears on the right-hand side at both stages, as do county and year fixed effects. The

20 Foster (1997) coined the term *functional breadth*, although she did not use it as an instrumental variable and computed it for only one year. I tabulated the variable myself for every COG year from 1957 through 2002.

21 See Wooldridge (2002, ch. 5) and Baum, Schaffer, and Stillman (2003) for an explanation of IV estimation. Although described as a *two-stage* process, in practice the model can be estimated in one step, which is how the procedure is implemented in most software packages.

advantage of this approach is that the second-stage model uses only the variation in jurisdictional overlap that can be explained by state laws to predict contemporary taxation. If the institutions do not matter, then using laws for creating them as a source of identification should not yield significant results in the second-stage model.

Second-stage results from the 2SLS model are shown in Table 4.8.[22] In specification (1), which uses five-year lagged values of functional breadth as an instrument, jurisdictional overlap remains positive and significant. In fact, the estimated effect of jurisdictional overlap is larger than in the original results, suggesting that endogeneity, if anything, was biasing the coefficients downward. This result is consistent with the idea that high-demanding interest groups turn to special districts to provide services when general-purpose governments spend less than they would like. Of course, without data on local interest group activity, this account is largely speculative. In any event, the more important point is that using state laws as an exogenous source of variation demonstrates that it is the existence of jurisdictional overlap itself that is responsible for the increased spending.

To address any possible concern that interest groups manipulate the state laws themselves—a tall order since county interest groups would have to influence the state legislature—model (2) uses functional breadth from 1957 as an instrument for jurisdictional overlap from 1972 to 2002. It seems very safe to assume that state laws in 1957 are not influenced by the spending demands of interest groups in the future. Because there is no over-time variation in the instrument, I cannot include county or state fixed effects in model (2). Nevertheless, the estimated effect of jurisdictional overlap in model (2), using the 1957 value of functional breadth as an instrument, remains highly significant and somewhat larger than the OLS estimates. The coefficients for jurisdictional overlap (or any of the control variables) cannot be directly compared between models (1) and (2) of Table 4.8 due to the differences in the use of fixed effects. Nevertheless, in both cases the results indicate that it is the institutions themselves that matter.

Finally, perhaps the connection between overlap and budget size is just the product of some unobserved "shock" in the county. If the correlation between changes in jurisdictional overlap and changes in the budget is merely the by-product of a local demand shock, then contemporary taxes and spending should not be correlated with historically predetermined levels of jurisdictional overlap. Therefore, using historical values of overlap

---

22 Results of the first-stage model are shown in the Methodological Appendix, Section A.2.2.

Table 4.8. *Instrumental Variables Analysis, State Laws*

	IV	IV
	Five-Year Lagged State Laws	1957 State Laws
	(1)	(2)
Jurisdictional overlap	365.7**	188.7***
	(168.70)	(36.65)
FPI	0.916***	1.410***
	(0.04)	(0.0535)
Per capita income	0.0249***	0.0854***
	(0.00)	(0.00379)
ln(population)	1.635	−226.4***
	(45.51)	(14.62)
Five-year change in	−262.8***	−686.1***
population	(90.58)	(87.02)
Percent nonwhite	−84.26	−69.78
	(150.60)	(70.80)
Percent age ≤18	352.7	279.0
	(489.80)	(418.7)
Percent age ≥65	−32.43	−1,368***
	(504.40)	(401.9)
Federal aid, five-year lag	0.0144	0.296*
	(0.03)	(0.155)
State aid, five-year lag	−0.113***	0.0104
	(0.04)	(0.0323)
Constant		−1738***
		(230.9)
Observations	21,198	21,198
# of clusters	3,032	3,032
R-squared	0.324	0.423

Notes: The dependent variable is general own-source revenue per capita. All dollar values are CPI-adjusted to year 2002 dollars. The instrument in model (1) is the number of special-district functional types authorized by state law, lagged by 5 years. The instrument in model (2) is the number of special district functional types authorized by state law in 1957. Model (1) includes county and year fixed effects (not reported). Model (2) includes year fixed effects (not reported). The R-squared reported for model (1) is the within R-squared. Standard errors, clustered by county, are reported in parentheses.
*significant at 10%, **significant at 5%, ***significant at 1%.

to instrument for current values should break any spurious connection between overlap and spending that is the result of unobservable shocks.

To implement this 2SLS model, I use data from the two end points of my study period. That is, I use the 1972 value of jurisdictional overlap as an instrument for the 2002 value. With a lag of 30 years, this instrument is unlikely to be correlated with demand shocks in 2002. The second-stage model uses the estimated value of overlap, and contemporary values of the other control variables, to predict total own-source revenue in 2002. Because I use only one year of data in this exercise, it is not possible to include county-level fixed effects. Instead I use state fixed effects, so the resulting coefficients are based on variation between counties within the same state.

To establish a baseline relationship between jurisdictional overlap and own-source revenue in 2002, I begin by estimating an OLS model (that is, entering the contemporary value of jurisdictional overlap directly). The results are shown in model (1) of Table 4.9. Jurisdictional overlap is significantly associated with own-source revenue, with the coefficient of $185, which suggests that increasing from the 25th to the 75th percentile of jurisdictional overlap in 2002 results in an increase of $176 in own-source revenue. In 2002, the median value of own-source revenue is $1,481, so the overlap effect represents about a 12 percent increase, consistent with the results from the panel models shown previously. The significant findings in both the panel and cross-sectional models indicate that there is a positive relationship between jurisdictional overlap and the size of local budgets both between counties and within the same county over time.

Model (2) presents the second stage of the IV analysis. The complete first-stage results are reported in the Methodological Appendix, Table A12. It is clear that the results are virtually unchanged when historically predetermined values of overlap are used to instrument for the contemporary values. The coefficient of $151 is somewhat smaller than the noninstrumented coefficient, but the substantive effects are of comparable magnitude. These results contradict the notion that the connection between jurisdictional overlap and own-source revenue is driven by demand shocks or, more generally, that some unobservable factor causes an increase in both local taxation and the number of layers of government. Rather, local areas that had more overlapping jurisdictions in 1972 continue to spend more in 2002, consistent with the existence of an ongoing common-pool problem.

As an aside, it is worthwhile to note the differences in the estimated effects of some of the control variables in the cross-sectional model compared to the panel model. The coefficients for nearly all of the control variables are larger in absolute terms in the cross-sectional models

Table 4.9. *IVs Analysis, Lagged Values*

	OLS	IV
	(1)	(2)
Jurisdictional overlap	184.67	151.12
	(52.04)***	(53.50)***
FPI	1.30	1.32
	(0.10)***	(0.09)***
Per capita income	0.05	0.05
	(0.01)***	(0.01)***
ln(population)	−1,290.48	−1,253.76
	(267.03)***	(272.95)***
ln(population)^2	49.71	48.31
	(11.67)***	(11.85)***
Five-year change in population	−559.64	−635.42
	(509.51)	(496.44)
Percent nonwhite	25.03	5.14
	(166.30)	(167.64)
Percent age ≤18	−2054.84	−1975.99
	(1284.47)	(1,291.65)
Percent age ≥65	−3,173.91	−3,065.96
	(1,276.21)**	(1,298.82)**
Federal aid, five-year lag	0.23	0.23
	(0.14)*	(0.14)*
State aid, five-year lag	−0.15	−0.14
	(0.18)	(0.18)
Observations	3,027	3,022
# of clusters	48	48

Notes: The dependent variable is general own-source revenue per capita in 2002. In model (2), year 2002 jurisdictional overlap is instrumented with 1972 jurisdictional overlap. All dollar values are CPI-adjusted to year 2002 dollars. Both models include state fixed effects (not reported). Standard errors, clustered by state, are reported in parentheses.
*significant at 10%, **significant at 5%, ***significant at 1%.

(Table 4.9) than in the comparable panel models (Table 4.3, model (1)). This differential suggests that the control variables are correlated with unmeasured, time-invariant attributes of counties that influence the level of local taxes and spending; the county fixed effects wipe out such unmeasured factors, whereas the cross-sectional models do not.

Together, these 2SLS models using state laws and historically predetermined values as instruments provide strong evidence that the relationship between jurisdictional overlap and local taxation is causal. More extensive 2SLS analyses are presented in Berry (2008) and confirm the basic results shown here.

4.4.7 Functional Form

The inflationary effect of jurisdictional overlap on local taxes and spending is robust and cannot be explained away by functional performance, fiscal constraints on general-purpose governments, infrastructure investment, temporary demand shocks, or unobservable, time-invariant heterogeneity across counties. Indeed, the results presented previously provide resounding support for the fiscal common-pool model set forth in Chapter 3. Given the strong support for the model's prediction of a positive relationship between jurisdictional overlap and taxes and spending, it is worthwhile to explore the magnitude and functional form of this relationship in greater detail. All of the models presented thus far make parametric assumptions; in particular, all are linear in the parameters. With respect to jurisdictional overlap, as I explained earlier, I transformed the ratio of overlapping jurisdictions to municipalities into log form in order to account for the long right tail of the distribution. I then fit a linear relationship between this log-transformed variable and own-source revenue per capita. Does this parametric fit approximate the true relationship in the data?

In this section, I investigate whether using a more flexible functional form in the model yields roughly comparable estimates of the relationship between jurisdictional overlap and own-source revenue. If I reach a similar conclusion with a more flexible model, I will have additional support for the functional form assumptions used elsewhere in the book.

To model own-source revenue as a flexible function of jurisdictional overlap, I use a generalized additive model (GAM), in which I estimate the effect of overlap with thin-plate regression splines.[23] The GAM includes all of the covariates used previously, which enter the model linearly. Estimation of county-level fixed effects proved computationally infeasible in the GAM.[24] Instead, I estimate the model using state and year fixed effects, which should suffice for the task of recovering the approximate functional

---

23 The seminal reference on GAMs is Hastie and Tibshirani (1990). Beck and Jackman (1998) provide an accessible introduction. My implementation follows Wood (2006) and the associated *R* package, *mgcv*. I refer to this implementation of the model as *semiparametric* because jurisdictional overlap is measured nonparametrically via thin-plate regression splines, while the remaining covariates are modeled parametrically (linearly).

24 The county fixed effects imply the estimation of nearly 3,000 additional model parameters. Memory constraints prevented me from estimating the GAM with county fixed effects.

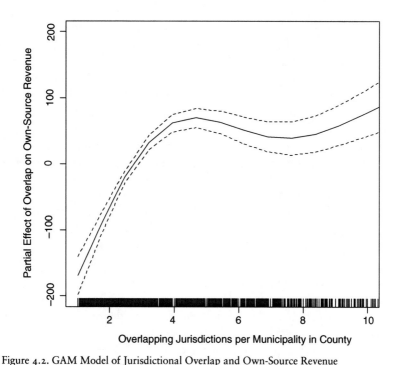

Figure 4.2. GAM Model of Jurisdictional Overlap and Own-Source Revenue

Notes: The graph depicts results from a GAM model in which the number of overlapping jurisdictions per municipality is fit with thin-plate regression splines. The dependent variable is own-source revenue per capita. The model includes all control variables shown in Table 4.2, modeled linearly, as well as state and year fixed effects. The unit of observation is county-by-year, and there are 21,198 observations. The solid line represents the predicted values, and the dashed lines demarcate the 95 percent confidence interval. The x-axis is truncated at the 95th percentile value to improve readability.

form of the relationship. The dependent variable is county aggregate own-source revenue per capita. The nonparametric portion of the GAM model does not yield a neat set of model parameters that can be reported in the usual tabular form. As such, common practice is to report the fitted relationship graphically (Wood 2006), which I do for jurisdictional overlap and own-source revenue in Figure 4.2. With state fixed effects included, the point estimates can be interpreted as deviations from statewide average own-source revenue, which is the y-axis in Figure 4.2.[25]

Judging from the figure, the relationship between jurisdictional overlap and revenue is not strictly linear. Roughly, it appears that spending

---

25 The x-axis in Figure 4.2 is truncated to improve readability. The maximum value is 74, and plotting the entire range of the data makes the graph virtually unreadable in the range where most of the data lie. Truncating the axis at 10 retains 95 percent of the data and allows a clear depiction of the fitted relationship.

increases steeply with overlap up to about four layers of government, then increases less dramatically. There appears to be a plateau between five and seven layers. However, it is important to note that five is the 75th percentile of the data, and 95 percent of counties have fewer than 10 overlapping jurisdictions per general municipality. Thus, I do not wish to overinterpret the plateau-and-peak pattern at the upper tail of the distribution.

Substantively, the estimated sizes of the effects comport nicely with those reported in the previous parametric models. Increasing the number of overlapping jurisdictions from two to five—that is, from the 25th to the 75th percentile—results in roughly $150 more in own-source revenue according to the GAM results. While this figure is slightly larger than the $134 implied by the equivalent parametric model (model (1) of Table 4.3), given the confidence intervals around both estimates the results are remarkably similar.

As a final check on functional form, I estimate a comparable GAM model using a different measure of jurisdictional overlap: the number of functional special district layers in the county. The dependent and control variables are unchanged. Figure 4.3 presents the results. Increasing from the 25th to the 75th percentile of the data—from two to five layers—is associated with roughly a $90 increase in spending. The magnitudes between the two models are not directly comparable due to their different scales, but the substantive implications are similar: Moving from a relatively small to a relatively large degree of jurisdictional overlap results in a spending increase in the range of $90 to $150, which is a range that contains most of the estimates presented earlier in the parametric models. Thus, regardless of how I measure jurisdictional overlap—in terms of territorial overlap of functional layering—and regardless of how I model it—parametrically or nonparametrically—I get results that are in the same ballpark, at least for the range of values at which most counties are found.

I conclude that the parametric model approximates the underlying relationship sufficiently well, and offers additional advantages, to justify its use. In particular, the parametric model offers the possibility of computing county-level fixed effects and clustered standard errors, in addition to its overall greater familiarity to applied researchers.

4.5   SUMMARY

My aim in this chapter has been to test the central prediction of the fiscal common-pool model: that the vertical layering of specialized jurisdictions causes public budgets to be larger than when the same services

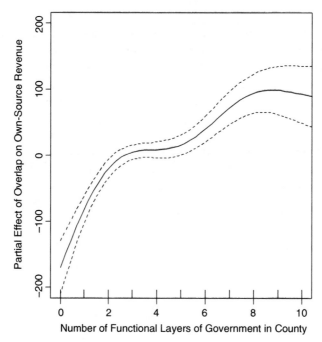

Figure 4.3. GAM Model of Functional Layering and Own-Source Revenue

Notes: The graph depicts results from a GAM model in which the number of functional layers of government in a county is fit with thin-plate regression splines. The dependent variable is own-source revenue per capita. The model includes all control variables shown in Table 4.2, modeled linearly, as well as state and year fixed effects. The unit of observation is county-by-year, and there are 21,198 observations. The solid line represents the predicted values, and the dashed lines demarcate the 95 percent confidence interval. The *x*-axis is truncated at the 95th percentile value to improve readability.

are provided by a general-purpose government. Because I could not run a field experiment to randomly create special-purpose jurisdictions, I employed several econometric strategies to identify the causal effect of jurisdictional overlap on local taxes and spending. Throughout, I used fixed effects to account for any observable or unobservable time-invariant attributes of counties that could be correlated with both jurisdictional overlap and the size of local budgets. At the same time, I controlled for a set of time-varying county attributes suggested by the prior literature to influence local government fiscal behavior. Furthermore, I supplemented these analyses with 2SLS models in which state laws governing the creation of special districts and historically predetermined values were used as instruments. In every case, the estimated relationship between jurisdictional overlap and local taxes and spending was strongly positive and statistically significant.

Having identified the effect of jurisdictional overlap on local taxes and spending, I sought to demonstrate that it could not be accounted for by alternative theories. In a series of subsequent analyses, I showed that the relationship cannot be explained by functional performance, capital investment, user charges, fiscal constraints on municipalities, geographic flexibility of special-purpose districts, or shocks to local demand for public services.

While it is possible to question any one of these results in isolation, taken together they powerfully suggest that fiscal externalities from concurrent taxation cause significant increases in local taxes and spending in the way predicted by the fiscal common-pool theory.

5

Specialization and Quality

The common-pool model of local politics put forth in this book is based on the idea that special interest groups have disproportionate influence in special-purpose jurisdictions compared to general-purpose governments. The result is that special-purpose jurisdictions spend more on their particular services than a general-purpose government would spend when performing the same functions. In the aggregate, this leads to the prediction that the total size of the local budget will be larger when a given bundle of services is provided by many single-function governments than when it is provided by one general-purpose government. The empirical results in the preceding chapter support this prediction, providing strong evidence that taxes and spending are higher in counties where there are more special-function jurisdictions for each municipality, all else equal.

The fiscal common-pool model, as developed in Chapter 3, does not make specific predictions about how special-function jurisdictions will spend their budgets. I merely postulate that there is an interest group that cares strongly about the service provided by each jurisdiction and prefers more spending on that service than other voters do. In considering the social desirability of special-function jurisdictions, however, an important question is whether they spend their additional revenue on providing higher-quality services or whether their inflated budgets simply reflect waste and inefficiency. Ultimately, the answer to this question hinges on the demands of the relevant interest groups. For example, return to Moe's (2006) argument about selective participation by teachers' union members in school board elections. Union members may prefer higher spending in ways that result in better education, such as smaller classes. On the other hand, union members may demand particularistic benefits that provide little value to other taxpayers, such as less rigorous tenure standards or earlier retirement. Or, in park district politics, local nature buffs may demand better maintenance of facilities, which would benefit all park visitors, or they may demand elaborate facilities for rock climbing or wind surfing, which benefit only a few. In any special-function domain, it is possible to imagine ways in which additional revenue could be spent to improve quality or to provide particularistic benefits to interest groups or employees, or both.

Without making additional assumptions about the motivations of local interest groups, the common-pool theory is silent on whether larger budgets for special-function jurisdictions result in better quality or wasteful spending. Indeed, either outcome would be perfectly consistent with the theory laid out in Chapter 3. Empirically, however, the distinction is important. On the one hand, if inflated budgets are devoted to particularistic spending, there is a strict utility loss for other voters. On the other hand, if larger budgets result in higher quality, some of the negative consequences of higher taxation by special-function jurisdictions would be offset. Of course, higher quality cannot *completely* offset the negative effects of overtaxation when spending is set higher than the point where marginal costs exceed the sum of marginal benefits. In other words, it is important to remember that it is possible to *overprovide* quality in local government, as in anything else, given that quality is costly. However, overproviding quality is more desirable, from a social welfare standpoint, than wasteful or particularistic spending.

Whether or not special-function jurisdictions deliver superior services is an empirical question. In this chapter, I attempt to shed light on that question by analyzing the performance of special districts relative to general-purpose governments in one particular domain: public libraries. Libraries offer a number of advantages for this purpose compared to other public services. First, there is variation both within and between states in the provision of library services by special districts versus general-purpose governments. By contrast, while education accounts for a much larger share of local expenditures, schools are almost always provided by special districts, and there are very few cases in which public education is provided by both school districts and municipalities within the same state, making it difficult to compare outcomes under the two institutional regimes. In addition, while measuring the quality of schools remains controversial, assessing the quality of libraries is relatively straightforward, as will be explained later. Finally, the decision to focus on libraries is partly opportunistic: Compared to many other types of local public services for which systematic data are hard to find, public libraries have been the subject of regular and comprehensive data collection by the National Center for Education Statistics (NCES) since the early 1990s.

The remainder of this chapter is organized as follows. First, I provide a brief overview of the historical development and geographic diffusion of library districts. Next, I analyze the performance of libraries in library districts relative to libraries operated by general-purpose governments along three dimensions: financing, collections and staffing, and utilization and efficiency. I then compare my findings with those from studies of other types of districts in the literature. Finally, I discuss the implications of these results for my fiscal common-pool theory of jurisdictional overlap.

5.1 BACKGROUND[1]

Public libraries existed in the United States as early as the mid-1800s, but special-purpose government provision of library services did not become commonplace until the 1950s and 1960s. The leader in the development of library districts was Indiana, where a statewide system of library districts evolved organically from the state's original system of city and town public libraries. A 1901 state law enabled all cities and incorporated towns to establish public libraries with independent appointed boards. Between 1899 and 1917, well over 100 libraries were built in the state thanks to grants from the Carnegie Corporation, which were provided on the condition that the community receiving the library facility would support its operations with a local tax. By the 1940s, a statewide system of public library districts coterminous with one or more general-purpose local governments had evolved, numbering 188, which accounted for nearly all library districts in existence nationwide at the time.

Perhaps because of their small number, few early-twentieth-century scholarly accounts of special municipal corporations mentioned library districts at all (e.g., Guild 1918; Kettleborough 1914). Library districts were discussed in Kirk H. Porter's early appraisal of special districts, in which he disapprovingly referred to them as a kind of "disguised" special district, meaning one coterminous with a city or county (Porter 1933). According to Porter, advocates of library district creation in the 1930s typically argued that the establishment of independent library governments would remove library administration from the negative influences and constant fluctuations of local politics. Library districts also grew increasingly appealing during the 1930s because their independent taxing powers assured local libraries a reliable stream of funding. During the Great Depression, city and county libraries experienced drastic budget cuts and, in many cases, struggled to meet the increases in demand for their services that resulted from soaring unemployment (Martin 1998).

At the same time, the number of professional librarians with formal education and training was increasing dramatically. Supported by the

---

1 Sarah Anzia cowrote this section on the historical development of library districts.

already well-established American Library Association (ALA), the growing class of library professionals was committed to the provision of free,
high-quality, uninterrupted library service, achieved through the proliferation of library districts. In 1956, the ALA's lobbying in Washington
paid off: Congress passed the Library Services Act, which established a
$7.5 million federal grant program to the states to enhance library ser-
vice in rural areas. In 1964, the enticements for expanding library services grew even stronger when Congress passed the Library Services and
Construction Act (LSCA), which authorized $73 million in its first year to
strengthen state library agencies, help local libraries finance construction,
and assist libraries in communities of any size in the provision of services
(Martin 1998).

The push for a universal minimum level of library service nationwide,
the increasing acceptance of special-purpose government as a way to
accomplish that goal, the passage of state enabling legislation, and the
lure of state and federal financial support ignited an upsurge in the creation of public library districts beginning in the 1950s and continuing
steadily up to the present. As shown in Table 5.1, the number of library
districts in the United States increased from 207 in 1942 (of which all but
19 were in Indiana) to 1,580 in 2002. In the latter year, library districts
had spread to 26 states and nearly 850 counties. The rapid pace of library
district creation across the country has not slowed in recent years. Texas,
for example, has only recently opened the door to public library districts
(O'Connor 2004).

In their institutional and fiscal parameters, library districts comport
with the picture of other special-purpose jurisdictions presented in
Chapter 2. In all the states that enable creation of public library districts, an independent government can be established when enough signatures are gathered to place a proposition on the ballot. The district
is formed when a majority (of those who turn out) vote in favor of
the proposed jurisdiction and a new tax rate to fund its operations.
Beyond this commonality, library district design differs from state to
state. Library districts can cross municipal and county lines or be coterminous with existing government boundaries. They can serve populations of anywhere from a few hundred to a few hundred thousand and
may or may not provide their own library collections. Typically, library
districts are governed by an elected board of trustees, but there are
several districts in which governing board members are appointed by
other government officials.[2] Most districts depend on property taxation

---

2 For example, trustees of Indiana library districts are appointed by county, municipal, town, township, or school board officials.

Table 5.1. *Library Districts, 1942–2002*

Year	Library Districts	States Where Present
1942	207	4
1952	269	7
1957	322	9
1962	349	9
1967	410	10
1972	498	11
1977	586	12
1982	638	13
1987	830	15
1992	1,043	17
1997	1,496	26
2002	1,580	26

Source: Census of Governments.

for their operating revenue, but some districts rely on a special sales tax instead (O'Connor 2004). Depending on a district's size, service population, and revenue stream, it might offer a traditional book collection, audio and visual materials, access to cooperating network libraries, bookmobile distribution, books-by-mail service, children's reading programs, and other services.

5.2 ANALYSIS: DO LIBRARY DISTRICTS PERFORM BETTER?

In this section, I compare the performance of public libraries operated as special districts with the performance of libraries operated by general-purpose governments. My data on the performance of public libraries come from the Public Libraries Survey (PLS) conducted by the NCES. The PLS collects data on the finances, employment, collections, and operations of all public libraries in the United States. Annual public use data files from the PLS are available for 1992 through 2004 and contain data on roughly 8,900 public libraries each year. After merging the annual data files and matching individual libraries across years, I was able to assemble a panel data set of 114,756 observations.

For PLS purposes, a public library is defined as an entity established under state enabling laws to serve a specific geographic constituency, supported in whole or in part with public funds, and providing at least the following: a collection of printed or other library materials; paid

employees; a time when the library is open to the public; and facilities
to support the collection and staff. A library may have only one main
outlet, or it may be a system with multiple branches. The vast majority
of public libraries operate under one of three *legal bases*: operation by
a general-purpose local government, such as a city or county; operation
by a special district; or operation by a nonprofit organization. My aim
is to compare the performance of special district libraries with that of
municipal and nonprofit libraries. The PLS contains a variety of performance outcomes, ranging from the size of the collection to the number
of circulation transactions, as will be explained later. Another important advantage of the PLS, compared to the COG, is that it reports the
total population contained in the service area of each library, enabling
me to normalize many of the performance measures to an accurate *per
capita* basis. In addition, because the same area may be served by multiple overlapping library districts, the PLS contains information on *duplicated population*, or the population in a library's service area that is also
served by one or more other libraries. On average, only about 3 percent
of a library's population is duplicated in this way, but the figure is as
high as 50 percent in some cases.

My basic empirical strategy is to regress measures of library performance on indicators for institutional type, demographic controls, and
state and year fixed effects. Because the boundaries of library service
areas often do not conform to standard U.S. Census geographies, relatively few demographic controls are available. Lacking a source of
demographic data aggregated to library service areas, I utilize several
county-level control variables, the smallest level of geographic aggregation by which each library could be matched to an existing demographic
data set. From the Regional Economic Information System (REIS) of the
Bureau of Economic Analysis, I obtained estimates of the county's annual
per capita income, with the expectation that libraries in more affluent
counties will provide more elaborate collections and services. County
income will also capture local cost-of-living differentials that might
affect the costs of operating public libraries, most notably employee
salaries. From the 1990 U.S. Census, I obtained information on the fraction of the adult population with a college degree, the fraction under age
18, and the fraction over age 65. I expect each of these variables to be
positively associated with demand for library services. Year fixed effects
capture any secular changes in library performance over time due to, for
example, fluctuating national economic conditions. With the inclusion
of state fixed effects, identification in these models comes from differences between special district and municipal libraries within the same
state. This approach controls for any (measurable or unmeasureable)

time-invariant difference across states, such as statewide preferences or institutional features.[3]

Finally, I control for the libraries' administrative structure, based on PLS classifications. Specifically, I include a dummy variable for libraries with multiple service outlets (18 percent of cases) and a dummy variable for libraries with multiple service outlets *and* multiple administrative offices (1.5 percent of cases). The omitted category is for libraries with one service outlet and one administrative office, which account for the remaining 80 percent of the cases.

One notable weakness of the PLS is that the data appear not to have been "cleaned" or checked for coding errors. Whatever the cause, many of the relevant variables have a few extreme values that are clearly implausible. For example, one library with 8 full-time employees reports that there are only 18 people in its service area; another reports $23,000 per capita in annual operating expenditures; still another reports more than 1,000 annual visits per person in its service area. There are several instances in which the largest value for a particular variable is more than 1,000 times larger than the 99th percentile value. Many of the outlandish values appear to stem from errors in the population variable. In order to purge the data of these potentially influential outliers, I implemented the following protocol. For each model, I excluded all cases in which the reported value for the dependent variable was greater than 1.5 times the 95th percentile value or less than 0.5 times the 5th percentile value. Alternative approaches, such as taking logs of the dependent variables or winsorizing the data, yield results comparable to those presented later. Summary statistics for all of the variables are provided in Table A.16 of the Methodological Appendix.

The analysis proceeds in three stages. First, I compare taxing and spending by library districts relative to municipal and nonprofit libraries. Second, I analyze library collections and staffing. Finally, I examine several measures of utilization and operational efficiency.

5.2.1 Library Finances

I begin by comparing per capita revenue and expenditures for library districts relative to libraries operated under alternative institutional regimes, either municipal or nonprofit. This analysis of the finances of individual districts is an important complement to the analysis of

---

3 An ideal design for this analysis would include unit-level fixed effects for individual libraries over time. However, it is exceedingly rare for a library to change from municipally run to a special district or vice versa.

aggregate county area finances presented in the preceding chapter. The preceding aggregate-level analysis provided evidence for the prediction that aggregate taxes and spending will be higher when more jurisdictions have access to a shared tax base. The following analysis addresses the hypothesis that special districts will spend more on the services they provide than will a general-purpose government fulfilling the same function.

Table 5.2 presents three models of fiscal outcomes. Model (1) demonstrates that library districts raise roughly $5 per capita more in local revenue than do libraries operated by general-purpose governments (the omitted category). While $5 is not large in absolute terms, it amounts to a 28 percent increase for the average library, which obtains $18 per capita in local revenue. In fact, the relatively small per capita amount but large proportional increase points to one of the important elements of local fiscal politics suggested in Chapter 3: fiscal illusion. That is, a series of small tax increases by a large number of overlapping jurisdictions may arouse less of a reaction from voters than would an equivalent increase levied by a single government. In the aggregate, a series of small, incremental tax increases by multiple overlapping jurisdictions can add up to a fiscally consequential growth in the public sector, as demonstrated in the preceding chapter.

Models (2) and (3) show, respectively, that library districts also spend more on operating costs and capital expenditures than libraries operated by general-purpose governments. These results are consonant with findings from the preceding chapter (see Section 4.4.3) indicating that, while special districts do have higher capital expenditures per capita than general-purpose governments, this is not the primary explanation for districts' overall larger budgets. Rather, most of the difference in spending between district libraries and general-purpose libraries is attributable to operating expenditures. In addition, note that the sum of the operating and capital expenditure differentials between district libraries and general-purpose libraries is less than the differential in revenue; library districts on average raise $4.88 per capita in additional revenue but spend $4.24 more than municipally run libraries. This apparent discrepancy is consistent with the observation from at least one other study (Little Hoover Commission 2000) that special districts often tax more than they spend and accumulate large surpluses. However, given the confidence intervals around each of the estimates, I cannot reject the hypothesis that the sum of the coefficients in models (2) and (3) is equal to the coefficient in model (1)—in other words, that the sum of the operating and capital expenditure differentials is equal to the revenue differential between library districts and libraries operated by general-purpose governments.

Table 5.2. *Library Finances*

	Local Revenue per Capita	Operating Expenditures per Capita	Capital Expenditures per Capita
	(1)	(2)	(3)
Special district dummy	4.880***	3.190***	1.047***
	(0.903)	(0.783)	(0.209)
Nonprofit dummy	−7.835***	−3.020**	0.340***
	(1.069)	(1.357)	(0.110)
ln(service area population)	0.311	−0.954	0.072
	(0.473)	(0.639)	(0.075)
ln(duplicated population)	−0.0824	−0.00795	−0.0375
	(0.126)	(0.142)	(0.031)
County per capita income	0.931***	0.891***	0.0457***
	−0.24	−0.236	−0.0151
County pct BA (1990)	11.03	20.80*	1.357
	(9.671)	(10.890)	(1.206)
County pct age under 18 (1990)	9.813	19.57	4.11
	(19.340)	(18.750)	(3.158)
County pct age over 65 (1990)	5.069	16.76	0.541
	−9.058	−12.19	−1.423
Multiple admin. offices	−1.58	1.529	0.305
	(1.463)	(1.491)	(0.297)
Multiple outlets	0.484	2.304***	0.14
	(0.541)	(0.832)	(0.165)
Constant	−12.16	−3.957	−1.986
	(10.410)	(10.230)	(1.790)
Observations	106,203	106,959	105,430
R-squared	0.248	0.197	0.019

Notes: Observations are a panel of public libraries from 1992 to 2004. Robust standard errors clustered by state are in parentheses. All models include state and year fixed effects (not reported). For each model, observations where the dependent variable is greater than 1.5 times the 95th percentile value or less than 0.5 times the 5th percentile value are dropped (see text).
*** $p < 0.01$, ** $p < 0.05$, * $p < 0.1$.

In additional analyses, I estimated comparable models (not reported) wherein the dependent variables were federal and state aid received by public libraries. I found no difference between the aid received by library districts and by libraries operated by general-purpose governments. The larger sums of local revenue raised by library districts, therefore, cannot be attributed to a shortfall in state or federal aid relative to other public libraries.

Relatively few of the control variables evince a significant relationship with library finances. Nonprofit libraries receive less public funding than libraries operated by local governments and spend less on library operations. However, nonprofit libraries spend somewhat more on capital investments than libraries run by general-purpose governments, though less than library districts. County-level income is robustly, and unsurprisingly, positively related to all three of the dependent variables in Table 5.2. Each additional $1,000 of per capita income is associated with $0.93 in additional revenue, $0.89 in operating expenditures, and $0.05 in capital expenditures per capita. This relationship may indicate that more affluent citizens demand better library services, or it may reflect cost-of-living differentials that make public services more expensive in high-income areas. The county-level education and age variables are positively associated with library taxes and spending, as predicted, but the relationships are not highly significant statistically. Library systems with multiple outlets or administrative offices also appear to spend more per capita on current operations and capital investment, although the relationship is significant in only one of the models.

The results shown in Table 5.2 reinforce the findings from the preceding chapter, now showing that special-function jurisdictions spend more than general-purpose governments providing the same service. The remaining question is whether special-purpose jurisdictions—in this case, library districts—also provide higher-quality services.

5.2.2 Library Collections and Staffing

While some aspects of library quality are difficult to observe—for instance, the expertise of the reference librarian—the heart of the matter is the quality of a library's collection. The PLS contains several variables regarding library collections, and I begin with the most basic: the number of books. Model (1) of Table 5.3 shows that library districts provide significantly fewer books per capita than libraries operated by general-purpose governments. Specifically, the coefficient indicates that library districts provide roughly one-half book less per person than municipally run libraries, which amounts to a difference of about 9 percent relative to the average library's 5.4 books per capita.[4] In addition, the PLS contains

---

4 The average (median) library holds 84,000 (26,000) books and serves a population of 30,000 (6,700). See Table A.16 of the Methodological Appendix for additional details.

Table 5.3. *Library Collections and Staffing*

	Books per Capita (1)	Employees per Capita (2)	Percent Librarians (3)	Avg. Library Wage/ Avg. County Wage (4)	Percent Other Expenses (5)
Special district dummy	-0.477**	0.259	-0.120**	-0.0026	0.255***
	(0.183)	(0.170)	(0.048)	(0.012)	(0.036)
Nonprofit dummy	-0.0122	-0.848***	0.0651	-0.0444***	0.330***
	(0.218)	(0.265)	(0.106)	(0.009)	(0.040)
ln(service area population)	-2.005***	-1.094***	-0.530***	0.0483***	-0.0321***
	(0.175)	(0.237)	(0.033)	(0.007)	(0.012)
ln(duplicated population)	0.0101	-0.00512	0.0210**	0.00321***	-0.000701
	(0.035)	(0.033)	(0.010)	(0.001)	(0.003)
County per capita income	0.0481***	0.140***	-0.00824***	-0.00734***	-0.00575***
	(0.014)	(0.038)	(0.003)	(0.002)	(0.001)
County pct BA (1990)	5.035***	5.980***	0.334	0.264	0.108
	(1.519)	(1.905)	(0.369)	(0.160)	(0.168)
County pct age under 18 (1990)	2.414	6.112	-0.314	0.0645	0.293
	(2.825)	(4.345)	(0.843)	(0.339)	(0.318)

(continued)

Table 5.3. (continued)

	Books per Capita	Employees per Capita	Percent Librarians	Avg. Library Wage/ Avg. County Wage	Percent Other Expenses
	(1)	(2)	(3)	(4)	(5)
County pct age over 65 (1990)	9.234**	7.233**	1.014*	0.967***	0.509
	(3.629)	(3.071)	(0.570)	(0.265)	(0.321)
Multiple admin. offices	3.134***	1.662***	0.636***	−0.0424**	0.0743
	(0.408)	(0.611)	(0.102)	(0.019)	(0.057)
Multiple outlets	1.845***	1.215***	0.206***	−0.0193*	0.0243
	(0.241)	(0.363)	(0.037)	(0.011)	(0.017)
Percent librarians				0.0860***	
				(0.018)	
Constant	18.70***	8.840***	5.367***	0.148	−1.047***
	(1.343)	(2.373)	(0.418)	(0.166)	(0.208)
Observations	106,574	106,641	107,484	64,812	64,393
R-squared	0.346	0.101	NA	0.104	NA

Notes: Observations are a panel of public libraries from 1992 to 2004. Robust standard errors clustered by state are in parentheses. All models include state and year fixed effects (not reported). For each model, observations where the dependent variable is greater than 1.5 times the 95th percentile value or less than 0.5 times the 5th percentile value are dropped (see text). Models (3) and (5) are estimated by fractional logit; all other by linear regression. Note that there was significant item nonresponse for the dependent variables in models (4) and (5) (see text).

***p < 0.01, **p < 0.05, *p < 0.1.

data on many other components of a library's collection and services: audio books, videos, serial subscriptions, Internet access, and bookmobiles. To conserve space, I will not report the results of all of these models. Suffice it to say that the only significant difference I found in any of these models is that library districts provide significantly more *videos* than libraries operated by general-purpose governments, a differential that is equivalent to about 14 percent of the average number of videos. While it might be tempting to conclude from this result that library districts are more technologically advanced, the null findings for Internet access and audio books run counter to this intuition.

If not excelling in its collection, a library may achieve excellence in its staffing. Model (2) of Table 5.3 suggests that library districts do not have any more employees than municipally run libraries. The estimated coefficient is statistically insignificant and relatively small—equivalent to about 4 percent of the average district's employment. It does not appear, therefore, that library districts compensate for their smaller collections by providing more staffing.[5] Could it be that districts provide *better* staffing? The quality of a library's staff is not directly observable, but the PLS does contain data on the fraction of employees who are actually librarians. Presumably, patrons rely on librarians, rather than administrators or maintenance workers, to provide services that enhance their satisfaction with the library. Model (3) shows that library districts have a significantly lower proportion of librarians among their employees compared to libraries operated by general-purpose governments. Because the dependent variable is a proportion, the model is estimated as a *fractional logit* (Papke and Wooldridge 1996), so the coefficients are not directly interpretable. To put the size of the effect in context, the marginal effect of being a library district on the proportion of staff who are librarians, holding other values at their means, is 3 percentage points. This is a relatively small effect, as the average library has 57 percent librarians among its staff.

The results shown thus far present a bit of a puzzle: Library districts have fewer books and comparable staffing levels, though relatively fewer librarians, than municipally run libraries. Yet, library districts have significantly larger budgets. So, where does the extra money go? The money does not appear to go into employee salaries. Model (4) of Table 5.3

---

5 An implication of the results from models (1) and (2) is that library districts have a significantly higher ratio of employees per book than libraries operated by general-purpose governments. In other words, library districts have a significantly higher labor-to-capital ratio. This difference is consistent with disproportionate influence of labor unions in library districts, although I have no direct evidence of union influence.

shows that the average wage for library employees, relative to the average wage in the county, is no different for library districts than for libraries operated by other kinds of governments. If libraries do not have bigger collections, larger staffs, or more generous employee compensation, then their additional money must be going elsewhere. Model (5) shows that such is indeed the case, as the districts have a significantly higher fraction of their expenditures classified as *other*, defined as expenditures not devoted to collections or staff. Again, because the dependent variable is a proportion, I have used a fractional logit model, whose coefficients are not easily interpretable. The marginal effect is fairly large, as the coefficient indicates that library districts devote 4.5 percentage points more of their budgets to other spending categories. The average library allocates roughly 21 percent of its budget to items other than staff and collections, so 4.5 percentage points would represent more than a 20 percent increase. One caveat with respect to models (4) and (5) is that there is significant item nonresponse for some of the detailed financial questions in the PLS—which explains the smaller sample sizes in these models compared to the others—so the results must be interpreted with appropriate caution.

Unfortunately, the PLS data do not permit me to decompose the *other* category into any finer detail, so it is impossible to know how exactly that money is put to use. It is worth noting that in the literature on school districts, the fraction of spending on administration is one oft-used, though not uncontroversial, indicator of inefficiency (see Hanushek 1986). By extension, one might imagine that library district spending on administration—that is, *other*—is an indication of inefficiency. Without further information, however, it is not possible to say that such spending does not produce something of value to patrons. Still, it would be very hard to argue, on the basis of the results shown in Table 5.3, that library districts perform *better* than other types of libraries.

The control variables in Table 5.3 perform more or less as expected. The results show that nonprofit libraries have fewer employees than other types of libraries and pay them less. That said, nonprofit libraries have collections as large as those of municipal libraries and larger than those of special district libraries. Libraries located in counties with higher income or education levels tend to have more books and employees. The presence of children is not associated with the size of collections or staff, but libraries serving more elderly residents are better staffed and better stocked. Average salaries are higher when more of a library's employees are librarians.

5.2.3 Library Utilization and Efficiency

Of course, many aspects of a library's quality are not measured in the PLS data. For instance, one library building may be more beautiful than another or its staff friendlier. While I cannot directly observe these intangible aspects of library quality, it seems reasonable to expect that citizens will want to use a library more often when it is of better quality, and they will be less inclined to use a mediocre library, all else equal. If so, then one summary measure of a library's quality is its utilization, controlling for the demographics of its service area. In other words, given two libraries serving objectively similar populations, there is reason to believe that the one that is used more heavily is more desirable from the citizens' perspective. Models (1) and (2) of Table 5.4 estimate utilization rates for library districts relative to other types of libraries. Model (1) estimates library circulation per capita, which measures the number of circulation transactions per person in the service area. Of course, if libraries provide programs or services that patrons value, such as children's reading groups, then citizens may visit the library without checking out materials, making circulation an underestimate of library utilization. Therefore, model (2) estimates library *visits* per capita. However, the differences between special districts and other types of libraries are not statistically significant according to either measure. The point estimates are negative, suggesting that, if anything, district libraries are underutilized relative to libraries operated by general-purpose governments.

That library districts spend more but do not appear to provide more books or better services, or achieve higher utilization by patrons, suggests that they are less efficient than other types of libraries. By *less efficient*, I mean that it costs more to provide a comparable level of service. Models (3) and (4) of Table 5.4 test this proposition directly by estimating the average cost per circulation transaction and the average cost per library visit for districts relative to municipally run libraries. Model (3) indicates that it costs roughly 40 cents more for each circulation transaction in a library district. This 40-cent premium amounts to about 12 percent of average library costs, which run $3.34 per circulation transaction. The average cost per visit—again, to capture the possibility that desirable services may lure patrons to visit the library without necessarily checking out materials—is also higher in library districts. According to model (4), library districts spend 52 cents more per visit, which is equivalent to roughly 10 percent of the average cost per visit, $5.37.

Again, the control variables appear to operate in sensible ways. Nonprofit libraries are more efficient than special district libraries,

Table 5.4. *Library Utilization and Efficiency*

	Circulation per Capita	Visits per Capita	Cost per Circulation	Cost per Visit
	(1)	(2)	(3)	(4)
Special district dummy	−0.219	−0.0488	0.396***	0.515***
	(0.196)	(0.0881)	(0.130)	(0.131)
Nonprofit dummy	−0.323	−0.420***	−0.368	−0.178
	(0.271)	(0.140)	(0.239)	(0.232)
ln(Service area population)	−0.432**	−0.176*	−0.0413	−0.112**
	(0.168)	(0.0913)	(0.0544)	(0.0498)
ln(Duplicated population)	−0.0520*	−0.0219	0.0541***	0.0279
	(0.0300)	(0.0250)	(0.0194)	(0.0256)
County per capita income	0.0924***	0.0764***	0.0504*	0.0736**
	(0.0166)	(0.00946)	(0.0300)	(0.0317)
County pct BA (1990)	12.18***	4.799***	−0.745	−0.638
	(2.860)	(1.041)	(1.330)	(1.477)
County pct under age 18 (1990)	4.707	0.324	3.264	0.387
	(5.818)	(2.460)	(3.342)	(2.720)
County pct over age 65 (1990)	10.04**	4.359**	−2.011	−3.036**
	(4.680)	(1.756)	(1.340)	(1.398)
Multiple admin offices	0.342	−0.352	0.311*	1.314***
	(0.460)	(0.277)	(0.176)	(0.390)
Multiple outlets	0.0546	−0.141	0.396***	0.823***
	(0.222)	(0.126)	(0.0883)	(0.0998)
Constant	5.197	3.077**	0.992	4.039***
	(3.260)	(1.386)	(1.143)	(0.957)
Observations	106,716	106,213	106,868	106,288
R-squared	0.050	0.047	0.106	0.064

Notes: Observations are a panel of public libraries, 1992 to 2004. Robust standard errors clustered by state are in parentheses. All models include state and year fixed effects (not reported). For each model, observations where the dependent variable is greater than 1.5 times the 95th percentile value of less than 0.5 times the 5th percentile value are dropped (see text).
***$p < 0.01$, **$p < 0.05$, *$p < 0.1$.

although no different from municipally operated libraries. There is weak evidence of economies of scale, as the average cost per visit is declining in service area population, although the result for average cost per circulation transaction fails to attain statistical significance. Libraries in high-income counties experience more visits and more circulation transactions, consistent with the idea that more affluent citizens have higher demand for library services. At the same time, the average cost per visit and per circulation transaction is higher in more affluent counties, which may reflect higher operating costs. The relationship between education and library utilization is highly significant, as expected. Somewhat surprisingly, the presence of children is not significantly related to library utilization, although the presence of the elderly is. Finally, libraries that operate multiple outlets are significantly more expensive (per visit and per transaction) and fail to attain higher utilization.

5.2.4   Summary

Collectively, the results presented in Tables 5.2 to 5.4 paint a fairly clear picture. Library districts do spend significantly more than other types of libraries. But library districts have fewer books. Districts have a comparable number of employees, although their employees are less likely to be actual librarians, relative to libraries operated by general-purpose governments. Unsurprisingly, given that districts spend more but offer fewer books and have no more employees than other libraries, the share of district budgets allocated to other expenditures is also significantly higher. Despite spending more, library districts do not attract more visitors or have higher circulation than municipally run libraries. In spending more while failing to provide a larger collection or attain higher utilization, library districts are significantly less efficient than other types of libraries, at least according to the two simple measures used previously. Library districts spend roughly 10 percent more per circulation transaction and per visit than libraries operated by general-purpose governments. Overall, these results are entirely consistent with the common-pool model, as well as with the empirical results presented in the preceding chapter. Finding similar results using different data sources, units of aggregation, and modeling strategies is reassuring.

5.3   RELATED STUDIES

Results from the preceding analysis are fairly clear and compelling, but libraries are only one of the many services provided by local governments. Is there any evidence to suggest that the library results are typical of the differences between special-function and general-purpose jurisdictions providing the same services? Unfortunately, relatively few studies have attempted to assess the quality or efficiency of public services provided by special-purpose governments compared to those of general-purpose governments. The study most similar to my analysis of library districts is that of Emanuelson (2008), who compared the performance of independent park districts to that of municipal parks and recreation departments in 10 midwestern states. He found that park districts spend on average nearly three times the amount per capita that parks and recreation departments spend. Yet, the average park district provides, on a per capita basis, fewer park facilities, fewer recreation programs, and fewer acres of parkland than the average parks and recreation department. Based on the information provided by the author, however, it is not clear whether these differences are statistically significant.

Several additional studies are confined to a single state. In a study of water utilities in Nevada, Bhattacharyya and colleagues (1995) found that utilities operated by water districts were significantly less efficient than those operated by county or municipal governments, although all three types of public utilities were less efficient than utilities operated by private firms.

Thompson (1997) conducted a survey of citizen satisfaction with various public services in Michigan. He found that citizens were more satisfied with library and fire services provided by general-purpose governments than with those provided by special districts; for the remaining five services he investigated, satisfaction was not significantly related to the type of jurisdiction providing them. Thompson also found that vast majorities of respondents expressed a preference for having services delivered by a city or town, whereas less than 3 percent of respondents preferred that a special district provide any given service. At the same time, many citizens did not understand which type of jurisdiction was actually providing their services at present.

Based on a survey of Illinois residents, Chicione and Walzer (1985, ch. 6) found that the perceived quality of public services is negatively associated with the number of single-function governments per capita in a county. Park and school districts were exceptions, where citizen satisfaction was positively correlated with the per capita number of special-purpose jurisdictions.

In sum, the weight of the evidence from other studies is generally consistent with the results from my analysis of public libraries suggesting that special-function districts are less efficient and provide no better quality than general-purpose governments. That said, this is clearly an area in which more research would pay high dividends.

5.4   DISCUSSION

Based on the results of my analysis of library districts, as well as the few existing related studies, it would be difficult to sustain the argument that special districts justify their higher budgets by providing higher-quality services than general-purpose governments. Along every measurable dimension of performance, specialized districts do no better—and often do worse—than municipalities performing the same function. Therefore, it appears unlikely that the negative welfare consequences of higher taxes due to jurisdictional overlap are offset by better quality due to functional specialization.

From the perspective of my theory of special interest politics and selective participation, the results shown in this chapter suggest that function-specific interest groups demand from specialized government something other than higher levels of the same services provided by municipalities. They may demand specialized services that cater to preference outliers— for example, heated swimming pools for park districts or elaborate computer facilities at public libraries. Based on the available data, I cannot rule out the possibility that specialized governments excel along some less tangible dimensions such as these. At the very least, however, the burden shifts to proponents of special-purpose jurisdictions to provide convincing evidence of some dimension on which these institutions outperform, rather than merely outspend, general-purpose governments.

Taken together, the results of this chapter and the preceding one establish the case that jurisdictional overlap with concurrent taxation leads to a fiscal common-pool problem, resulting in overexploitation of the shared tax base, compared to a general-purpose government. There is no evidence suggesting that higher spending by specialized governments can be attributed to higher-quality services. Establishing the existence of a fiscal common-pool problem is not the end of the story, however. The literature is replete with examples of successfully managed common-pool resources. The next chapter explores the potential for "governing the fiscal commons" that is the shared local tax base.

6

Governing the Fiscal Commons

The preceding chapters have demonstrated that when local governments overlap, the shared tax base takes on the character of a fiscal common-pool resource (CPR), leading to a familiar result; namely, "overfishing." The aim of the present chapter is to investigate another dimension of jurisdictional overlap. In particular, one of the striking themes in the CPR literature is that institutions often develop, deliberately or organically, to mitigate the potential tragedy of the commons. What, then, are the institutions, if any, that govern the local fiscal commons? I argue that local political parties can play this role by coordinating the policies of multiple overlapping governments.

The chapter proceeds as follows. I begin by briefly reviewing the literature on successful CPR management. The remainder of the chapter focuses on the role of local political parties in managing the fiscal commons. I discuss parties first theoretically, exploring their means and motives in fiscal policy. Next, I provide an empirical test of the interaction between party organizational strength and jurisdictional overlap. The results indicate that counties with strong party organizations are able largely to overcome the fiscal common-pool problem of overlapping jurisdictions.

6.1 COMMONS KNOWLEDGE

In her seminal study of institutions governing CPRs, Elinor Ostrom observes that "At the most general level, the problem facing CPR appropriators is one of organizing: how to change the situation from one in which appropriators act independently to one in which they adopt coordinated strategies to obtain higher joint benefits or reduce their joint harm" (1990, p. 39). Even when collective benefits may be obtained through organizing, however, appropriators face a number of hurdles. Ostrom (1990) identifies three types of collective action problems that principals must solve in a CPR situation. First is the problem of institutional supply: Although there may be demand for an institution to govern the commons, supplying the institution is equivalent to creating another public good, subject to the same incentive problems that led to the CPR problem itself. Second is the problem of credible commitment: Although the collective welfare may be higher when all follow the rules, each has an incentive to deviate for short-term gain if monitoring and sanctions are not strong. Finally, and closely related, is the problem of monitoring: Monitoring and imposing sanctions are costly actions, and each actor has an incentive to free-ride on the efforts of others, suggesting yet another nested collective action problem.

In spite of these and other seemingly formidable obstacles, an ever-growing body of empirical research shows that many actors have been able to create institutions to successfully manage CPRs (Ostrom 1990; Ostrom, Gardner, and Walker 1994). Ostrom (1990, ch. 3) provides a useful summary of some of the common characteristics of successful, long-lived CPR institutions. Among the features she emphasizes are the following. The individuals affected by the institution are able to participate in creating and modifying the rules. Clearly defined boundaries denote who has the right to withdraw resources and how much. Monitoring is done either by the appropriators or by an outside party accountable to the appropriators. Conflict resolution mechanisms are available to quickly resolve disputes among appropriators or between appropriators and monitors. The CPR institution itself is accepted by external government authorities. In addition, outcomes are influenced by the number of appropriators, their discount rates, the presence of common interests and interactions outside the CPR situation, and the availability of strong leadership in the group (Ostrom 1990, p. 188).

With this background, what, if any, CPR institutions can be identified in the arena of local government finance? Many candidates present themselves. Metropolitan or regional governance institutions, both formal and informal, may help to coordinate policies among the many local governments serving an area (Rusk 1993). Revenue-sharing agreements among governments may cause individual jurisdictions to internalize the effects of their policies on the common tax base (Orfield 1997). Similar to revenue sharing, centralization of revenue collection by the state government, which would then redistribute funds to local jurisdictions, would amount to a form of vertical integration of the taxing authority. More direct approaches include various constitutional and statutory limitations on the revenue-raising or expenditure authority of local governments (Ladd and Tideman 1981). As such, tax and expenditure limitations do not alter the *incentives* of local governments as CPR appropriators, but simply restrict their *access* to the common tax base.

Each of the examples mentioned, and no doubt many others, warrant analysis from a fiscal CPR management perspective. In this chapter, however, I will focus on one particularly promising institution for coordinating the fiscal policies of overlapping local governments: political parties.

6.2 POLITICAL PARTIES, MULTILEVEL GOVERNMENT, AND COLLECTIVE ACTION PROBLEMS

The argument that local political parties, or "machines," function to informally organize and centralize fragmented urban power structures dates back at least to Banfield (1961, 1970) and Wilson (1973). A number of later scholars have applied these ideas to large-n studies of state and local politics as well as to case studies of particular cities or political machines; prominently, see Jones (1983), Shefter (1985), Erie (1988), and Fuchs (1992). A central theme of this literature is that the presence of a strong party constrains public spending because politicians are able to resist the demands of interest groups when they can rely on electoral majorities delivered by the party organization. Miranda (1994) finds that public budgets are smaller in cities with a strong party organization, while Mayhew (1986) and Primo and Snyder (2007) produce the same finding at the state level.

Although the aforementioned studies address the role of parties in suppressing interest group spending demands—an obvious connection with the theory I put forth in Chapter 3—none of them explicitly discusses how parties coordinate the policies of territorially overlapping jurisdictions in a multilevel government. A more direct precedent for the argument I intend to make is found in Riker's (1964) early work on federalism. More so than any constitutional provision or explicit policy decision, Riker saw the political party organization as the most important factor determining the extent to which the activities of different levels of government in a federation are integrated or centralized. When the same party controls multiple layers of government, it can serve to informally coordinate their policies. As Riker wrote, "the federal relationship is centralized according to the degree to which parties organized to operate the central government control the parties organized to operate the constituent governments. This amounts to the assertion that the proximate cause of variations in the degree of centralization (or peripheralization) in the constitutional structure of a federation is the variation in degree of party centralization" (1964, p. 129).

Riker's argument about the fundamental integrative role of political parties in a federal system has received renewed attention recently, for example in the work of Filippov, Ordeshook, and Shvetsova (2004), Kramer (2000), and Rodden (2005).

Filippov, Ordeshook, and Shvetsova (hereafter FOS), are concerned broadly with the provision of collective goods and the regulation of externalities in federations. They frame the federal system as a multiplayer prisoners' dilemma, in which all states share in the collective benefits of union but each individual state would be better off if it could unilaterally "defect" by not contributing to the collective costs. Because the game is one of repeated interactions, FOS invoke the folk theorem to suggest that many equilibria are possible, including stable cooperative equilibria. In essence, their focus is on the same type of collective action problem that I identified with respect to overlapping jurisdictions in Chapter 3. FOS seek to identify particular institutions that increase the likelihood of arriving at stable, socially desirable equilibria. Their chief candidate to fill such a role is the political party.

Like Riker, FOS see the party as an institution with the potential to integrate otherwise independent units of government. The party creates relationships of mutual dependence among politicians in different units of government through two primary mechanisms. First, party labels link the electoral prospects of copartisan politicians in different units of government. Second, parties provide ladders of advancement for politicians as their careers progress through different units and levels of government. In each situation, being a member of a party makes the individual politician better off than if she were not a member. Therefore, FOS argue, copartisans are more likely to be able to reach cooperative equilibria than completely independent politicians would be. In other words, even when an individual politician may, all else equal, prefer to defect by pursuing a policy that benefits her current constituents at the expense of those in other units, she will refrain from doing so because it is more important to preserve alliances with copartisans in the long run.

Rodden (2005) has done the most important empirical work on the role of parties in influencing the fiscal policy of federations. He is concerned with situations in which state or local governments can borrow money with an expectation that the debt will be repaid by the central government, which creates common-pool incentives for excessive borrowing. Rodden (2005, ch. 5) finds that overall deficits are lower in federal countries when larger proportions of the leaders of state and local governments are members of the same party that controls the central government. He concludes that vertically integrated parties "create links between central and provincial politicians, creating 'electoral externalities' that give provincial politicians incentives to be concerned with national collective goods rather than purely local interests" (p. 11).

The basic argument that political parties can serve to unite politicians involved in different facets of government is, of course, not unique to problems of federalism.[1] The quintessential explanation of parties as solutions to collective action dilemmas is provided by Aldrich (1995), who also emphasizes the importance of party labels and career ladders. Within Congress specifically, Cox and McCubbins (1993) and Kiewiet and McCubbins (1991) portray parties as cartels that centralize and orchestrate the legislative process for the benefit of their members. Indeed, the argument of Kiewiet and McCubbins that parties coordinate various committees and "subgovernments" in the appropriations process to mitigate fiscal externalities is very similar to—and partly the inspiration for—the argument I will make about the role of parties in coordinating fiscal policy among overlapping local governments.

6.2.1   Local Parties: Means and Motives

I contend that political parties often play a role in local politics analogous to their role in federal and congressional politics, described previously. At the simplest level, each U.S. county can be thought of as a "mini-federation" with multiple overlapping layers of government. Seen from this perspective, the argument of Riker, Rodden, FOS, and others that political parties integrate or centralize policy across governmental units translates more or less directly to the local sector. For such arguments to apply in this setting, however, local parties must have both the *motive* and the *means*—using the terminology of FOS—to play the integrative role assigned to them in theory.

The party's motive is grounded in electoral competition. Nearly all the theories mentioned previously rely on the assumption that politicians are fundamentally motivated by reelection and that their electoral prospects are enhanced when they band together as a party. The electoral motive for local political parties can be seen clearly by returning to the theoretical model introduced in Chapter 3.

With specialized jurisdictions and selective political participation, the collective policy outcome involves overspending on all goods. An individual politician operating independently has a chance to be elected only

---

1 Nor is the argument unique to politics. As explained in Chapter 1, the overlapping-governments problem in local public finance is analogous to the double-marginalization (or chain-of-monopolies) problem familiar in the economic theory of monopoly (Spengler 1950; Tirole 1988). Vertical integration is one way that private firms are able to overcome the double-marginalization problem, and I contend that the same principle applies in the case of overlapping governments, where parties play the role of a single owner of the integrated "firm."

if his platform is x^*_{sj} on the good within his jurisdiction. Notice, however, that if a party ran one candidate for each office, and if these candidates collectively offered the socially optimal policy vector, the party could defeat an opposing group of candidates who ran proposing x^*_{sj} on all goods. In other words, *if voters selected candidates as groups rather than as individuals*—which is to say, as parties—then, the group offering efficient policies would dominate any other group. The reason is that when voters choose a party, rather than choosing individual candidates office by office, they are effectively in the same position as voters choosing a candidate for the general-function government, and I have already shown that the vote-maximizing policy for such a candidate is the (weighted) social welfare-maximizing policy vector. Thus, electoral competition provides a motive for parties to propose more efficient aggregate spending packages than individual independent politicians would propose.

If electoral competition provides the motive, then by what means can parties induce voters to select candidates as a group rather than independently, issue by issue? The primary mechanism is *slating*, which, according to Mayhew, "carries an implication of generating or adding to an official field of candidates by inducing people to enter it, and perhaps also limiting it by inducing others to stay out" (1986, pp. 19–20). Party control of slating is especially important for local elections, where few candidates have the personal resources or reputation to run without party support. Mayhew notes that in Gary, Indiana, for example, at the time of his writing, "Party control of nominations is so strong that any serious candidate pays a slating fee to the party in order to be considered for the slate" (1986, p. 98). Thus, with control over slating, a party can ensure that it puts forth a set of candidates with a collective vote-maximizing platform.

In conjunction with slating, options available to the party for rewarding cooperation or punishing defection from the party platform include recruiting those likely to cooperate (e.g., careerists), providing or withholding funding and personnel resources for campaigns, and encouraging or forestalling primary challenges. As explained later, these attributes are in fact fundamental components of Mayhew's (1986) definition of a *traditional party organization*.

Several other aspects of the situation suggest that this setting is likely to support the local party as a strong CPR institution, according to the criteria identified by Ostrom (1990). First, monitoring is nearly costless, since government budgets are publicly known. Thus, it is relatively easy for the monitor (party) to know exactly who is extracting from the tax base and how much. Second, institutional supply is not a major obstacle; political parties do not have to be created specifically for this purpose, since they generally already exist to serve other functions (Aldrich 1995). Third, because parties presumably have a longer life than any individual politician, they should be more willing to incur the costs of enforcement today in order to receive an increased stream of benefits from cooperation in the future. Finally, parties share many of the characteristics that Ostrom associates with successful, long-lived CPR institutions: Officeholders are also party members and presumably have some influence in creating and modifying its rules; the party provides a forum for resolving conflicts between appropriators; party members presumably have common interests and interactions outside of the fiscal arena; and access to the tax base is clearly defined and limited.

It is by no means obvious that every local political party will have the means to play the integrative role just described. On the one hand, because most local elections are nonpartisan—meaning that voters do not see a candidate's party affiliation printed on the ballot—the party label may not play as important a role in local elections as in national contests (Hawley 1973). On the other hand, because local offices are less visible, individual candidates are less likely to be able to rely on their own name recognition, significant campaign resources, or media coverage to win election without the resources of a party. While the importance of local parties no doubt varies from place to place, Oliver and Ha (2007) have shown that voters often name party affiliation as an important driver of vote choice *even in nonpartisan elections*. Regardless, it is not safe to simply assume that all local parties will be able to fullfil the coordination function; it is an empirical question.

Whatever the challenges, in order to succeed electorally with a socially efficient policy platform, the party must be able to obtain at least one of the two following outcomes. First, the party must be able to induce enough voters who are not members of the special interest group at stake in the specialized election to vote so that a candidate proposing lower spending can win. Second, the party must be able to induce special interest voters to cast a party line vote, even when the party's candidate proposes lower spending on their own good. Note that while it is in each group's immediate interest to defect by electing the higher-spending candidate, it may be in their long run interest to cooperate by voting the party line. As explained in Chapter 3, the situation is a repeated prisoners' dilemma, and cooperative equilibria are possible—not guaranteed, but possible. If the party can achieve one of these two goals, then the collective outcome will approximate the one that would have occurred if there were only one general-purpose government.

This argument suggests that where parties are strong—that is, where they are able to achieve one or both of the electoral outcomes just described—there should be smaller differences between the tax rates charged by general-purpose governments and those charged by a collection of special-purpose governments providing the same services. In other words, the effects of jurisdictional overlap in inflating local tax rates should be smaller where party organizations are stronger.

As noted previously, several existing studies have found that taxes and spending are significantly lower in areas with strong political parties—for example, Mayhew (1986), Miranda (1994), and Primo and Snyder (2007). My theory provides a different explanation for the observed effect of parties on the size of the budget. Fortunately, the explanation I am suggesting is observationally distinct: All of the existing studies focus on the *main effect* of party organization, while I expect an *interaction* between the number of overlapping governments and the presence of strong parties.

6.3   DATA AND METHODS

My empirical strategy is to incorporate variables measuring party organizational strength into the models of taxing and spending developed in the preceding chapters. I begin with Mayhew's (1986) *traditional party organization* (TPO) score. In what he describes as a sort of party organization "census," Mayhew reviews a remarkable range of sources—from the usual scholarly books and journal articles to local newspapers and even unpublished undergraduate course papers—to evaluate party organizations in the lower political units (usually counties) of each state. Based on this evaluation of the local party organizations, Mayhew assigns a TPO score of 1 (low) to 5 (high) to each state according the extent to which its *local* parties satisfy the following criteria:[2]

1. *It has substantial autonomy.* The local party acts substantially independently of public officials and party organizations at higher levels of government, as well as independently of corporations and labor unions.
2. *It lasts a long time.* The party has endured for decades and survived leadership changes.
3. *Its internal structure has an important element of hierarchy.* Local party leaders exert substantial influence in the promotion of candidates and in other party affairs.
4. *It regularly tries to bring about the nomination of candidates for a wide range of public offices.* The range ordinarily includes multiple

---

2 Items in italics are directly quoted from Mayhew (1986, pp. 19–20); all else is loosely paraphrased.

levels of government and multiple offices at each level. Often the effort involves slating candidates, which implies both recruiting some candidates and limiting access by others.

5. *It relies substantially on "material" incentives, and not much on "purposive" incentives, in engaging people to do organization work or to supply organization support.* Local parties rely on tangible rewards, such as money, appointive positions, and government contracts to maintain their supporters, rather than ideology or policy commitments.

These five criteria, not coincidentally, resemble many of the attributes that Ostrom (1990) ascribes to successful CPR institutions, as discussed previously. Thus, Mayhew's TPO scores provide a reasonable approximation of the party characteristics likely to be necessary for exerting control over a vertical structure of local governments. A complete list of state TPO scores is presented in the Methodological Appendix, Table A.17.

There are (at least) two limitations of Mayhew's TPO scores for present purposes. First, the scores were developed in 1986 to represent party characteristics in the 1950s and 1960s. The public finance data I will rely on cover the period from 1972 on. On the one hand, because the party scores are from an earlier period, they are plausibly exogenous to current spending decisions, which is desirable. On the other hand, to the extent that state party organizations have changed since the time of Mayhew's analysis—and in particular, to the extent that some state party organizations have become notably weaker (Besley, Persson, and Strum 2006)—the TPO scores will not reflect the contemporary party capacity to coordinate the behavior of local governments. However, Mayhew himself argues that party organization changes glacially (1986, esp. ch. 8). Indeed, he writes in his Introduction that "I came to think of American local-level electoral environments (in their structural aspects) as enduring independent variables, so to speak, settings capable of outlasting events, issues, individual politicians, ethnic groups, unions, and private corporations operating in politics, and even particular political parties, and able to shape to an appreciable degree what happens in politics and government as these things or actors happen, operate, or come and go" (p. 9). If Mayhew is correct about the longevity of party organizations, then his TPO scores should remain reasonably good proxies for party strength during the time period under study here. Nevertheless, as a robustness exercise, I extend the analyses using an alternative, more recent measure of party organizational strength, described later.

The second limitation is that Mayhew reports state-level TPO scores, which represent a rough average of the scores for each state's local political units.[3] Because my unit of analysis will be the county, TPO scores for this level would be ideal. However, Mayhew argues that "cities located in the same state almost always bear a family resemblance to each other in organizational forms" (1986, p. 23), which provides some comfort in using state-level scores here. In any event, both of these limitations should bias the results *against* finding a significant effect for the TPO score and its interaction with jurisdictional overlap.

I note that because the TPO score is a time-invariant state-level variable, it is not possible to estimate its main effect in models that use county-level fixed effects. This is not a serious concern, since the main effect of party organization is not a quantity of primary interest in my analysis. The important point is that it is possible to estimate the *interaction* between the TPO score and jurisdictional overlap even when county-level fixed effects are included. The interaction term reveals whether changes in jurisdictional overlap have different effects on spending depending on the level of party organizational strength, which is the central question of this chapter.

Finally, so as not to conflate party strength with partisanship or ideology, I add the Democratic Party's county-level presidential vote share as a control variable. I match each county-year observation to the vote share from the preceding presidential election. The presidential vote share variable should capture the county's partisan leanings, leaving the TPO score free to reflect party organizational strength.

6.4 RESULTS

Table 6.1 shows three specifications that extend the basic panel regression model developed in Chapter 4. In model (1), I simply add the TPO score as a covariate. As mentioned previously, because the TPO score is a time-invariant state-level variable, I cannot include state or county fixed

3 Mayhew (1986, pp. 21–22) explains that "In principle the score for each state is an average of scores for each of its lower political units (counties in most states) weighted appropriately according to population size, and each contributory score for a lower unit registers the incidence and influence of TPOs in its own electoral politics: minimal scores for locales with no TPOs at all, somewhat higher scores for locales where TPOs have exercised decisive influence in nominating processes for some lower-level offices some of the time (and where the TPO nominees have subsequently won election), and on up to maximal scores where TPOs have exercised decisive influence in nominating processes for major and minor offices year after year (and again nominees have won election). This is the plan in principle. In practice, given the evidence, it is impossible to be anywhere near so exact. My fallback procedure is to circumvent arithmetic and make scoring judgments about states as wholes, basing them on whatever evidence there is but staying as close as possible to the logic of positing scores for locales and then weighting and averaging them."

effects if I want to estimate the main effect of the TPO score. I do so in model (1) primarily for curiosity's sake, for the main effect of the TPO score is not a central issue here. That said, the results shown in Table 6.1 provide striking support for Mayhew's (1986) analysis of the relationship between party organization and the size of the public sector. The TPO effect is negative and significant, consistent with Mayhew's state-level cross-sectional results. A movement of one point on the TPO scale is associated with a decrease of $61 per capita, or roughly 5 percent of own-source revenue for the median county. It bears reemphasizing that while the TPO score is a state-level variable, the units of analysis here are counties, so that the proper interpretation of the coefficient is that counties in a state with a TPO score of, say, 1 collect about $60 more from each person in own-source revenue than counties in a state with a TPO score of 2, all else equal.

In many respects, the results shown here represent an ideal out-of-sample test of Mayhew's theory. His analysis covers the years 1953 through 1980, while I use data through 2002. In addition, Mayhew analyzes state-level data and finds that TPO scores are negatively associated with *combined* state and local revenue. Table 6.1 extends the analysis to the county level, thus confirming Mayhew's findings at a smaller level of aggregation. Moreover, the analysis here includes a much richer set of control variables than Mayhew's original analysis, which included only per capita income and an indicator variable for Confederate states. Perhaps most impressive, the size of the effects reported in Table 6.1 is roughly equivalent to the size of the effects reported by Mayhew. Across different years and a variety of specifications, Mayhew (1986, pp. 265–267) finds that a 1-point increase in the TPO score is associated with about a 2 to 6 percent decrease in revenue, well in line with the 5 percent effect reported here.

Mayhew offers five possible explanations for why having traditional party organizations is associated with having smaller public economies (1986, pp. 292–295). First, the types of people attracted to organization politics are unlikely to have program-building ambitions. Second, interest groups likely to desire ambitious governmental programs exercise less influence. Third, organization politics tends to be issueless and nonideological, removing some of the impetus for governmental action. Fourth, patronage tends to ward off bureaucracy, and the latter may be more expensive. Fifth, organization politics may foster a political culture skeptical of the government's ability to handle money responsibly. Mayhew provides case studies with some evidence supporting each of these lines of argument.

A different view of the TPO effect has been put forth recently by Primo and Snyder (2007). They contend that strong party organizations

Table 6.1. *Party Organization*

	(1)	(2)	(3)
Jurisdictional overlap	199.30	227.45	173.83
	(14.05)***	(48.48)***	(40.58)***
Mayhew TPO score	−60.57		
	(5.62)***		
Dummy = 1 if strong-party state		−62.01	
		(48.58)	
Jurisdictional overlap* Strong-party state dummy		−122.75	−209.07
		(37.27)***	(57.72)***
FPI	1.39	1.37	0.91
	(0.05)***	(0.05)***	(0.04)***
ln(population)	−171.52	−168.65	12.00
	(15.24)***	(15.26)***	(37.74)
Per capita income	0.08	0.08	0.02
	(0.00)***	(0.00)***	(0.00)***
Percent nonwhite	−321.89	−387.96	−208.50
	(67.54)***	(68.07)***	(152.97)
Five-year change in population	−833.63	−874.37	−244.86
	(92.94)***	(94.63)***	(88.14)***
Percent age ≤18	−818.34	−778.61	−328.27
	(425.26)*	(423.68)*	(470.53)
Percent age ≥65	−2,088.09	−2,069.62	−616.95
	(427.74)***	(427.44)***	(518.08)
Federal aid, five-year lag	0.29	0.29	0.02
	(0.15)*	(0.15)*	(0.03)
State aid, five-year lag	−0.01	−0.01	−0.10
	(0.03)	(0.03)	(0.04)***
Democratic presidential vote share	−3.86	−3.76	0.44
	(0.91)***	(0.91)***	(0.50)
Constant	−1,396.83	−1,503.31	−343.81
	(236.58)***	(234.25)***	(416.04)
R-squared (within)	0.40	0.40	0.33
Observations	21,184	21,196	21,196
# of clusters	3,030	3,032	3,032
Includes county fixed effects?	No	No	Yes

Notes: The dependent variable is general own-source revenue per capita. All dollar values are CPI-adjusted to year 2002 dollars. Standard errors, clustered by county, are reported in parentheses. All models include year dummies (not reported).
*significant at 10%, **significant at 5%, ***significant at 1%.

constrain pork-barrel spending. Primo and Snyder suggest that politicians seek spending to provide benefits to their constituents, which will enhance the prospects of reelection, a view that is consistent with the model I presented in Chapter 3. However, these authors argue that a strong political party alleviates legislators' demands for spending because politicians can rely on the party's reputation and organization, rather than on particularistic constituent benefits, to enhance their reelection goals. Therefore, overall government spending should be lower, and more efficient, in states with a strong party organization. Using a panel of state data from 1957 to 2000, Primo and Snyder also find that Mayhew's TPO score continues to have a significant negative relationship with spending.

I will not attempt here to evaluate or test these various explanations for the TPO main effect. However, such robust reaffirmation of Mayhew's findings does suggest that additional research into the mechanism underlying the TPO effect is warranted.

Returning to the main questions at hand, note that the effect of jurisdictional overlap holds even after controlling for party organization in model (1) of Table 6.1. The central hypothesis that there is an interaction between jurisdictional overlap and party strength is tested in models (2) and (3). To test this hypothesis, I estimate the interaction between the TPO score and jurisdictional overlap. First, I divide the counties into two groups: those in what Mayhew identifies as organization states (TPO scores of 4 or 5) and those in nonorganization states (TPO scores of 3 or less).[4] I then estimate the interaction between this TPO dummy variable and jurisdictional overlap. I begin by estimating the model without county fixed effects, which recovers the TPO main effect as well as the interaction term. As predicted, the interaction term is significant and negative. The proper interpretation of the coefficients is that jurisdictional overlap has a slope of $227 where the TPO dummy is 0 and a slope of $104 where the TPO dummy is 1.[5] The difference between the two slopes is statistically significant. Put differently, the overlap effect is about half as large in TPO states as in non-TPO states. The main effect of the TPO dummy is negative but not significant.

---

4 This same dichotomization of the TPO scale is used by Mayhew (1986) and Primo and Snyder (2007). Given that there is only one state with a TPO score of 3 (Louisiana), there does appear to be a natural grouping into these two categories. Furthermore, if I run equivalent models with dummy variables for all five TPO categories, my results regarding the interaction with jurisdictional overlap are substantively unchanged.

5 To recover the effect of jurisdictional overlap where the TPO dummy equals 1, simply add the two coefficients: $227 + -$123 = $104. The standard error is $34.

In model (3), I include county-level fixed effects, so that the specification mirrors that in Chapter 4 (e.g., model (1) of Table 4.3), plus the inclusion of the TPO interaction term. Differences in the TPO main effect (intercept) are picked up by the fixed effects.[6] The interaction remains highly significant and in the direction predicted. Specifically, the slope of jurisdictional overlap is estimated to be $174 in non-TPO states and –$35 in TPO states. In fact, I cannot reject the hypothesis that the effect of jurisdictional overlap is insignificant in TPO states (p = 0.38). Furthermore, when I run a fully interacted model—that is, a model allowing *all* the coefficients to differ for TPO and non-TPO states—the results with respect to jurisdictional overlap are nearly identical: Overlap has a positive effect on spending in weak-party states but not in strong-party states. Moreover, none of the other variables has a significantly different effect in TPO and non-TPO states.[7]

It also bears emphasizing that the magnitude of the overlap effect in non-TPO states is substantially larger than the results presented in Chapter 4 suggest. The coefficient of $174 for non-TPO counties in equation (3) indicates that increasing jurisdictional overlap from the 25th to the 75th percentile results in an increase of $160 per capita in own-source revenue. With median own-source revenue of $1,200 for non-TPO counties, this represents nearly a 15 percent increase in revenue collections. The models used in Chapter 4 pooled TPO and non-TPO counties together and thus underestimated the effect of jurisdictional overlap in weak-party states (and overestimated it in strong-party states).

In short, jurisdictional overlap does not have the inflationary effect on the public budget in areas with strong party organizations that it does elsewhere, consistent with the theory that strong parties coordinate the behavior of independent overlapping governments in order to mitigate overexploitation of the common tax base.

The other new variable used in this chapter is Democratic presidential vote share, which is significant and negative in models (1) and (2) of Table 6.1. This result is contrary to the conventional wisdom that the Republican Party is the party of fiscal conservatism. However, when county fixed effects are added in model (3), the Democratic vote share becomes insignificant, suggesting that Democratic partisanship is correlated with time-invariant county omitted variables that lead to lower spending.

---

6 A rule of thumb when using interaction terms is that the main effects of both components should also be included (Kam and Franzese 2007). I emphasize that this condition is satisfied here because the TPO main effect is subsumed in the county-level fixed effects.

7 Results of the fully interacted model are shown in the Methodological Appendix, Table A.13.

6.4.1 *Sensitivity Analysis*

Table 6.2 presents a set of sensitivity analyses. First, I show results separately for southern and nonsouthern states. As Besley et al. (2006) emphasize, the South underwent a substantial transformation from one-party dominance to two-party competition beginning in the 1950s. One may wonder, therefore, whether the party organization effect merely reflects a difference in the effect of jurisdictional overlap in southern states. Models (1) and (2), which respectively present results for nonsouthern and southern states, suggest that the TPO–overlap interaction is not unique to the South. The main effect of jurisdictional overlap is positive, and the interaction with the TPO dummy is negative in both models. The magnitude of the effects is comparable, although the interaction term is larger for southern states. So, party organizations in the South may be somewhat more effective in constraining overspending by overlapping jurisdictions, but the basic pattern is the same across both groups of states.

Next, models (3) and (4) use common-function spending and current spending, respectively, as dependent variables, for reasons suggested in Chapter 4. In both cases, there remains a strong positive effect of jurisdictional overlap on spending, as well as a negative interaction between jurisdictional overlap and party organizational strength. Indeed, in these two spending models, party organization appears to *more* than offset any positive effect of jurisdictional overlap on spending, such that spending appears to decline with the number of overlapping jurisdictions where parties are strong. Perhaps special districts fulfill their proponents' claim of efficiency when strong parties are available to prevent capture by issue-specific interest groups.

Finally, I investigate the correlation between the presence of strong party organizations and overlapping jurisdictions. Does the null result for strong-party states arise simply because there are not many single-function jurisdictions to begin with? The answer is no. The average value of jurisdictional overlap is actually slightly higher in strong-party states than in weak-party states—3.4 versus 3.3 overlapping jurisdictions per municipality, respectively—but the difference is hardly statistically significant ($p = 0.89$). In other words, the failure to find a fiscal common-pool effect in strong-party states is not due to a scarcity of overlapping jurisdictions.

6.4.2 *An Alternative Measure of Party Organizational Strength*

The preceding sections have demonstrated that across a variety of fiscal outcomes, the inflationary effects of jurisdictional overlap are mitigated

Table 6.2. *Sensitivity Analysis*

	Non-South	South	Common Spending	Current Spending
	(1)	(2)	(3)	(4)
Jurisdictional overlap	142.15	195.80	136.43	179.06
	(61.86)**	(49.66)***	(28.89)***	(29.72)***
Jurisdictional overlap* Strong-party state dummy	−142.19	−260.83	−301.96	−282.55
	(86.86)*	(72.28)***	(52.97)***	(40.39)***
FPI	0.81	1.03	0.08	0.83
	(0.05)***	(0.05)***	(0.03)***	(0.03)***
ln(population)	1.13	−40.95	−169.48	−293.26
	(65.19)	(50.52)	(29.72)***	(27.49)***
Per capita income	0.03	0.03	0.02	0.01
	(0.01)***	(0.00)***	(0.00)***	(0.00)***
Percent nonwhite	−850.24	303.32	946.31	434.58
	(248.95)***	(193.96)	(129.95)***	(111.54)***
Five-year change in population	−278.89	−190.71	−186.41	−447.16
	(153.66)*	(82.94)**	(63.00)***	(48.07)***
Percent age ≤18	−1,285.73	1,003.30	1,219.13	1,348.46
	(756.92)*	(579.82)*	(425.72)***	(343.77)***
Percent age ≥65	−1,707.45	1,039.52	1,791.92	867.71
	(717.39)**	(795.53)	(459.41)***	(378.91)**
Federal aid, five-year lag	0.10	0.00	0.07	0.08
	(0.06)*	(0.02)	(0.04)*	(0.04)**
State aid, five-year lag	−0.09	−0.05	0.27	0.26
	(0.05)**	(0.06)	(0.04)***	(0.03)***
Democratic presidential vote share	−1.03	−1.26	−3.98	−1.64
	(0.76)	(0.81)	(0.46)***	(0.41)***
Constant	668.42	−1,751.36	1,038.90	2,317.41
	(725.89)	(528.43)***	(354.73)***	(317.19)***
R-squared (within)	0.29	0.41	0.84	0.69
Observations	11,631	9,565	21,196	21,196
# of clusters	1,664	1,368	3,032	3,032

Notes: The dependent variable is general own-source revenue per capita for models 1 and 2; common-function spending per capita for model 3; and current expenditures per capita for model 4. Model 1 is estimated using only nonsouthern states. Model 2 is estimated using only southern states. All dollar values are CPI-adjusted to year 2002 dollars. Standard errors, clustered by county, are reported in parentheses. All models include county and year fixed effects (not reported).
*significant at 10%, **significant at 5%, ***significant at 1%.

where there are strong political parties. One concern with the results shown thus far is that Mayhew's TPO measure reflects party organizations as they existed in the 1950s and 1960s, whereas my analysis covers the period 1972 through 2002. In principle, if the TPO scores were out of step with contemporary party organizational capacity, this should have biased me against finding significant results. Nevertheless, to corroborate the results based on Mayhew's TPO scores, I also replicated each analysis using a second, more recent measure of party strength, Clark and Hoffmann-Martinot's (1998) strong party organization (SPO) scores.

The SPO scores are based on surveys of mayors of U.S. cities with a population greater than 25,000 conducted in the 1980s by Terry Clark. Specifically, the SPO measure is derived from mayors' responses to three questions concerning party activity in the campaign, mention of party affiliation in the campaign, and the frequency with which the mayor met with local party officials while in office (see Miranda 1994). I aggregated the mayoral responses from each state to produce state-level SPO scores. The complete list of state scores is contained in the Methodological Appendix, Table A.17.

Relative to Mayhew's TPO scores, the SPO scores have advantages and disadvantages. An advantage is that the SPO scores are more recent. Indeed, the survey was conducted roughly in the middle of my study period, meaning that the scores are more likely to capture contemporaneous party strength. In addition, the SPO scores are based on the responses of mayors, who presumably have inside knowledge of their local parties. A disadvantage is that while SPO scores tap general information about party activity, they do not specifically capture all of the information assessed by Mayhew, such as candidate slating. Another disadvantage is that the survey on which the SPO scores are based has a response rate of about 40 percent, and there is no reason to believe that the response probability is uncorrelated with party organizational capacity. Finally, SPO scores could not be computed for eight states because there were no completed mayoral surveys.[8] Despite the limitations of both the TPO and SPO scores, however, finding consistent results using these two independent measures should bolster confidence in the conclusions reached from the analysis.

I begin by examining the relationship between Mayhew's TPO scores and the state-level average of Clark's SPO scores. The simple correlation between the two measures is 0.53 ($p < .001$). A more revealing picture is

---

8 The missing states are North Dakota, Nebraska, New Mexico, Nevada, Oregon, South Carolina, South Dakota, and Virginia.

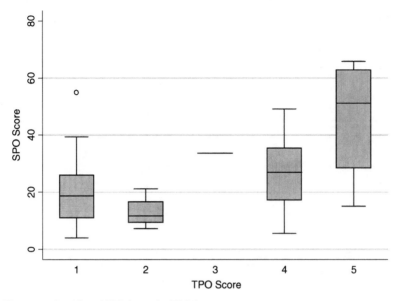

Figure 6.1. Box Plot of SPO Scores by TPO Score

Note: There is only one state with a TPO score of 3: Louisiana. The outlying observation with a TPO score of 1 and an SPO score of 55 is Alabama.

provided in Figure 6.1, which shows a box plot of SPO scores for each level of the TPO score. Despite their different methodologies and time periods, the two sets of scores are in considerable agreement as to the relative strength of party organizations. There is not much differentiation in SPO scores for states with a TPO score of 1 versus 2. However, the distinction between the strongest and weakest party organization states is clear under both coding systems. In particular, the dichotomization into strong and weak-party states used in the preceding analysis—that is, TPO scores below and above 3—is also evident in the SPO scores. The strong TPO states have a median SPO score of 36, while the weak TPO states have a median SPO score only half as large, 18. One notable exception is Alabama, which scores 1 (low) on the TPO scale but 55 (high) on the SPO scale.

In Table 6.3 I replicate several of the preceding models, substituting the SPO score for the TPO score. Model (1) shows the basic interaction model of party strength and jurisdictional overlap where the dependent variable is own-source revenue per capita. As was the case using the TPO score, the result is a significant negative interaction between SPO and jurisdictional overlap. This interactive relationship is depicted in Figure 6.2, which shows the marginal effect of jurisdictional overlap at different values of the SPO score. The effect of overlap is strongest where parties are weakest and declines as party organizational strength

Table 6.3. *An Alternative Measure of Party Organizational Strength, Clark's SPO Score*

	Base Model	Non-South	South	Common Spending	Current Spending
	(1)	(2)	(3)	(4)	(5)
Jurisdictional overlap	263.63	350.72	253.07	219.95	210.47
	(70.86)***	(147.05)**	(86.90)***	(45.02)***	(47.58)***
Jurisdictional overlap*SPO Score	−5.84	−4.83	−8.35	−5.88	−4.39
	(2.12)***	(3.14)	(2.99)***	(1.60)***	(1.46)***
FPI	0.97	0.86	1.07	0.07	0.87
	(0.04)***	(0.06)***	(0.05)***	(0.03)*	(0.03)***
ln(population)	25.11	36.47	−39.70	−159.05	−313.44
	(42.96)	(81.94)	(52.73)	(33.01)***	(30.29)***
Per capita income	0.03	0.03	0.03	0.03	0.01
	(0.00)***	(0.01)***	(0.00)***	(0.00)***	(0.00)***
Percent nonwhite	−37.62	−840.86	379.54	967.87	496.75
	(180.27)	(354.73)**	(206.21)*	(144.12)***	(128.69)***
Five-year change in population	−174.45	−192.22	−165.26	−166.88	−412.71
	(103.50)*	(193.90)	(91.35)*	(69.45)**	(52.91)***
Percent age ≤18	−454.38	−1,338.04	781.64	762.81	1,548.60
	(561.52)	(949.08)	(651.27)	(490.75)	(408.93)***

Percent age ≥65	−952.87	−1,989.85	494.29	1,471.40	921.38
	(631.66)	(915.61)**	(895.26)	(517.28)***	(438.25)**
Federal aid, five-year lag	0.02	0.11	−0.00	0.06	0.07
	(0.03)	(0.07)	(0.02)	(0.04)	(0.04)*
State aid, five-year lag	−0.13	−0.12	−0.08	0.24	0.23
	(0.04)***	(0.06)**	(0.06)	(0.04)***	(0.03)***
Democratic presidential vote share	−0.24	−1.63	−1.25	−3.70	−2.62
	(0.55)	(0.96)*	(0.84)	(0.51)***	(0.45)***
Constant	−1,410.33	125.71	−897.79	2,260.29	2,342.17
	(462.06)***	(934.48)	(520.52)*	(371.62)***	(345.01)***
R-squared (within)	0.334	0.296	0.398	0.847	0.696
Observations	18,142	9,612	8,530	18,142	18,142
# of clusters	2,595	1,375	1,220	2,595	2,595

Notes: The dependent variable is general own-source revenue per capita for models 1, 2, and 3; common-function spending per capita for model 4; and current expenditures per capita for model 5. Model 2 is estimated using only nonsouthern states. Model 3 is estimated using only southern states. All dollar values are CPI-adjusted to year 2002 dollars. Standard errors, clustered by county, are reported in parentheses. All models include county and year fixed effects (not reported).

*significant at 10%, **significant at 5%, ***significant at 1%.

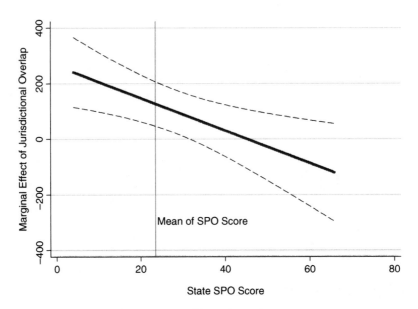

Dashed lines give the 95% confidence interval.

Figure 6.2. Interaction between Party Organization and Jurisdictional Overlap

Note: This figure shows the marginal effect of jurisdictional overlap on own-source revenue across different values of the SPO score. Point estimates (solid line) and confidence intervals (dashed lines) are based on model (1) of Table 6.4. The vertical line marks the SPO score for the average county.

increases. At the highest levels of party strength, the effect of overlap cannot be distinguished from zero, and the point estimates are even negative.

The remaining columns of Table 6.3 replicate the sensitivity analyses from Table 6.2 with SPO substituted for TPO scores. In every case, the main effect of overlap remains positive and the interaction with SPO scores is negative. In model (2), restricted to nonsouthern states, the interaction term is less precisely estimated ($p = 0.12$). Otherwise, the results are in harmony with the same models using TPO scores. The consistency between the results using these two completely independent and temporally disjoint measures enhances the argument that the interaction between party organizational strength and jurisdictional overlap is genuine, not the artifact of a particular coding decision or idiosyncratic evaluation of local parties. Moreover, TPO scores and SPO scores yield comparable results in all of the analyses to be reported in the remainder of this chapter, although to conserve space I will not continue to report two versions of every model.

6.4.3 Party Competition

The preceding sections establish that the interaction between party organization and jurisdictional overlap is as predicted: Spending is higher where jurisdictions overlap and parties are weak but not where parties are strong. But might there not be some other characteristic of strong-party states—however defined—that interacts with jurisdictional overlap to suppress the common-pool problem? Omitted variables are always a concern, and the data available on local party organizations will not enable me to show definitively that the relationship is causal. Having said that, I emphasize that the county fixed effects absorb any time-invariant omitted variables. Furthermore, recall that as revealed in the fully interacted model, no other variable in the model *except* jurisdictional overlap exhibited different effects between strong and weak-party states. Any counterexplanation for my findings would have to invoke an omitted variable correlated with party strength that influences not the level of spending in a county, but the effect of changes in jurisdictional overlap on spending.

One concern is that there is some attribute of political parties themselves, other than organizational strength, that dampens the connection between jurisdictional overlap and spending. In this regard, perhaps the most commonly invoked attribute of a party system is *competitiveness*. The classic Chicago School argument is that competition in politics, as in markets, promotes efficiency.[9] This view is most persuasively argued in a recent paper by Besley et al. (2006), who analyze the breakdown of the Democratic Party's near monopoly in the South beginning in the 1950s to shed light on the effects of party competition. The authors conclude that increases in political competition have quantitatively important, positive effects on economic performance and the quality of elected politicians. More relevant to the present inquiry, these authors find that greater political competition leads to lower overall state taxes.

The argument advanced by Besley and his coauthors pertains to the main effect of party competition, while the issue here is the interaction between competition and jurisdictional overlap. Returning to the theoretical framework of Chapter 3, party competition can be envisioned as a force that enhances turnout propensity and voter responsiveness, the φ and θ terms of the probabilistic voting model. Alternatively,

---

9 Classic statements on political competition from the Chicago School of political economy are found in Stigler (1971, 1972) and Peltzman (1998). The argument reaches its apotheosis in Wittman (1995).

"competitiveness" may be just another way of labeling the values of voter turnout and responsiveness. In either case, the important point is that competitiveness may interact with jurisdictional overlap, because in areas where voters' turnout propensity or responsiveness is higher, my model suggests that overspending by single-function governments will be constrained.

Note that the Besley et al. (2006) argument does not necessarily contradict the Mayhew (1986), Miranda (1994), and Primo and Snyder (2007) arguments that a strong party constrains spending. It is possible to conceive of party strength and party competition as two distinct, though not necessarily independent, aspects of a party system. If so, and if both variables are important in the way suggested by the respective authors, then party strength and party organization may be either complements or substitutes. For example, a state with both strong party organizations and a more competitive electoral environment may experience stronger constraints on spending than one with either factor operating alone.

To explore the possible effects of party competition, I rely on county-level electoral returns for gubernatorial elections from 1950 to 1990.[10] Unfortunately, there is no national data source on electoral returns for local government offices. Instead, I adopt as my measure of electoral competition the average vote share for the party that won most often from 1950 to 1990.[11] In other words, I compute each party's average share of the vote in all the gubernatorial elections over the study period and then take the leading party's average vote share as my measure of competitiveness. Conceptually, this measure is bounded by 50 percent and 100 percent in a two-party system.[12] If one party consistently wins a large share of the vote, the county is less competitive. On the other hand, if the leading party's average vote share is close to 50 percent, the county can be considered more competitive.

Although this measure of competition is based on statewide elections, it varies within states due to differences in party vote share across counties. In other words, it is a measure of the extent to which one party dominates gubernatorial elections *within the county* over time. While this is admittedly an imperfect proxy for party competition in local elections, it has the advantage of being plausibly exogenous to local fiscal decisions.

---

10 My data source is ICPSR study number 7757.

11 This is comparable to the measure used by Besley et al. (2006). However, they use the average vote share across elections for multiple statewide offices in a given year and allow the measure to vary over time.

12 In practice, there are a few counties with values less than 50 percent due to the presence of third parties. The minimum value observed in the data is 45 percent.

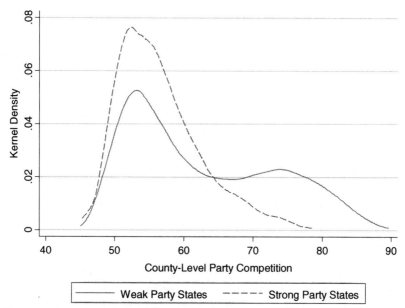

Figure 6.3. Party Organization and Party Competition

Note: The horizontal axis represents the average county-level vote share of the party that won the most gubernatorial elections from 1950 to 1990; therefore, lower values indicate greater party competition. Strong-party states are defined as those with a TPO score of 4 or 5; weak-party states are those with a TPO score of 3 or below.

It seems unlikely that citizens adjust their vote for governor in response to the spending of local governments, much less that the *average* party vote share over a 40-year period would be notably influenced by local spending in any given year.

I begin by examining the relationship between party organization and party competition. The average party competition index in TPO states is 56 percent, while the average in non-TPO states is 64 percent. The difference is statistically significant and equal to approximately three-quarters of a standard deviation in party competition. In other words, states with strong party organizations also have higher party competition, on average. This difference is demonstrated clearly in Figure 6.3, which shows overlaid kernel density plots (i.e., smoothed histograms) of party competition in TPO and non-TPO states. The distribution of party competition is concentrated more closely around the 50 percent threshold in strong-party states, while nearly all the cases in which one party wins 70 percent or more of the votes across time are found in weak-party states.

The significant positive relationship between party organization and party competition raises the question of which of these two mechanisms is at work in the interaction between TPO status and jurisdictional over-lap.[13] To answer the question, I add party competition to the spending models. In model (1) of Table 6.4 I enter both the TPO dummy and the party competition index, while excluding county fixed effects so that the main effects of these two party variables can be identified. Both vari-ables are significant, and the negative coefficient on the party compe-tition suggests that less competitive areas tax *less*. (Remember that a higher value on the competition index means less party competition.) However, when I add state fixed effects in model (2), the coefficient for party competition shrinks substantially and is no longer significant.[14] Thus, it appears that some underlying attribute of states with low party competition explains their smaller local government budgets, not party competition per se. Jurisdictional overlap, on the other hand, continues to demonstrate a positive, significant effect on spending regardless of the model specification.

The next two models in Table 6.4 show interactions between party competition and jurisdictional overlap. To facilitate interpretation, the party competition index is mean deviated in these models.[15] The inclu-sion of county fixed effects means that the main effect of party com-petition cannot be identified, but the interaction with jurisdictional overlap—the primary quantity of interest–is identified. In model (3) the interaction is positive, suggesting that jurisdictional overlap has a bigger effect on spending where parties are less competitive, but not statisti-cally significant. Model (4) jointly estimates the interactions between party strength and jurisdictional overlap and between party competi-tion and jurisdictional overlap. The main effect of jurisdictional over-lap remains positive and significant, while the interaction with the TPO dummy is negative and significant, consistent with the results reported in Table 6.1. The interaction between jurisdictional overlap and party competition remains insignificant. Based on these results, it appears that party organizational strength, but not party competition, mitigates the

---

13 Another interesting question is whether the relationship between party organiza-tion and party competition is causal or coincidental. For example, does a highly competitive electoral environment force parties to become more organized? Such questions are beyond the scope of the current investigation but clearly warrant further attention.

14 As a county-level variable, party competition can be identified in a model with state fixed effects, although the state-level TPO score cannot.

15 The main effect of jurisdictional overlap, therefore, can be interpreted as the effect at the average level of party competition (i.e., where the mean-deviated value equals zero). Without mean deviating party competition, the main effect of juris-dictional overlap would represent the effect when the leading party's vote share is zero, which is nonsensical.

Table 6.4. *Party Competition and Jurisdictional Overlap*

	(1)	(2)	(3)	(4)
Party competition index	−10.39 (1.21)***	−2.02 (1.56)		
Dummy = 1 if strong party state	−245.40 (19.56)***			
Jurisdictional overlap	190.79 (14.16)***	91.02 (22.88)***	121.93 (35.19)***	159.41 (43.04)***
Party competition index * Jurisdictional overlap			5.34 (4.19)	4.14 (4.27)
Strong party state dummy * Jurisdictional Overlap				−182.81 (63.83)***
Functional performance index	1.42 (0.05)***	1.31 (0.05)***	0.91 (0.04)***	0.91 (0.04)***
ln(Population)	−185.36 (15.22)***	−171.62 (15.28)***	29.90 (41.03)	19.16 (41.34)
Per capita income	0.08 (0.00)***	0.06 (0.00)***	0.02 (0.00)***	0.02 (0.00)***
Percent nonwhite	−95.12 (81.20)	215.97 (87.42)**	−156.82 (166.57)	−184.20 (166.92)
Five-year change in population	−772.62 (93.83)***	−604.79 (91.37)***	−266.63 (95.98)***	−263.56 (95.74)***
Percent Age ≤18	−799.56 (421.62)*	−1,725.66 (414.96)***	−356.78 (518.49)	−370.14 (516.43)
Percent Age ≥ 65	−2,173.91 (427.75)***	−2,774.81 (411.36)***	−669.40 (574.83)	−758.86 (574.65)
Federal aid, Five-year lag	0.23 (0.13)*	0.19 (0.10)*	0.02 (0.03)	0.02 (0.03)
State aid, Five-year lag	−0.04 (0.04)	−0.19 (0.05)***	−0.11 (0.04)***	−0.11 (0.04)***
Democratic presidential vote share	−2.94 (0.90)***	−1.55 (0.81)*	0.43 (0.55)	0.40 (0.55)

(continued)

Table 6.4. *(continued)*

	(1)	(2)	(3)	(4)
Constant	−702.90	−193.14	−1,280.87	−1,129.06
	(257.61)***	(280.27)	(444.40)***	(445.05)**
R-squared (Within)	0.41	0.49	0.33	0.33
Observations	20,568	20,568	20,568	20,568
# of Clusters	2,942	2,942	2,942	2,942
Fixed Effects?	No	State	County	County

Notes: The dependent variable is general own-source revenue per capita. All dollar values are CPI-adjusted to year 2002 dollars. Standard errors, clustered by county, are reported in parentheses. All models include year dummies (not reported).
*significant at 10%, **significant at 5%, ***significant at 1%.

common-pool problem among overlapping jurisdictions with concurrent tax authority.

As a final step in the analysis, I investigated the possibility that party competition and party organization are substitutes in constraining jurisdictional overlap. For example, perhaps party competition is an important constraint only where party organizations are weak. I separate the counties into two groups—TPO and non-TPO—and then estimate the interaction between party competition and jurisdictional overlap separately for each group.[16] Model (1) of Table 6.5 shows the results for weak-party states. The main effect of jurisdictional overlap is positive and significant, and there is still no evidence of a significant interaction with party competition. Model (2) is the equivalent model for strong-party states. Here the main effect of jurisdictional overlap is not significant, as expected. In addition, neither the main effect of party competition nor its interaction with jurisdictional overlap is significant. The interaction term between jurisdictional overlap and party competition is larger in strong-party states than weak-party states—suggesting that party competition is a stronger constraint on overspending where parties are strong—but the difference is not significant.[17]

Overall, the results from the party competition analysis provide no reason to amend the prior conclusion that a strong party *organization*

16 In other words, I am estimating a triple interaction including party organization, party competition, and jurisdictional overlap. The triple interaction can be estimated with the pooled sample, but presentation of the results is simpler with the split samples. The results do not change in either case. The party competition index is again mean-deviated in these models to facilitate interpretation.
17 The difference is tested by the pooled triple-interaction model (not shown).

Table 6.5. *Triple Interaction: Organization, Competition, and Overlap*

	Weak Parties	Strong Parties
	(1)	(2)
Jurisdictional overlap	158.68	35.57
	(42.56)***	(58.54)
Party competition index * Jurisdictional overlap	4.16	9.29
	(4.47)	(13.00)
FPI	0.94	0.75
	(0.05)***	(0.06)***
ln(population)	−16.26	141.44
	(45.92)	(82.55)*
Per capita income	0.02	0.02
	(0.01)***	(0.01)***
Percent nonwhite	−224.29	−223.35
	(182.79)	(392.22)
Five-year change in population	−284.16	−339.79
	(105.21)***	(189.36)*
Percent Age ≤18	−523.91	−157.59
	(613.02)	(583.93)
Percent Age ≥65	−1,242.24	344.77
	(662.42)*	(955.31)
Federal aid, five-year lag	0.02	−0.00
	(0.03)	(0.03)
State aid, five-year lag	−0.11	−0.06
	(0.05)**	(0.05)
Democratic presidential vote share	0.34	0.18
	(0.61)	(1.17)
Constant	37.92	−1,613.07
	(502.78)	(1,016.29)
R-squared (within)	0.30	0.47
Observations	15,309	5,259
# of clusters	2,190	752

Notes: The dependent variable is general own-source revenue per capita. Model 1 is estimated using only weak-party states (TPO ≤ 3). Model 2 is estimated using only strong-party states (TPO ≥ 4). All dollar values are CPI-adjusted to year 2002 dollars. Standard errors, clustered by county, are reported in parentheses. All models include county and year fixed effects (not reported).
*significant at 10%, **significant at 5%, ***significant at 1%.

helps to mitigate common-pool problems among overlapping jurisdictions. Jurisdictional overlap has a strong, positive effect on spending in weak-party states but a small, insignificant effect in strong-party states. Party competition, meanwhile, does not appear to play a significant role. Similar conclusions emerge when I substitute SPO scores for TPO scores in the models from Table 6.4 (not shown).

6.4.4   *Fiscal Constraints*

One may be concerned that there is some other aspect of the fiscal environment in strong-party states that prevents single-function jurisdictions from pumping up their budgets. The most obvious fiscal institutions are TELs. However, I demonstrated in Chapter 4 (see Table 4.6) that the effect of jurisdictional overlap on spending is unaffected by TELs. Moreover, if I regress my measure of TELs on the TPO or SPO score, I find no significant difference between strong- and weak-party states.[18] Nevertheless, as a robustness check, I assembled several additional measures of local government fiscal constraints and compared them across TPO and non-TPO states. First, Susan MacManus (1983) provides ratings of the severity of state restrictions on local government finance in three areas: property tax restrictions, nonproperty tax restrictions, and debt limitations. Second, the ACIR (1993a) provides data on whether states require balanced budgets for cities or counties.[19] Finally, another ACIR study (1981) ranks states according to the general degree of discretionary authority granted to local governments. Table 6.6 compares these institutional characteristics between TPO and non-TPO states.

For each of the seven variables just identified, Table 6.6 reports the mean values for TPO and non-TPO states, as well as *p*-values for the associated tests of differences. Across all of the variables, the values for TPO and non-TPO states are very similar, and I am unable to reject the hypothesis of no difference for any of the variables. Thus, there is no evidence here that local fiscal institutions vary significantly between TPO and non-TPO states, much less that such variation could account for the findings presented previously. The insignificant effects of jurisdictional overlap in TPO settings appear to be due to party organization, not TELs or other fiscal constraints.

---

18 Results are shown in the Methodological Appendix, Table A.14.
19 While all states but Vermont require a balanced *state* budget, only 11 states require balanced budgets for local governments. These are California, Colorado, Florida, Georgia, Kansas, Kentucky, Louisiana, Missouri, New Mexico, North Carolina, and Utah (ACIR 1993a).

Table 6.6. *Local Government Discretion in TPO and Non-TPO States*

Variable	Scale	Mean for TPO States	Mean for Non-TPO States	p-value[a]
Property tax restrictions on local governments (MacManus 1983)	Severity rated 1–4	2.31	2.7	0.2
Nonproperty tax restrictions on local governments (MacManus, 1983)	Severity rated 1–4	3.23	3.41	0.37
Borrowing restrictions on local governments (MacManus 1983)	Severity rated 1–4	2.92	2.76	0.55
Balanced budget required for cities or counties (ACIR 1993a)	Indicator 1/0	0.15	0.24	0.5
General discretionary authority granted to cities (ACIR 1981)	Rank 1–50	25.31	24.89	0.93
General discretionary authority granted to counties (ACIR 1981)	Rank 1–50	23.81	24	0.97
General discretionary authority granted to local governments (ACIR 1981)	Rank 1–50	23.69	26.14	0.61
Number of states		13	37	

[a]p-Value from test of difference of means or proportions, as appropriate.

6.5 SUMMARY AND CONCLUSIONS

The analysis presented in this chapter extends the common-pool model of local public finance by providing evidence of one of the institutions that governs the commons. I argued that, analogous to vertical integration in the private market, political parties integrate governance of multiple overlapping local jurisdictions, mitigating the overexploitation that results from uncoordinated taxation. The data support this view, revealing that greater jurisdictional overlap leads to larger public budgets where parties are weak, but that this effect is diminished or eliminated where strong party organizations are present. This interaction was demonstrated using two entirely independent measures of party strength and was shown to be robust to controls for partisanship, political competitiveness, and institutional fiscal constraints.

Although less important in the present context, these results also provide a forceful reaffirmation of Mayhew's (1986) original analysis of the relationship between party organization and public finance. Mayhew's finding of smaller public budgets in TPO settings is upheld here with a much richer set of control variables, including additional demographic, institutional, and political variables not considered in his analysis. Moreover, the results presented here represent out-of-sample tests for Mayhew's predictions, using a larger sample of observations from smaller units of analysis (counties) and a more recent time period. Finally, that the TPO scores Mayhew formulated in the 1980s continue to have predictive power and correlate significantly with a more recent measure is an endorsement of the accuracy both of his assessments and of his argument that organizational structures change very slowly. In short, the relationships Mayhew identified appear to be enduring, pervasive, and robust.

It should be emphasized that there is no inconsistency between Mayhew's argument that traditional party organizations are associated with smaller public budgets and the argument presented here that parties mitigate common-pool problems by coordinating the behavior of multiple overlapping governments. Mayhew's theory pertains to the overall size of the budget but says nothing about overlapping governments, while my theory predicts an interaction between parties and local governmental organization but yields no expectation about the main effect of parties on the size of the budget. The two views are not mutually exclusive and, in fact, may even be complementary. Indeed, one of the implications of this reaffirmation of Mayhew's findings is that additional research is in order to disentangle the various explanations for the strong TPO effect on local budgets.

7

Conclusion

The primary contribution of this book has less to do with any specific theoretical or empirical result and more to do with the attention it draws to an important but heretofore overlooked dimension of American politics: the vertical dimension. Where conventional horizontal theories suggest that the multiplication of jurisdictions enhances competition and efficiency, I contend that the proliferation of vertically overlapping jurisdictions is likely to have just the opposite effect. In large part, the failure of conventional theories to recognize the vertical dimension of governmental competition stems from the fact that jurisdictional layering on a large scale—that is, beyond the traditional federal-state-local overlay—is a relatively recent phenomenon; the majority of special-purpose jurisdictions that exist today were created after World War II. The workhorse theories of local political economy—beginning with Tiebout in 1956—have largely failed to keep pace with the institutional innovations that made vertically overlapping single-function jurisdictions the most numerous and fastest-multiplying American governments. Although single-function jurisdictions now outnumber and outspend all cities, and have more civilian employees than the federal government, scholars have yet to offer a working theory of their politics, much less a rigorous empirical investigation of such a theory. My aim in this book has been to begin filling that gap by providing a political theory of special-function government and testing that theory with comprehensive data and careful analysis.

I began by developing a formal model of the politics of overlapping special-function jurisdictions. I took established models of interest group competition with probabilistic voting and extended them to allow for multiple independently elected governments as well as selective participation by voters in each election. In my model, there are multiple public services and an interest group that benefits disproportionately from any given service. Politicians want only to be reelected and therefore enact policies that maximize their expected vote share. When there is only one general-purpose government, the politician must make trade-offs in the budget to account for the demands of the many competing groups that want higher spending on their preferred service while knowing that all voters dislike paying taxes. If all voters participate in the election, political competition leads to a socially efficient outcome, wherein the budget delivers each good at the level where the sum of marginal benefits equals marginal costs.

When each service is provided by an independent jurisdiction, however, the outcome may deviate substantially from the efficient benchmark. If all voters continue to participate in each election, there is no difference. Each politician makes the same trade-off she would have made under a general-purpose government, balancing the demands of one group for more spending on its favorite service against the reluctance of the other groups to pay taxes for it. But when there is *selective participation*—meaning that each group is most likely to turn out in the election of the jurisdiction that controls its preferred service—then the outcome will diverge from the case of general-purpose government. The single-function politician still wants only to be reelected, but she recognizes that the members of the relevant interest group are more likely to vote in the election than other citizens are. Therefore, she designs her policies to please the interest groups more than a general-purpose politician would. The result is that the single-function politicians provide higher spending on each service, and the aggregate budget is larger than it would be if there were only one government. This is the fiscal equivalent of a common-pool problem. Each interest group has disproportionate influence over a jurisdiction that can levy a tax on the general population. The interest group receives all the benefits from increased spending on its preferred service but pays only a fraction of the costs, which are spread over all the other voters. Therefore, the group has an incentive to demand more spending on its favorite service than it would actually be willing to pay for if it had to bear the full costs itself.

The extent of overspending by single-function jurisdictions is not unbounded, however. The main constraint is that the higher the budget goes, the more likely *other* groups are to turn out and vote against the increased taxes required to fund it. So, each specialized jurisdiction will spend more than a general-purpose government would, but only up to the point at which otherwise uninterested voters are drawn to the polls in protest. In Chapter 3, I solved for equilibrium spending under general-purpose government, as well as under special-purpose government with and without selective participation. The key result was that when there is selective participation, a special-purpose jurisdiction will spend more than a general-purpose government would when performing the same function. I also provided theoretical arguments and empirical evidence that selective participation is the norm. Finally, I showed that Tiebout competition may constrain overspending by special-function jurisdictions but will never eliminate it. Thus, the central prediction that emerged from my formal theory is that taxes and spending will be higher, all else equal, where there are more overlapping special-purpose jurisdictions.

In Chapter 4, I provided a test of this prediction using a panel of county-level public spending data with over 21,000 observations spanning 1972 to 2002. I regressed aggregate taxes and spending in various ways on the extent of jurisdictional overlap. My primary measure of overlap was the number of special-function jurisdictions in a county relative to the number of general-purpose governments, although I showed that the results were robust across a wide range of alternative measures. The unmistakable result is that increases in jurisdictional overlap lead to increases in the public budget. To put the result in perspective, increasing from a relatively low level of overlap (the 25th percentile) to a relatively high level (the 75th percentile) results in an increase of $130 in locally raised revenue, which is equivalent to roughly 11 percent relative to the mean. Moreover, the estimated impact of jurisdictional overlap was fairly large in comparison to other well-known correlates of spending—less than income but greater than virtually any demographic variable.

Having found the predicted positive relationship between jurisdictional overlap and aggregate taxation, I set about to distinguish my fiscal common-pool theory from other potential explanations for the observed finding. All of my empirical models included county fixed effects, which control for any (measurable or unmeasurable) time-invariant attribute of a county that could influence both the extent of jurisdictional overlap and the level of taxes and spending. Put differently, my models relate *changes* within counties over time in the level of jurisdictional overlap to *changes* within counties over time in taxes and spending. So, any feature of a county that does not change over time—specifically, that did not change between 1972 and 2002—cannot possibly be an explanation for my findings. Thus, I ruled out the possibility that there is some inherent attribute of counties with more overlapping jurisdictions that also causes them to spend more.

Nor can the observed connection between jurisdictional overlap and spending be explained by the bundle of services provided in a county. There was no significant relationship between changes in overlap and changes in the number of public services provided within a county. In addition, when I controlled for an index of functional performance or for a full set of dummy variables for each possible function, the estimated effects of jurisdictional overlap hardly changed. Lastly, when I restricted my analysis to expenditures on a set of common functions performed in virtually every county, I found that almost the entire overlap effect came through increased spending on these universal functions, rather than unusual services that would be provided only if a specialized jurisdiction were created to perform them. In short, the amplified spending associated with jurisdictional overlap comes through increased expenditures on a common bundle of services, not through expanding contents of the bundle itself.

I was able to rule out several competing explanations proposed in the literature for why specialized jurisdictions might spend more. The overlap effect is not due to increased capital spending or infrastructure construction; most of the spending increases are devoted to current operations. The overlap effect is not due to a switch to user charges in place of broad-based taxes; the lion's share of the increased revenue comes from property taxes. The overlap effect is not the result of using special districts to circumvent TELs on municipalities; the interaction between jurisdictional overlap and TELs is small and statistically insignificant. And the overlap effect is not due to the boundaries of special districts being tailored to small communities of interest that are willing to spend more for a specific public service; the effect remains even when I look only at the two in five districts whose boundaries are coterminous with an existing general-purpose government. While there was modest evidence supporting some of these arguments, none of them could explain more than a small share of the observed increases in taxes and spending that result from increases in jurisdictional overlap.

The final step in Chapter 4 was to pin down the causal argument. Nothing in my theory suggests or requires that the creation of overlapping jurisdictions is exogenous to local demands for spending. In fact, one implication of my theory is that local interest groups desiring increased spending on a particular service would do well to try to transfer the provision of that service from a general-purpose government to a special-function jurisdiction. It was important, therefore, to distinguish the effect of the institutions themselves from the effect of interest group influence generally. (Of course, to the extent that interest group influence within a county does not change much over time, this goal was already accomplished via the county fixed effects.) I concluded the chapter with an IV analysis using state laws governing the creation of special districts as an instrument for the level of jurisdictional overlap. Intuitively, the idea was to isolate sources of variation in jurisdictional overlap that could not be driven by short-run variation in the influence of county-level interest groups. I also used deeply lagged values of jurisdictional overlap as an instrument, isolating historically predetermined sources of variation that were plausibly exogenous from contemporary spending decisions. In both IV analyses, the estimated effects of jurisdictional overlap on local spending remained highly significant.

Collectively, the results shown in Chapter 4 provided resounding support for the fiscal common-pool model of jurisdictional overlap. While one might quibble with any one of the results taken in isolation, the robustness of the core relationship to a wide range of sensitivity analyses and falsification exercises cannot be easily dismissed. Moreover, the fiscal common-pool model appears to be the only theory that can plausibly explain the full array of results obtained across all the analyses.

With evidence in hand that jurisdictional overlap does indeed lead to increases in taxing and spending, my next step was to investigate whether the additional dollars result in higher-quality services. My theory makes no prediction in this regard: Interest groups may demand higher-quality services, or they may demand wasteful or particularistic benefits. But the answer could have important implications for interpreting the desirability of jurisdictional overlap, because higher-quality services would partially—only partially—offset the negative consequences of overtaxation. Therefore, in Chapter 5 I analyzed, as an illustrative case, the quality of the services provided by public libraries operated by special districts compared to libraries operated by general-purpose governments. The results were clear. Special-district libraries spent more but provided fewer books. Their employees were less likely to be actual librarians. Despite spending more, district libraries did not attract more patrons, and therefore their efficiency was significantly lower than that of municipally operated libraries. In other words, district libraries spent more per patron visit and more per circulation transaction. My review of the few other existing studies of special-district service quality turned up mostly similar results for other functions. While I could not reject the idea that districts outperform general-purpose governments on some other unmeasured dimension, the weight of my evidence suggested otherwise. At the very least, the burden must now shift to proponents of special-function jurisdictions to provide compelling evidence that they outperform, rather than merely outspend, general-purpose governments.

Showing the existence of a fiscal common-pool problem for overlapping jurisdictions was not the end of my story. In Chapter 6, I discussed the potential for establishing institutional solutions to common-pool problems and examined the impact of one particular institution: the political party. Inspired by previous work suggesting that political parties unofficially centralize the policies of state and national governments in a federation and solve collective action problems in legislatures, I reasoned that a strong local party could govern the fiscal commons by informally coordinating the policies of multiple overlapping jurisdictions in a local area. That is, if one party controlled the relevant offices in different jurisdictions, it could induce the officeholders to internalize the externalities arising from their taxing decisions. Drawing on the formal model presented in Chapter 3, I explained that a party's incentive for serving such a coordinating function is electoral: A slate of candidates offering efficient policies can defeat candidates pandering to special interests. Using data on party organizational strength from two independent sources—Mayhew's TPO score and Clark's SPO score—I found that, indeed, fiscal common-pool problems were mitigated by the presence of a strong political party. Specifically, jurisdictional overlap was seen to have a strong positive effect on local taxes and spending where parties were weak but only a small or null effect where parties were strong. Clearly, the political party is only one of many possible institutional responses to the fiscal common-pool problem, and additional research focusing on other approaches is surely in order.

7.1   SOCIAL WELFARE ANALYSIS

My empirical analysis showed that the creation of overlapping special-function jurisdictions leads to overspending *relative to the amount that would be spent by a general-purpose government.* Understanding the welfare implications of jurisdictional overlap—that is, whether citizens are better or worse off as a result—therefore requires assessing whether, in the *absence* of overlapping jurisdictions, general-purpose governments provide a desirable level of public services. In Chapter 3, I presented a model in which political competition leads general-purpose governments to provide socially efficient policies, where *socially efficient* meant maximizing a weighted Benthamite social utility function.[1] In this setting, increased spending resulting from common tax-pool exploitation by overlapping jurisdictions was social welfare-reducing; that is, citizens were made worse off because spending by special-function jurisdictions was set at a level where the sum of marginal benefits was less than the marginal cost.

Consistent with my argument, but approaching the problem from a very different perspective, another school of thought, originating with Tiebout (1956) and introduced to political science by Peterson (1981), argues that *interjurisdictional* competition forces local governments to adopt efficient policies. That is, whereas I focus on political competition

---

1 Recall that in my model the weights were based on political participation and responsiveness, so that groups with a higher propensity to turn out or change their vote in response to political platforms received greater weight.

within a jurisdiction, these scholars reach similar conclusions regarding the efficiency of general-purpose governments by focusing on competition between jurisdictions for mobile resources. In this view, interjurisdictional competition leads to marketlike efficiency in the provision of public goods. If it is correct that general-purpose governments can be expected to provide socially optimal tax-service bundles, then the proliferation of overlapping special-function jurisdictions makes citizens worse off due to overtaxation. On this point, at least, I am in agreement with the Tiebout school.

However, a related school of thought, inspired by Oates's (1972) work on fiscal federalism, contends that competition for taxable resources leads to inefficiently *low* tax rates. A major difference between the Tiebout model and the tax competition literature is the latter's focus on fiscal externalities through which one region's policies affect the tax bases of other regions.[2] In other words, a reduction in one region's tax rate to attract new businesses or residents generates a negative externality for other regions, which in turn lose those businesses or residents. According to Oates (1972, p. 143), "The result of tax competition may well be a tendency toward less than efficient levels of output of local services. In an attempt to keep taxes low to attract business investment, local officials may hold spending below those levels for which marginal benefits equal marginal costs. ..." If this view is correct—that is, if tax competition induces general-purpose governments to provide undesirably low levels of public services—then concurrent taxation by overlapping jurisdictions may be socially beneficial, leading to increases in tax rates that would otherwise be too low.

There are, thus, two conflicting answers to the question of whether jurisdictional overlap is socially harmful or beneficial. If my theory, or Tiebout's, is right that general-purpose governments with exclusive tax authority provide more or less efficient public services, then jurisdictional layering with concurrent taxation likely leads to taxes that are too high. On the other hand, if the tax competition literature is closer to the truth in predicting that general-purpose governments underprovide services, then the higher taxes associated with jurisdictional overlap may actually improve the welfare of local citizens. In Harberger's (1964) words, "An action which would take us away from a Pareto optimum if we were starting from that position can actually bring us toward such an optimum if we start from an initially distorted situation" (p. 59).

---

2 Wilson (1999) provides an excellent review of the tax competition literature and its conflicts with the Tiebout model. For a more extensive treatment, see Wellisch (2000).

This is a difficult problem to resolve empirically, as it would require a tractable measure of the social efficiency of general-purpose government policies. Moreover, as Oates (2001) himself acknowledges, the field has produced no systematic evidence of a fiscal race to the bottom, and existing evidence on this question is largely anecdotal. Being unable to definitively resolve this long-running dispute, I offer two considerations that point in favor of the negative view of jurisdictional overlap.

First, even if it were true that general-purpose governments spend too little, in order for increased spending by special-function jurisdictions to be an improvement, the additional spending would have to be accompanied by improved services. In other words, it is never welfare-enhancing merely to spend more, and by implication tax more, without also delivering more or better services. Yet, it has not been shown that special-function jurisdictions do, in fact, provide more or better services. Take the case of library districts examined in Chapter 5. There, it was shown that library districts spend significantly more, but provide fewer books and have no more employees than libraries operated by general-purpose governments. Even if it were shown that general-purpose governments spend too little on libraries—meaning that citizens are willing to pay higher taxes for better libraries—there is no reason to think that the increased spending by library districts would be welfare-enhancing since it does not appear to result in improvements in library service. In short, before one can argue that special districts enhance welfare by raising spending above an otherwise inefficiently low level, it would first have to be shown that higher spending by special-districts results in welfare-enhancing improvements to local services. The evidence shown thus far does not support that conclusion.

Second, even if it were shown that general-purpose governments underspend *and* that spending by special-function jurisdictions results in improved services, it would still remain to be shown that jurisdictional overlap does not result in spending that is too high. In other words, when a special district is established with the laudable goal of increasing the provision of a service that would otherwise be underprovided, what is to prevent an interest group, having established control over the new jurisdiction, from pumping up spending beyond the socially efficient level? Without some additional check, an institutional solution to one problem (underspending) may very likely create a new problem (overspending). It is not clear a priori which problem is worse from a social welfare perspective. But it should be clear that even when spending by a general-purpose government is agreed to be too low, there is no guarantee that establishing a special-function jurisdiction will produce a better outcome and plenty of reasons to worry that it will not.

Conclusion

In summary, I believe the weight of the evidence suggests that the increased spending by overlapping special-function jurisdictions, relative to a general-purpose government, is unlikely to be welfare-enhancing. First, there is relatively little evidence that general-purpose governments underspend. Second, there is equally little evidence that special-function jurisdictions provide better services. And, finally, there is nothing to stop special-function jurisdictions, once formed, from overspending, effectively solving one problem while creating another. That said, the case is far from closed. The key question is whether general-purpose governments provide a socially efficient level of services. Like many questions of social welfare, this one is inherently difficult and may be empirically intractable. There are plausible theories providing contrary answers and not enough solid evidence on either side to reach a firm conclusion.

7.2 CONNECTIONS WITH OTHER LITERATURES

The results of my analysis have obvious implications for the study and practice of specialized local government and public finance. They also have implications for related areas of research, including the Tiebout literature, fiscal federalism and multilevel government, and political parties.

7.2.1 Tiebout

Recognizing the fiscal common-pool problems of overlapping jurisdictions substantially undermines the Tiebout-inspired notion of the local public sector as an efficient marketplace. The primary incentive for government efficiency in the Tiebout model is the elasticity of the tax base. That is, inefficient policies result in decrements to the tax base, due either to mobile assets exiting the jurisdiction or to a decline in the value of local property.[3] Governments seeking to preserve or expand their tax base, therefore, have an incentive to adopt policies that maximize voter welfare. However, as explained in Chapter 3, the common-pool problems associated with concurrent taxation weaken these incentives because any negative consequences arising from undesirable policies are also spread among the various governments sharing the tax base. That is, when the tax base declines as a result of the actions of one government, all the overlapping jurisdictions feel the adverse effect. The culprit government suffers only a fraction of the costs associated with its actions. By contrast, a unitary government must internalize all the costs of its actions. The

---

3 The debate over capitalization in the Tiebout model is beyond the scope of this analysis. See Hamilton (1983) and Fischel (2001, ch. 3) for surveys.

incentives for efficiency become weaker as more governments share the same tax base.

If the fiscal common-pool model is a challenge to the Tiebout tradition, it is more an empirical challenge than a theoretical one. That is, I have no qualms with the Tiebout model as theory. But I am suggesting that the actual world of local government diverges in important ways from the world envisioned by Tiebout. While the institutional foundations of Tiebout's original model are unspecified, most scholars working in this tradition assume (often implicitly) that governments are general-purpose and nonoverlapping. The Tiebout model, in other words, is a theory of one level of government operating in isolation. While such a simplification might have been tenable in the institutional climate of Tiebout's time (1956), the emergence of jurisdictional overlap as a central feature of contemporary local governance challenges any theory that ignores the vertical dimension of intergovernmental competition.

The lack of attention to specialized jurisdictions—despite their numerical, political, and fiscal significance—is symptomatic of a broader inattention within the discipline to the institutional underpinnings of local political economy. While the *new institutionalism* has swept through political science and economics in recent years, the study of *local* institutions has lagged markedly behind the rest of the field. Consider, for example, how much is known about the budgetary politics of Congress relative to the city council, or how much is known about the workings of almost any federal bureaucracy in comparison with the workings of local school boards. The near-hegemony of the Tiebout model is at least partly to blame. In equilibrium, institutional variation has no effect on policy outcomes in a pure Tiebout world. Any institutional feature that would cause one government to perform differently from the (unique) optimum would be competed away, so that any institutional variation that remains in equilibrium must make no difference in the relative performance of local governments. From this perspective, it is no surprise that institutionalists have, for the most part, directed their attention away from the local public sector. This is unfortunate, because the local sector offers an ideal laboratory for exploring institutional variation.

Let me be clear that I am not arguing against the importance of interjurisdictional competition as envisioned by Tiebout and his disciples. Nor am I suggesting that models of interjurisdictional competition ought to be supplanted by models of vertical layering. Rather, interjurisdictional competition must be understood within the context of a more complex set of intergovernmental fiscal relationships. Tiebout competition is one important dimension of intergovernmental competition but it is not the only dimension, nor is it always and everywhere the most important dimension. The next generation of progress in our understanding of the local public sector is likely to come from a better appreciation of the complex interplay between vertical and horizontal relationships. Keen and Kotsogiannis (2002) have made important contributions along these lines, as has Volden (2005), but this literature is in its infancy.

Finally, some have seen Tiebout's model as an effort to eliminate politics from the theory of the local public sector (Epple and Zelenitz 1981; Helsley 2004; Rose-Ackerman 1983). As long as the option to vote with your feet keeps local governments accountable, voting at the ballot box is unnecessary. While many critiques of the Tiebout model have focused on its heroic assumptions about the attributes and behavior of individuals—homogeneity, costless mobility, perfect information, and exogenously endowed income—I believe that Tiebout's assumptions about government are most problematic. The complex vertical layering of fiscally and politically interacting governments defies Tiebout's institution-free model of local nonpolitics. With each special-function government being able to provide concentrated benefits with diffuse costs, opportunities and incentives abound for interest group mischief. In this setting, the ideal of a unitary government operating as an apolitical efficiency-seeker is particularly hard to swallow. Mobility is undoubtedly an important complement to politics at the local level, but it is no substitute.

7.2.2 Fiscal Federalism and Multilevel Government

Federalism is again at the top of the research agenda for political scientists, economists, and constitutional scholars (see Weingast 2009). In settings as diverse as the European Union (EU), Russia, Iraq, and South Africa, the design of federal institutions is at the forefront of political debate. If, as Oates argues, the study of federalism is essentially the study of "the vertical design and functioning of the public sector" (1991, p. xi), then the fiscal externalities of multilevel government demonstrated here are relevant to federal systems generally. Indeed, the analysis presented in this book can be thought of as a sort of comparative politics applied within U.S. borders, and there is no reason why the analysis could not be extended to other countries or regions. The basic hypothesis that vertical externalities arise when multiple layers of government share a common tax base is easily portable to other settings. Indeed, cross-national analysis of jurisdictional overlap, and its effect on fiscal outcomes, may be one of the most fruitful avenues for extending the theoretical and empirical models developed here.

In the field of comparative politics, related questions of institutional design have garnered increasing attention under the rubric of *multilevel governance.*[4] In this literature, scholars debate the relative merits of what Hooghe and Marks (2003) have labeled *Type I* and *Type II* governance, where Type I is represented by general-purpose governments as I have described them and Type II is characterized by special-function jurisdictions. Frey (1996, 2001) and Frey and Eichenberger (1999) promote a form of Type II government they call *functional, overlapping, and competing jurisdictions (FOCJ)*, which bear a family resemblance to U.S. special districts. While much of the multilevel governance literature is focused specifically on the EU, the net is cast broadly to include federal systems as well as nations whose constitutions are not federal but whose governance is to one degree or another decentralized (Bache and Flinders 2004).

Proponents of Type II jurisdictions (e.g., Frey and Eichenberger 1999; Schmitter 2000) often invoke the U.S. experience with special districts as a successful example. Yet, my analysis suggests that these scholars may be too sanguine in their assessment. The great virtue of Type II jurisdictions from the perspective of their advocates is that they are efficient. The primary source of their efficiency is said to be that they cause externalities across jurisdictions to be internalized by tailoring the boundaries of individual jurisdictions to encompass the full costs and benefits of the services they provide (Marks and Hooghe 2004). However, this literature essentially ignores the vertical fiscal externalities that are created when Type II jurisdictions with tax authority are layered on top of one another. Again, this is a case where an institution intended to solve one problem (internalizing horizontal externalities) may create a new problem (creating vertical externalities), and the net benefits are at best ambiguous.

Type II jurisdictions are also said to promote competition among jurisdictions by lowering barriers to exit (Hooghe and Marks 2003). As I have shown, however, it is no more or less costly for a citizen to exit the jurisdiction of a special-function government than it is to exit that of a general-purpose government. Because citizens ultimately must choose a single housing location rather than an à la carte menu of jurisdictions, exit in either case involves moving, which is relatively costly. Type II jurisdictions are a wash on this account.

A last point in favor of Type II jurisdictions is that they are said to be impermanent and "are discontinued when their services are no longer demanded ..." (Frey and Eichenberger 1999, p. 18). Once again, the U.S. experience with special districts suggests otherwise. Special districts are notoriously difficult to eradicate (see Little Hoover Commission 2000). In Illinois, as in many other states, enabling legislation makes no

---

4 The contributions to Bache and Flinders (2004) provide a sampling of this literature.

provision for the termination of most types of jurisdictions, meaning that eliminating even a single district requires a special act of the state legislature (Illinois General Assembly, Commission on Intergovernmental Cooperation 2003).[5] If U.S. special districts are any indication, Type II districts should be considered semipermanent rather than temporally flexible.

7.2.3   Political Parties

With a few notable exceptions, the major theme of the literature on political parties in the 1970s and 1980s was decline and decay (e.g., Broder 1972; Polsby 1983). Depending on their orientation, scholars lamented or celebrated the deteriorating role of political parties generally, including the relative insignificance of local parties (Peterson 1981). Political parties have been resuscitated to some extent in political science beginning in the 1990s, as a new wave of scholarship (e.g., Aldrich 1995; Cox and McCubbins 1993) drew attention to their role in solving collective action problems of one sort or another. Much of this literature has been devoted to parties in the U.S. Congress and other legislatures. In a small way, the work presented here may suggest a similar revitalization of our conception of the role of *local* political parties.

Granted, there are some respects in which political parties are of less use in the local context than in the national one. Because the majority of local elections are nonpartisan—meaning that the candidates' party affiliations do not appear on the ballot— party labels are less easily used as heuristics or informational "shortcuts" by voters. And if the old adage that "there is no Republican or Democratic way to clean a street" is correct (Lowi 1967, p. 85), then local politics may be fundamentally less ideological, making party labels less informative cues about candidates' policy positions.

Yet, in other respects, the political party may be even more important in the local context than in the national one. Because the local institutional landscape is so much more fragmented, the role of an organization that can coordinate various centers of power is especially vital. Of course, the idea that parties help to coordinate behavior across related institutions, such as congressional committees or branches of government, is well known in the national context. But these ideas have not received

---

5 The case of the Cook County Tuberculosis Sanitarium District, which survived— and continued to raise millions of dollars in revenue—until 2006, despite years of opposition from county officials and good government groups, is a case in point (The Civic Federation, 2003).

as much attention in the local context. The work presented in this book provides some of the first evidence that political parties play a central role in harmonizing vertically overlapping local governments. But I have only scratched the surface of the potentially important coordinating activities of local parties.

My analysis has been restricted to the realm of public finance. It seems equally likely that political parties help to coordinate other types of policies across jurisdictions. For example, regional transportation policy might flow more smoothly when multiple connected jurisdictions are in the hands of the same party. Educational materials might be better coordinated when the school board and the library district share partisan ties.

Similarly, while the focus here has been on vertical coordination across overlapping jurisdictions, it is conceivable that political parties contribute to *horizontal* coordination, that is, facilitating cooperation among competing governments in a more traditional Tiebout context. Returning to an issue raised previously, it is possible to imagine that partisan collusion across jurisdictions could make citizens worse off if it means reducing healthy interjurisdictional competition. On the other hand, when competing jurisdictions are engaged in a destructive race to the bottom in competition for businesses, partisan coordination across governments might improve matters.

The major obstacle to further study of these and related issues is the lack of readily available data on local parties and elections. Due to the decentralized nature of election administration in the United States, there is no central repository of local election returns or partisan affiliations of officeholders. In most cases, scholars must still collect such data one county at a time. This problem is especially acute for data relating to special-function jurisdictions. The mayoral elections database assembled by Ferreira and Gyourko (2009) is a major step in the right direction, but far more work remains to be done. Until systematic data become available, the study of local political parties is likely to remain mired in a morass of conjecture and conflicting case studies.

7.3 POLICY IMPLICATIONS

As explained in Chapter 2, the debate over local government structure in the United States has centered around two sharply contrasting schools of thought. A regionalist, or "reform," camp has argued that the proliferation of local governments leads to inefficiency, unaccountability, and destructive competition. On the other side, the public choice school has promoted the proliferation of local governments for the efficiency benefits of interjurisdictional competition. The results of my study suggest that both sides of the debate have gotten something right but that each has also ignored crucial institutional design issues.

While I obviously share the reformers' concern over the proliferation of special-purpose jurisdictions, I emphatically do not share their enthusiasm for regional government. And while I share the public choice school's belief in the benefits of interjurisdictional competition, I do not believe that the multiplication of jurisdictions per se enhances competition. Likely pleasing neither group, my results would seem to favor the promotion of a large number of territorially exclusive local government jurisdictions, that is, a large number of general-purpose governments rather than single-purpose districts. The existence of many competing governments *having exclusive tax authority* within their own boundaries appears to be the desirable structure for the local public sector, promoting both competition between jurisdictions and political accountability within jurisdictions.

Assuming that a wholesale reconstruction of local government institutions is not in the offing, are there more modest policy recommendations that can be derived from this study? Perhaps the most obvious one is to remove taxing authority from special-function jurisdictions without eliminating the jurisdictions themselves. General-purpose governments would have the sole authority to levy taxes within their territory, but they could contract with specialized jurisdictions for the provision of particular services. This system would have the advantage of granting one authority sole responsibility for the bottom-line tax bill, forcing it to make trade-offs among competing interests. At the same time, specialized jurisdictions could remain flexible in their geographic contours, tailoring themselves to regional or very local problems as need be. This proposal, which separates taxation from service provision, is close in spirit to the contracting approach described by Miller (1981) and would capture many of the advantages of Frey and Eichenberger's (1999) idealized FOCJ.

Another modest proposal would simply tinker with the electoral calendar, moving special-district races to coincide with those of more prominent state and national offices. Recall that the underlying source of fiscal externalities among overlapping governments is selective participation, allowing interest groups with parochial concerns to dominate the elections for specialized jurisdictions. Selective participation is encouraged when elections for specialized jurisdictions are held on separate dates from elections for major offices, as is common practice. Of course, moving special-purpose elections to coincide with major elections would not guarantee the participation of average voters, as ballot rolloff would remain a possibility. But consolidating election dates would go a long way toward reducing the costs for general-interest voters to participate in special-purpose elections, especially if bond and tax referenda were also consolidated. As a general matter, the effect of election timing on selective participation, interest group influence, and government policy is an area ripe for additional research.

7.4 AMERICAN DEMOCRACY IN 3-D: TOO MUCH OF A GOOD THING?

The most deeply troubling implication of this study is one that is difficult to quantify or formalize. I am referring to the implication to be drawn from the fact that the multiplication of governments has been accompanied by a diminution of public participation in them. Turnout in the elections for special-purpose jurisdictions is among the lowest for any office, even as these institutions are the most numerous American governments. I see two possible interpretations of this relationship, both of which are perverse and disheartening.

The first interpretation is that the lack of engagement in the politics of local special-function jurisdictions reflects deep satisfaction with their performance. Frey and Eichenberger are typical of this perspective in writing that "a low rate of voter participation is not a problem as such. Rational citizens do not vote as long as they are satisfied with the services provided" (1999, p. 10). In other words, *lack of participation is the hallmark of a successful democracy*. If this is true, then special-purpose governments are successful indeed.[6] But this is an impoverished notion of democracy.

The idea that low participation in local elections arises from voter satisfaction is contradicted by the great impact of election timing on turnout. For example, participation increased from 17 to 45 percent after Sacramento County, California, moved special-district elections from odd years to even years to coincide with other state and local races (Little Hoover Commission 2000). Are we to believe that the incremental 28 percent of voters were simply more satisfied with their governments in odd years? Or recall Nassau County, New York, where special-district elections take place on 24 different days spread throughout 11 of the 12 months of the year—but none in November (Suozzi 2007). Can anyone seriously maintain that the 2 to 14 percent turnout in these elections reflects nothing more than voter contentment?

---

6 Perhaps none has been more successful than the South Mississippi County School Board, which in 2003 held an election where no on turned out to vote, not even the candidates (Giuffrida 2003).

The second interpretation, though more plausible, is no less perverse: The proliferation of governments and elected officials may actually undermine democratic participation and accountability. In other words, *too many elections are bad for democracy*. The idea that the jurisdictions that are the smallest and, in some sense, "closest" to the people are also the least participatory and deliberative runs counter to generations of "small is better" democratic theory, from Tocqueville (1835) to Frug (2002).[7]

Not only is the level of participation in special-function elections troubling, but so too is the nature of that participation. It appears—and I emphasize *appears*, because good data are not available, so my argument is necessarily more speculative on this point—that the competitive pluralism of general-purpose governments (Dahl 1956) is being displaced by a sort of *hiving pluralism* characteristic of jurisdictional specialization. That is, rather than engaging with each other in a broad-ranging contest over collectively decided priorities and purposes, local interest groups are increasingly withdrawing into a collection of narrower, well-partitioned realms of influence that intersect only on the tax bill.

I hope the Panglosses are right when they say that the proliferation of jurisdictions and the concomitant decline of voting reflect a political system that is maximizing both governmental efficiency and citizen happiness. The evidence put forth in this book, however, suggests that they are profoundly wrong.

---

7 For his part, Frug is well aware of the problems for local democracy posed by special districts, writing that "the multiplicity of entities and their technical nature generate an unusual amount of voter confusion and apathy" (2002, pp. 1783–1784).

Methodological Appendix

This appendix serves two purposes. First, I provide additional details regarding data issues, definitions, and case selection. Second, I present a variety of additional analyses supporting the main findings in the text and discuss more technical econometric issues. The reader who is not concerned with the data and econometric details can skip this appendix without missing any important substantive content.

A.1 DATA ISSUES

A.1.1 COG Data on Special Districts

The primary source of data for the government finance and organization variables used in my analyses is the COG. Like any data source, this one has strengths and weaknesses. The strengths of the COG are its comprehensive coverage of U.S. local governments, its historical comparability from the 1970s on, and the breadth of its coverage of government finance variables. The weaknesses of the COG are a matter of some dispute, as evidenced in the exchange between Leigland (1990) and Sacks (1990). Foster (1997, pp. 81–84) also reviews data quality issues related to the COG.

Leigland (1990) is highly critical of the COG and raises two primary concerns about the data on special districts. First, he argues that the Census Bureau overcounts special districts that are functionally inactive. For example, he shows that in the 1982 COG, 24 percent of special districts reported no expenditures, but the Bureau classified only 1.5 percent of districts as inactive. Leigland concludes that "The Bureau overcounts certain kinds of districts by being unreasonably conservative in keeping functionally inactive entities in its 'universe file of governments'" (1990, p. 377). Second, Leigland argues that the Bureau undercounts other types of districts by incorrectly attributing their activities to parent general-purpose governments. In particular, even when a parent government has relatively weak fiscal or administrative control over a special district, the Bureau is prone to classify the district as a dependent entity and attribute its fiscal activities to the general-purpose government that oversees it. The problem is especially acute for public authorities that have been created to finance major public works projects. Leigland writes that "the Census Bureau's definition and classification scheme may involve a bias against recognizing and counting the largest and most financially active special districts" (1990, p. 373). In fact, his analysis suggests that as much as 42 percent of special district debt is erroneously attributed by the Bureau to general-purpose governments.

In essence, the concerns about the COG data on special districts are that some small or inactive districts are overcounted, while some large districts are undercounted. While the appropriateness of the Bureau's practices has been defended (Sacks 1990), the most important issue in the present context is not the absolute accuracy of the data, but how any weaknesses in the data could bias the analyses presented previously. In this respect, accepting for the sake of argument that Leigland is right on both counts about the COG data, the problems should, if anything, bias me *against* finding my predicted results. That is, if many functionally inactive districts are mistakenly included, then it should be less likely that I will find a positive association between the number of special districts per municipality and aggregate taxes and spending. By the same token, if a large fraction of special district fiscal activities is mistakenly attributed to municipalities, then I should also be less likely to observe an increase in taxing and spending associated with an increase in the ratio of special districts to municipalities. In other words, if the COG data on special districts are inaccurate in the ways suggested, then the results from my models are actually *underestimates* of the true effects of jurisdictional overlap. Not being in a position to resolve the debate over COG data quality, I suggest that my results be interpreted as lower bounds on the effects of jurisdictional overlap on local taxes and spending.

A.1.2   *Case Selection*

In this section, I provide additional documentation of the process through which I arrived at the 21,198 observations used in the preceding analyses. I began with the complete set of 21,903 county-area records contained in the COG from 1972 to 2002.[1] I excluded Washington, D.C. (seven

---

1 The number of county-area records in the COG varies slightly across the study period. In 1972 there were 3,115 cases; in 1977, 3,118; in 1982, 3,131; in 1987, 3,132; in 1992, 3,135; and in 1997 and 2002, 3,136.

Methodological Appendix

cases) because it is not a state and has no counties. I excluded all cases from Alaska (147), because the state uniquely relies on boroughs rather than counties and boroughs do not cover the entire land area of the state. When I merged the COG data with county-level data from the CPH, I lost an additional 102 records that do not have a match. Of these, 68 cases are from Virginia, which has a unique entity known as *independent cities*, which are classified as county-areas by the COG but as cities by the CPH. Outside Virginia, there were an additional seven counties from the COG that did not have a match in the CPH in one or more years. The complete list of cases that did not match between the COG and CPH is contained in Table A.1. Among the records that were lost in the COG-to-CPH merge, the only county of notable size is Miami-Dade. In the CPH schema, the county changes from Dade (FIPS code 12025) to Miami-Dade (FIPS code 12086) in 1990. In the COG, this entity is always known as the Miami-Dade (GOVS code 10013) county-area. In addition to the cases that do not match between the COG and the CPH, I lost two additional records when I computed the five-year lagged population change variable: Bristol and Washington counties in Rhode Island both have missing values in 1972. Collectively, these case selection and data merging procedures reduced my sample from 21,903 to 21,645 county-year records.

Recall that I defined jurisdictional overlap in terms of the ratio of overlapping jurisdictions per municipality. Because division by zero is undefined, I lose cases where there are no incorporated municipalities within a county. Specifically, there are a total of 447 cases from 69 counties in which there was no municipality in the county, and hence my measure of jurisdictional overlap is undefined. Again, a plurality of these cases (161) come from Virginia and represent entities considered to be independent cities by the CPH and county areas by the COG. A complete list of the observations that are lost due to the absence of an incorporated municipality is contained in Table A.2. Unsurprisingly, most of the counties are rural, and the median population among these 447 observations is 9,200, compared with a median population of 21,000 among the remaining observations. One might be concerned that dropping counties with no municipalities systematically biases the analysis of jurisdictional overlap in some way. However, I note that several alternative measures of jurisdictional overlap *are* well defined for cases where there are no municipalities, and when I use any of these alternative measures the results are remarkably similar, as demonstrated in Table A.6.

Based on the case selection, data merging, and exclusion of cases without incorporated municipalities, I have a total of 21,198 county-year

Table A.1. *COG Receords That Did Not Match CPH Data*

Area Name	State	Total Cases	Years
La Paz County	AZ	4	1987 to 2002
Broomfield	CO	1	2002
Dade County	FL	3	1992 to 2002
Ste. Genevieve County	MO	7	All
Cibola County	NM	5	1982 to 2002
Carson City	NV	7	All
Bedford City	VA	7	All
Chesapeake City	VA	7	All
Emporia City	VA	7	All
Fairfax City	VA	7	All
Franklin City	VA	7	All
Lexington City	VA	7	All
Manassas City	VA	6	1977 to 2002
Manassas Park City	VA	6	1977 to 2002
Nansemond	VA	1	1972
Poquoson City	VA	6	1977 to 2002
Salem City	VA	7	All
Menominee County	WI	7	All
TOTAL		102	

observations used in Chapter 4, which includes 3,025 cases in 1972, 3,027 in 1977, 3,030 in 1982 and 1987, 3,029 in 1992 and 1997, and 3,028 in 2002.

Finally, in Chapter 6, I add the Democratic Party's county-level vote share in presidential elections. Doing so causes me to lose two observations, as I could not obtain the returns for Muscogee, Georgia, in 1972 or 1976. For the analysis of party competition in Chapter 6, I lost 19 observations—7 from Honolulu, Hawaii, and 6 each from Bristol and Washington, Rhode Island—for which I could not obtain the necessary historical gubernatorial vote shares. In addition, I exclude Minnesota (348 observations) from the party competition analyses, because the Democratic-Farmer-Labor Party is tabulated separately from the two major parties according to my Inter-University Consortium for Political and Social Research (ICPSR) data source, making the state an outlier in my party competition metric. With these additional case selection and data merging steps, I have a total of 21,196 observations used in most of the analyses in Chapter 6 and 20,568 used in the party competition analysis (Tables 6.4 and 6.5).

Table A.2. *Counties with No Incorporated Municipalities in the COG*

Area Name	State	Total Cases	Years
Alpine County	CA	7	All
Mariposa County	CA	7	All
Mono County	CA	3	1972 to 1982
Trinity County	CA	7	All
Tolland County	CT	3	1992 to 2002
Echols County	GA	7	All
Hawaii County	HI	7	All
Kauai County	HI	7	All
Maui County	HI	7	All
Wichita County	KS	1	1987
Martin County	KY	2	1972, 1977
McCreary County	KY	7	All
Cameron Parish	LA	7	All
Plaquemines Parish	LA	7	All
St. Bernard Parish	LA	7	All
St. Charles Parish	LA	7	All
St. John the Baptist	LA	7	All
Baltimore County	MD	7	All
Howard County	MD	7	All
Oscoda County	MI	7	All
Issaquena County	MS	2	1972, 1977
Camden County	NC	7	All
Currituck County	NC	7	All
Hyde County	NC	7	All
Banner County	NE	7	All
McPherson County	NE	7	All
Catron County	NM	2	1972, 1977
Los Alamos County	NM	7	All
Douglas County	NV	7	All
Esmeralda County	NV	7	All
Eureka County	NV	7	All
Lander County	NV	7	All
Mineral County	NV	7	All
Storey County	NV	7	All
Borden County	TX	7	All
Crockett County	TX	7	All
Glasscock County	TX	7	All

(continued)

Table A.2. *(continued)*

Area Name	State	Total Cases	Years
Jeff Davis County	TX	1	1972
Jim Hogg County	TX	7	All
Kenedy County	TX	7	All
King County	TX	7	All
Loving County	TX	7	All
McMullen County	TX	7	All
Terrell County	TX	7	All
Zapata County	TX	7	All
Amelia County	VA	7	All
Arlington County	VA	7	All
Bath County	VA	7	All
Bedford County	VA	7	All
Bland County	VA	7	All
Charles City County	VA	7	All
Chesterfield County	VA	7	All
Cumberland County	VA	7	All
Gloucester County	VA	7	All
Goochland County	VA	7	All
Henrico County	VA	7	All
James City County	VA	7	All
King and Queen County	VA	7	All
King George County	VA	7	All
Mathews County	VA	7	All
Nelson County	VA	7	All
New Kent County	VA	7	All
Northumberland County	VA	7	All
Powhatan County	VA	7	All
Prince George County	VA	7	All
Spotsylvania County	VA	7	All
Stafford County	VA	7	All
York County	VA	7	All
Essex County	VT	6	1977 to 2002
TOTAL		447	

A.1.3 Defining Common Functions

As one element of my effort to separate the overlap effect from functional performance, I identified a set of *common functions*, which I defined as those functions provided in at least 90 percent of cases. Table A.3 lists

Table A.3. *Common-Function Spending Categories*

Function	Frequency (%)
Police protection	99.9
Financial administration	99.8
Elementary and secondary education	99.7
Central staff services	99.6
General expenditure—NEC	99.6
Regular sighways	99.4
Interest on general debt	98.4
Fire protection	97.2
General public buildings	94.9
Health	93.7
Natural resources	93.6
Parks and recreation	90.4
Solid waste management	89.4
Sewerage	89.4
Libraries	88.0
Public welfare—NEC	85.8
Corrections	85.0
Judicial and legal	70.8
Housing and community development	59.1
Air transportation	55.6
Protective inspection and regulation—NEC	48.1
Own hospitals	40.8
Parking facilities	28.8
Public welfare—vendor payments, medical	27.1
Public welfare—other assistance programs	25.5
Public welfare—vendor payments, other	23.5
Public welfare—categorical assistance programs	19.1
Higher education	14.9
Other hospitals	10.0
Water transport and terminals	7.6
Misc. commercial activities	6.1
Transit subsidies	2.8
Public welfare—institutions	0.4
Toll highways	0.2
Education—NEC	0.05

Notes: Frequency is defined as the percentage of county-year observations with positive spending on a given function. Functions with a frequency of at least 90 percent are defined as *common functions.*

all the functional spending items contained in the COG and the proportion of county-year observations in which there was positive spending.[2] The 90 percent threshold is admittedly somewhat arbitrary. For instance, one could argue that there is a "natural break" in the data at around 85 percent. However, lowering the threshold will only increase the amount of spending included and therefore will make this measure more similar to total spending. Under the current definition, common functions account for roughly 80 percent of total spending. Since I have already shown that the overlap effect is present for total spending, I am not concerned that the definition of common functions is insufficiently inclusive. Because common-function spending is one of several strategies I use to address functional performance, and because all produce similar results, I am satisfied with the 90 percent threshold as a rough definition of functions that are provided almost universally.

A.2 METHODOLOGICAL ISSUES

A.2.1   *Results from Chapter 2*

In Chapter 2, I explained that the existing literature has yielded mixed findings on the question of whether special districts are created to circumvent TELs imposed on other local governments. A major limitation of past studies is that most are cross-sectional and therefore relate the number of special districts in existence at a given time with the contemporaneous existence of TELs. Such analyses cannot show whether TELs cause the formation of special districts, whether the existence of special districts leads to the enactment of TELs, or whether the relationship is merely coincidental. To illustrate this difficulty, Table A.4 presents a series of state-level panel regressions of the number of special districts against the number of TELs. The number of special districts by state is taken from the COG for the years 1942 and 1952–2002 at five-year intervals. The number of TELs is taken from ACIR (1995) and Mullins and Wallin (2004), the details of which are explained in greater detail in Chapter 4.

In model (1) of Table A.4, I simply pool the data and regress the log of the number of special districts on the number of TELs, in the style of the cross-sectional analyses used in the existing literature. There is a significant, positive relationship, and the point estimate indicates that an increase of one TEL is associated with roughly a 10 percent increase

---

2 Table A.3 lists all the functional spending categories that are included under the rubric of "general expenditures." Additional items, such as utility, retirement, and insurance trust spending, are not included.

Table A.4. *Special Districts and TELs*

	(1)	(2)	(3)	(4)
Total number of fiscal restrictions on all local governments	0.11 (0.05)**	−0.02 (0.03)		
Total number of fiscal restrictions on county governments				0.13 (0.11)
Total number of fiscal restrictions on municipal governments				−0.21 (−0.11)*
Property Tax Revenue Limit—county			0.19 (0.20)	
Assessment increase limit—municipality			0.14 (0.24)	
Assessment increase limit—county			0.00 0.00	
Overall property tax rate limit—county			−0.06 (0.18)	
Specific property tax rate limit—county			−0.11 (0.58)	
General revenue limit—county			0.69 (0.75)	
General expenditure limit—county			−0.26 (0.35)	
Full disclosure—county			0.06 (0.29)	
Overall property tax rate limit—municipality			0.00 0.00	
Specific property tax rate limit—municipality			−0.10 (0.20)	
Property tax revenue limit—municipality			−0.33 (0.16)**	
General revenue limit—municipality			0.00 0.00	
General expenditure limit—municipality			−0.19 (0.20)	
Full disclosure—municipality			0.00 (0.29)	

(continued)

Table A.4. *(continued)*

	(1)	(2)	(3)	(4)
Constant	3.80	3.93	3.99	3.91
	(0.28)***	(0.16)***	(0.25)***	(0.17)***
Fixed effects?	No	Yes	Yes	Yes
R-squared	0.20	0.57	0.58	0.57
Observations	595	595	595	595
# of clusters	50	50	50	50

Notes: Observations are state aggregates for 1942, and 1952 through 2002 at five-year intervals. The dependent variable is ln(number of special districts) in the state. Standard errors, clustered by state, are reported in parentheses. All models include year dummies (not reported).
*significant at 10%, **significant at 5%, ***significant at 1%.

in the number of special districts. Clearly, states with more TELs have more special districts. But when state fixed effects are added in model (2), the relationship between TELs and special districts becomes negative and insignificant. In model (3), rather than using a *count* of TELs, I include an indicator variable for the existence of each type of TEL tracked in ACIR (1995). Only one type of TEL is significant—namely, property tax revenue limits for municipalities—and here the relationship is negative, exactly the opposite of what would be expected if TELs caused the formation of special districts. Finally, in model (4), I count the number of TELs separately placed on counties and municipalities. The number of municipal TELs is negatively associated with the number of special districts, and the relationship is significant at the 6 percent level. Together, these findings suggest that time-invariant state attributes account for having more TELs and more special districts, but there is no evidence that the number of special districts increases within states over time in response to changes in TELs.

A.2.2 Results from Chapter 4

Correlations among Alternative Measures of Overlap. There are several plausible measures of jurisdictional overlap, and the choice among them is not clear-cut on theoretical grounds alone. As emphasized in the text, the results of my analysis do not hinge on the choice of any particular metric. Table A.5 shows correlations among the various measures of jurisdictional overlap. All of the bivariate correlations are statistically significant. In this discussion, I will focus on the correlations between the variable I used in the main analysis—the log of the number of overlapping jurisdictions per municipality—and the alternative

Table A.5. *Correlations among Measures of Jurisdictional Overlap*

	ln(Overlapping Districts per GP Government)	Functional Layers	1/Layers	ln(Special Districts and Overlapping Towns per GP Government)	ln(Special Districts per GP Government)	Overlapping Jurisdicitons as % of All Gov'ts in County	Average Unit's Share of County-Area Revenue	Special Districts' Share of County-Area Revenue	Municipalities' Share of County-Area Revenue	ln(Overlapping Jurisdictions)
Functional layers	0.44	1.00								
1/layers	-0.45	-0.72	1.00							
ln(special districts and overlapping towns per GP government)	0.96	0.48	-0.48	1.00						
ln(special districts per GP government)	0.83	0.57	-0.53	0.86	1.00					
Overlapping jurisdictions as % of all governments in county	0.93	0.42	-0.55	0.87	0.75	1.00				
Average unit's share of county-area revenue	-0.28	-0.43	0.58	-0.26	-0.14	-0.32	1.00			

(continued)

Table A.5. *(continued)*

	ln(Overlapping Districts per GP Government)	Functional Layers	1/Layers	ln (Special Districts and Overlapping Towns per GP Government)	ln(Special Districts per GP Government)	Overlapping Jurisdicitons as % of All Gov'ts in County	Average Unit's Share of County-Area Revenue	Special Districts' Share of County-Area Revenue	Municipalities' Share of County-Area Revenue	ln(Overlapping Jurisdictions)
Special districts' share of county-area revenue	0.18	0.32	-0.29	0.20	0.29	0.19	-0.11	1.00		
Municipalities' share of county-area revenue	-0.08	0.06	-0.01	-0.07	-0.04	-0.07	0.18	-0.14	1.00	
ln(overlapping jurisdictions)	0.59	0.69	-0.66	0.58	0.41	0.61	-0.70	0.12	0.03	1.00
ln(number of cities)	-0.34	0.33	-0.28	-0.30	-0.36	-0.32	-0.57	-0.05	0.09	0.53

measures of jurisdictional overlap, which are shown in the first column of Table A.5. One alternative approach is simply to count the number of types of special districts that exist in a county, which I call the number of *functional layers*. I also compute the reciprocal of the number of layers, and these two variables are correlated at 0.44 and −0.45 with the number of overlapping jurisdictions per municipality.[3] Next, I compute the number of overlapping jurisdictions, excluding school districts, per municipality. To be specific, I sum the number of special districts, territorially overlapping townships, and the county and divide this sum by the number of municipalities and territorially exclusive townships. This measure is correlated at 0.96 with the original measure of jurisdictional overlap, which indicates that school districts are not disproportionately influencing my analysis of jurisdictional overlap as reported in the text. Another plausible measure of jurisdictional overlap is the fraction of all governments in the county that have the capacity for territorial overlap; this variable is correlated at 0.93 with the number of overlapping jurisdictions per municipality. Next I compute three variables that reflect the distribution of revenue authority across types of local governments: the fraction of aggregate local revenue accounted for by the average local government, the fraction accounted for by special districts, and the fraction accounted for by municipalities. These variables have the lowest correlation with my primary measure of jurisdictional overlap, suggesting that the ratio of special districts to municipalities does not translate directly into districts' share of revenue. The average government's share of revenue is negatively correlated at −0.28 with the number of overlapping jurisdictions per municipality. Following the formal model in Chapter 3, a government's share of all local revenue may be an indication of the extent to which it internalizes the full social value of its tax activities. Finally, I seperate the numerator and the denominator from my primary measure of overlap, which are correlated with it at 0.59 and −0.34, respectively.

Alternative Measures of Overlap Generate Comparable Results. The significant correlations among the various measures of jurisdictional overlap suggest that all are tapping into common institutional patterns across counties, although the different variables are far from being perfectly

---

3 Taking the reciprocal effectively reverses the sign of the correlation between the variable; a higher value indicates *less* jurisdictional overlap. For instance, where there is only one layer of government, jurisdictional overlap is equal to $1/1 = 1$. As the number of layers increases, $1/\text{layers}$ becomes smaller: With two layers, we have $1/2 = .5$; with three layers, $1/3 = .33$; and so on. Thus, the negative correlation is expected.

interchangeable. In this section, I demonstrate that using *any* of these alternative measures in the main models of Chapter 4 leads to substantively similar findings with respect to the positive relationship between jurisdictional overlap and local taxation. These results should ease any concerns that support for my argument is sensitive to a particular definition of the main variable of interest.

To conserve space, Table A.6 presents only the coefficients for the jurisdictional overlap variables, although each model includes the full set of control variables used in Table 4.3 of Chapter 4, as well as county and year fixed effects. Because the jurisdictional overlap variables are measured on different scales, I also present standardized coefficients for each model. The standardized coefficients should be interpreted as the number of standard deviations by which own-source revenue increases when jurisdictional overlap is increased by one standard deviation. The standardized coefficients allow more direct comparison of the magnitudes of the effects produced by the different measures of jurisdictional overlap.

First, note that all of the measures of jurisdictional overlap produce statistically significant results and all point in the direction predicted by the common-pool model: More jurisdictional overlap leads to higher own-source revenue.[4] The standardized coefficients range, in absolute size, from 0.06 to 0.17. The measure of jurisdictional overlap used in the text—the log of the number of overlapping jurisdictions per municipality (model 1)—produces a standardized coefficient of 0.10, which is roughly in the middle of the range. I conclude from these results that my findings are not sensitive to the use of any particular measure of jurisdictional overlap, that all of these measures produce effects that are in the same ballpark, and that the measure I have used throughout the text yields fairly middle-of-the-road estimates compared with other plausible measures.

Using Data Back to 1962 Does Not Change the Results. As explained in the text, detailed data on expenditures by function are available on a consistent basis from the COG beginning with 1972. Because functional expenditure data are necessary for computing the FPI, I use only the 1972 to 2002 data for the analyses presented in the text. However, basic fiscal data are available back to 1962. In Table A.7, I present results

---

4 Three of the overlap coefficients actually take on negative values—for 1/layers (model 2), the average government's share of revenue (model 7), and municipalities' share of revenue (model 9)—but note that in these cases higher values indicate *less* overlap, so the negative coefficients actually indicate that more overlap is associated with more revenue.

Methodological Appendix

Table A.6. *Base Model Using Alternative Measures of Jurisdictional Overlap*

(1)	(2)	(3)	(4)
Coefficient	Standardized Coefficient	Overall *R*-Squared	N

Model 1: ln (Overlapping Districts per Municipality)

133.73	0.10	0.27	21,198
(33.46)***	(0.02)***		

Model 2: 1/Layers

−272.44	−0.06	0.23	21,645
(67.13)***	(0.01)***		

Model 3: ln (Special Districts and Overlapping Townships per Municipality)

97.39	0.07	0.26	21,198
(31.75)***	(0.02)***		

Model 4: ln (Special Districts per Municipality)

98.75	0.07	0.25	21,198
(30.04)***	(0.02)***		

Model 5: Overlapping Jurisdictions as % of All Local Governments

374.41	0.10	0.26	21,645
(85.10)***	(0.02)***		

Model 6: ln (Layers)

79.61	0.06	0.23	21,645
(21.78)***	(0.01)***		

Model 7: Average Unit's Share of County-Area Revenue

−779.86	−0.17	0.22	21,645
(160.87)***	(0.03)***		

Model 8: Special Districts' Share of County-Area Revenue

1,041.45	0.15	0.21	21,645
(83.66)***	(0.01)***		

Model 9: Municipalities' Share of County-Area Revenue

−285.25	−0.05	0.23	21,645
(170.68)*	(0.03)		

Notes: The dependent variable is general own-source revenue per capita. All dollar values are CPI-adjusted to year 2002 dollars. Standard errors, clustered by county, are reported in parentheses. All models include county and year fixed effects and the standard set of controls (not reported).
*significant at 10%, **significant at 5%, ***significant at 1%.

Table A.7. *Using the Full Panel Back to 1962*

	(1)	(2)	(3)
Jurisdictional overlap	75.90		
	(23.95)***		
Overlapping jurisdictions as % of all local governments		260.07	
		(60.45)***	
ln(special districts and overlapping townships per municipality)			100.29
			(28.36)***
ln(population)	−48.56	−115.35	−48.76
	(31.89)	(45.59)**	(31.60)
Per capita income	0.03	0.04	0.03
	(0.00)***	(0.01)***	(0.00)***
Percent nonwhite	568.51	769.13	543.73
	(142.00)***	(178.69)***	(141.67)***
Percent age ≤18	608.75	718.63	537.05
	(442.30)	(522.78)	(438.06)
Percent age ≥65	696.39	791.23	649.85
	(463.69)	(482.76)	(464.84)
Federal aid, five-year lag	23.00	19.60	22.62
	(4.69)***	(5.32)***	(4.67)***
State aid, five-year lag	−146.35	−206.74	−149.54
	(30.52)***	(41.49)***	(30.71)***
Constant	1,808.97	2,656.08	1,042.90
	(433.46)***	(591.24)***	(384.15)***
R-squared (within)	0.39	0.39	0.39
Observations	27,248	27,692	27,249
# of clusters	3,036	3,085	3,036

Notes: The dependent variable is general own-source revenue per capita. All dollar values are CPI-adjusted to year 2002 dollars. Standard errors, clustered by county, are reported in parentheses. All models include county and year fixed effects (not reported).
*significant at 10%, **significant at 5%, ***significant at 1%.

using the extended county-level panel from 1962 on. These models necessarily exclude the FPI as a control. Using three measures of jurisdictional overlap that I was able to compute based on the pre-1972 data, I find that adding the additional data from 1962 and 1967 leads to substantially similar findings. These results indicate that sacrificing the earlier years of data in order to obtain the FPI does not bias the results in any notable way.

Results Using Different Estimation Methods. Nearly all of the econometric models presented in Chapters 4 and 6 use county fixed effects, meaning that identification is based on changes within counties over time. As explained in the text, this approach has the advantage of controlling for the influence of any (observable or unobservable) attribute of the county that does not change over time. In addition, all of the models in the text utilize clustered standard errors, which are robust to arbitrary forms of serial correlation. In this section, I test the robustness of my results to methodological alternatives to fixed effects and clustered standard errors.

All of the models reported in Table A.8 are versions of model (1) shown in Table 4.3 of Chapter 4 that use different estimation strategies. I begin by estimating the model via pooled OLS with clustered standard errors, which takes advantage of all within- and between-county variation but ignores unobservable heterogeneity. The estimate of the overlap effect, reported in model (1) of Table A.8, is notably larger and more precisely estimated. In model (2), I use first differences instead of fixed effects and recover roughly similar results.[5] Next, I estimate the model with random effects and clustered standard errors, which utilizes a weighted combination of within- and between-variation. Again, the estimated overlap effect is notably larger and more precisely estimated than in the fixed effects model. The random effects model assumes that the group-specific errors are uncorrelated with the explanatory variables, whereas the fixed effects model does not make this assumption.[6] If the assumptions of the random effects model are satisfied, then it is more efficient than the fixed effects model and would be the preferred approach. However, the additional orthogonality conditions of the random effects model can be tested with a Hausman-type test, and when I do so, the random effects model is resoundingly rejected.[7] In other words, although the main results hold up under a random effects specification, the evidence clearly favors the fixed effects model presented in the text.

Models (1) through (3) all use clustered standard errors to account for serial correlation in the errors. In models (4) and (5) I test alternative

5 The starting time period is dropped in the first differencing, which explains the smaller sample size for model (2).
6 See Wooldridge (2002, sect. 10.2) for a discussion.
7 See Wooldridge (2002, sect. 10.7.3) for an explanation of the use of the Hausman test to compare fixed and random effects estimators. In the present case, I use a heteroskedastic- and cluster-robust variant, the Sargan-Hansen test (see Baum, Schaffer, and Stillman 2003). The Sargan-Hansen test statistic is 862.05, which follows a chi-square distribution and has a p-value of less than 0.0001. A rejection of the null suggests that the orthogonality assumptions of the random effects model are not satisfied.

Table A.8. Comparing Different Estimation Methods

	(1) OLS	(2) First-Differences	(3) Random Effects	(4) Fixed Effects w/ AR(1) Disturbance	(5) Fixed Effects w/ Driscoll–Kraay SE
Jurisdictional overlap	181.04	87.16	199.58	116.89	133.73
	(13.49)***	(22.27)***	(15.30)***	(26.75)***	(15.55)***
FPI	1.41	0.73	1.06	0.79	0.92
	(0.05)***	(0.04)***	(0.04)***	(0.03)***	(0.04)***
ln(population)	−226.53	91.46	−135.41	34.23	34.51
	(14.77)***	(49.56)*	(14.38)***	(40.63)	(32.45)
Per capita income	0.09	0.02	0.04	0.03	0.02
	(0.00)***	(0.00)***	(0.00)***	(0.00)***	(0.00)***
Percent nonwhite	−75.94	−32.85	−239.40	−411.34	−15.38
	(69.03)	(157.82)	(66.05)***	(195.93)**	(155.22)
Five-year change in population	−683.85	−335.85	−366.61	−349.48	−282.26
	(87.16)***	(63.10)***	(74.61)***	(59.95)***	(90.26)***

Percent age ≤18	285.91	213.82	55.97	696.26	169.10
	(414.82)	(375.22)	(382.92)	(398.29)*	(291.10)
Percent age ≥65	−1,370.90	−709.94	−887.49	−459.17	58.47
	(404.50)***	(432.62)	(397.64)**	(449.06)	(174.68)
Federal aid, five-year lag	0.30	−0.01	0.06	−0.01	0.02
	(0.16)*	(0.02)	(0.05)	(0.02)	(0.04)
State aid, five-year lag	0.01	−0.02	−0.06	−0.04	−0.11
	(0.03)	(0.03)	(0.03)*	(0.02)*	(0.03)***
Constant	44.56	−99.61	−689.79	−1,388.20	0.00
	(247.56)	(16.10)***	(208.33)***	(301.63)***	0.00
R-squared	0.42	0.1	0.32	0.21	0.33
Observations	21,198	18,165	21,198	18,166	21,198
# of clusters	3,032	3,031	3,032	3,031	3,032

Notes: The dependent variable is general own-source revenue per capita. All dollar values are CPI-adjusted to year 2002 dollars. Standard errors are reported in parentheses; standard errors are clustered by county in columns 1, 2, and 3. All models include year dummies (not reported). *significant at 10%, **significant at 5%, ***significant at 1%.

approaches to estimating the standard errors; both models continue to include county and year fixed effects. Specifically, model (4) models the disturbance as AR(1). The results are roughly unchanged relative to the case with clustered standard errors. Finally, while all of the preceding results are robust to residual serial correlation (i.e., correlation within counties over time), there remains a possibility of spatial, or cross-sectional, correlation in the residuals (i.e., correlation among counties located near one another). Spatial correlation in the residuals might occur, for instance, if neighboring counties are subject to common regional economic shocks, demographic trends, or institutional changes. Model (5) uses Driscoll–Kraay (1998) standard errors, which are robust to arbitrary forms of serial *and* spatial correlation, as well as to heteroskedasticity. Again, the main results are upheld and the standard errors are, if anything, smaller than when county-level clustering is used.[8]

Based on the results presented in Table A.8, I conclude that the primary modeling strategy used in the text—namely, fixed effects with clustered standard errors—is appropriate and robust. Nearly every other approach produces larger estimated overlap effects, smaller standard errors, or both. Thus, the results presented in the text would appear to be relatively conservative estimates.

Intergovernmental Revenue. In modeling local taxing and spending decisions, it is important to control for intergovernmental revenue received from the state and federal governments. However, an obvious concern is that local budgets and intergovernmental aid are jointly determined, which presents an endogeneity problem. To deal with this problem, I used five-year lagged values of state and federal aid in the models presented in the text. In this section, I show that my results pertaining to jurisdictional overlap are essentially unaffected by the way in which I incorporate state and federal aid. In model (1) of Table A.9, I simply exclude state and federal aid altogether. In model (2), I use the contemporaneous (i.e., not lagged) values of state and federal aid. In model (3), I use 10-year lagged values of state and federal aid. Finally, in model (4), I instrument the current values of state and federal aid with their own 10-year lagged values. The estimated coefficients for jurisdictional overlap in models (1) through (3) are nearly identical, and the coefficient increases in magnitude in model (4). With respect to intergovernmental revenue, the estimated effect of state aid

---

8 Driscoll and Kraay (1998) use a Newey-West (1987) approach to serial correlation. The model reported in Table A.8 uses two lags in the autocorrelation structure. I have experimented with up to six lags and find that the standard errors become slightly smaller.

Table A.9. *Different Ways of Handling Intergovernmental Revenue*

	(1)	(2)	(3)	(4)
Jurisdictional overlap	129.99	133.00	136.57	179.64
	(33.54)***	(33.67)***	(33.67)***	(38.49)***
FPI	0.91	0.92	0.92	0.95
	(0.04)***	(0.04)***	(0.04)***	(0.04)***
ln(population)	57.20	42.94	29.41	−164.76
	(36.51)	(38.91)	(36.46)	(74.51)**
Per capita income	0.03	0.03	0.03	0.02
	(0.00)***	(0.00)***	(0.00)***	(0.00)***
Percent nonwhite	−90.48	−52.24	5.81	489.73
	(151.19)	(151.40)	(151.33)	(233.91)**
Five-year change in population	−306.92	−307.27	−291.80	−320.36
	(90.08)***	(90.20)***	(88.63)***	(98.51)***
Percent age ≤18	166.48	234.18	44.60	1,178.04
	(462.70)	(473.30)	(459.62)	(601.55)*
Percent age ≥65	79.07	92.24	34.05	334.88
	(504.48)	(505.30)	(503.81)	(548.96)
Federal aid		0.02		−0.11
		(0.03)		(0.35)
State aid		−0.06		−0.93
		(0.04)		(0.29)***
Federal aid, 10-year lag			0.00	
			(0.03)	
State aid, 10-year lag			−0.13	
			(0.03)***	
Constant	−1,981.37	−1,784.18	−1,024.75	
	(395.03)***	(423.49)***	(396.12)***	
R-squared (within)	0.33	0.33	0.33	
Observations	21,198	21,198	21,196	21,195
# of clusters	3,032	3,032	3,032	3,031

Notes: The dependent variable is general own-source revenue per capita. All dollar values are CPI-adjusted to year 2002 dollars. Standard errors, clustered by county, are reported in parentheses. All models include county and year fixed effects (not reported). In model (4), state and federal aid are instrumented with their own 10-year lagged values.
*significant at 10%, **significant at 5%, ***significant at 1%.

becomes notably larger and more significant in the IV model, suggesting that joint causation was a valid concern. Federal aid, on the other hand, is never a significant predictor of local own-source revenue.

Tax and Expenditure Limitations. In the models presented in Chapter 4, I measured fiscal limitations on local governments as simply a sum of the number of TELs in place in a state. In this section, I explore more complex measures. All of the TEL data are from ACIR (1995) and Mullins and Wallin (2004). I begin by entering a full set of dummy variables for each of the 21 different types of TELs tracked in the ACIR study. The results are presented in model (1) of Table A.10. The coefficient on jurisdictional overlap is essentially unchanged; if anything, it is slightly larger than the corresponding model (1) of Table 4.6 in Chapter 4. Next, I compute separate summary variables representing the number of TELs in place for counties, municipalities, and school districts, respectively. Again, the estimated effect of jurisdictional overlap does not change. Finally, I estimate models with interactions between each of the TEL summary variables and jurisdictional overlap, which corresponds to model (2) of Table 4.6 in Chapter 4. None of the estimated interaction terms is statistically significant and all are negative, exactly the opposite sign from what would be expected if special districts were being used primarily to circumvent fiscal restrictions on other types of local governments. The main effect of jurisdictional overlap remains significant (statistically and quantitatively) in all of the models. The results presented in Table A.10 provide further support for the idea that the overlap effect reflects a fiscal common-pool problem, not an institutional reaction to TELs.

State-Specific Time Trends. As previously discussed, the source of identification in the fixed effects models is change over time within counties. One concern with this identification strategy is that there might be some omitted county-level variable that changes over time and is correlated with both jurisdictional overlap and local taxes and spending. To a large extent, this concern should be assuaged by the 2SLS analysis presented in Chapter 4, which used deeply lagged values of jurisdictional overlap to instrument for current values. However, as an additional check, I also ran models that allow for a state-specific time trend. In other words, the model allows for a state-specific slope in spending over time. The estimated effect of jurisdictional overlap, shown in Table A.11, is virtually unchanged by the inclusion of the state-specific trends.

First-Stage IV Results. In Chapter 4, model (2) of Table 4.9 represents the second stage of a 2SLS model in which 2002 values of jurisdictional

Table A.10. *Tax and Expenditure Limitations*

	(1)	(2)	(3)	(4)	(5)
Jurisdictional overlap	141.61	136.94	195.00	212.18	187.50
	(51.68)***	(56.35)**	(76.47)**	(74.41)***	(72.35)**
Property tax revenue limit—county	139.84				
	(78.47)*				
Assessment increase limit—municipality	−8.14				
	(30.51)				
Specific property tax rate limit—county	285.18				
	(107.93)**				
General expenditure limit—county	−148.00				
	(79.90)*				
Full disclosure—county	−158.38				
	(52.73)***				
Specific property tax rate limit—municipality	−203.02				
	(99.84)**				
Property tax revenue limit—municipality	−196.83				
	(88.68)**				
General revenue limit—municipality	938.43				
	(202.12)***				

(continued)

Table A.10. (continued)

	(1)	(2)	(3)	(4)	(5)
General expenditure limit—municipality	-382.21				
	(86.81)***				
Full disclosure—municipality	214.14				
	(87.13)**				
Overall property tax rate limit—school district	-225.87				
	(35.97)***				
Specific property tax rate limit—school district	13.19				
	(50.23)				
Property tax revenue limit—school district	-12.62				
	(64.99)				
General revenue limit—school district	-244.65				
	(113.96)**				
General expenditure limit—school district	187.09				
	(62.15)***				
Full disclosure—school district	50.88				
	(83.52)				

	(1)	(2)	(3)	(4)	(5)
Total number of Fiscal restrictions on county governments		61.78 (86.22)	73.89 (44.21)		
Jurisdictional overlap * Total number of fiscal restrictions on county governments			−33.44 (31.04)		
Total number of fiscal restrictions on municipal governments		−26.18 (83.49)		86.57 (39.20)**	
Jurisdictional overlap * Total number of fiscal restrictions on municipal governments				−43.12 (28.72)	
Total number of fiscal restrictions on school district governments		−17.52 (43.12)			65.88 (43.82)
Jurisdictional overlap * Total number of fiscal restrictions on school district governments					−33.58 (30.59)
Constant	−1,736.43 (784.57)**	−1,571.06 (873.49)*	−1,859.09 (773.61)**	−1,913.59 (776.70)**	−1,868.50 (766.57)**
R-squared (within)	0.35	0.33	0.33	0.33	0.33
Observations	21,198	21,198	21,198	21,198	21,198
# of clusters	49	49	49	49	49

Notes: The dependent variable is general own-source revenue per capita. All dollar values are CPI-adjusted to year 2002 dollars. Standard errors, clustered by state are reported in parentheses. All models include county and year fixed effects and the usual controls (not reported). *significant at 10%, **significant at 5%, ***significant at 1%.

Table A.11. *State-Specific Time Trends*

	(1)
Jurisdictional overlap	132.91
	(33.33)***
FPI	0.91
	(0.04)***
ln(population)	−63.22
	(45.44)
Per capita income	0.03
	(0.00)***
Percent nonwhite	127.22
	(159.66)
Five-year change in population	−287.32
	(88.77)***
Percent age ≤18	898.08
	(462.76)*
Percent age ≥65	229.05
	(511.38)
Federal aid, five-year lag	0.01
	(0.03)
State aid, five-year lag	−0.08
	(0.04)**
Constant	−97.78
	(479.87)
R-squared (within)	0.37
Observations	21,198
# of clusters	3,032

Notes: The dependent variable is general own-source revenue per capita. All dollar values are CPI-adjusted to year 2002 dollars. Standard errors, clustered by county, are reported in parentheses. County and year fixed effects and state-specific time trends (not reported) are also included.
*significant at 10%, **significant at 5%, ***significant at 1%.

overlap are instrumented with 1972 values. For completeness, model (1) of Table A.12 in this appendix reports the corresponding first-stage regression. As expected, the 1972 values are strong predictors, yielding a coefficient of 0.79 and a t-statistic of more than 20. Controlling for jurisdictional overlap in 1972, several other variables also predict jurisdictional overlap in 2002. Specifically, counties that received more federal aid, that had fewer children, and that had a higher proportion of

Table A.12. *First-Stage IV Results and Reduced Form*

	(1)	(2)
1972 Jurisdictional overlap	0.79	117.38
	(0.04)***	(43.76)***
FPI	0.000	1.32
	0.000	(0.10)***
ln(population)	0.12	−1,225.37
	(0.09)	(286.54)***
ln(population)^2	−0.006	46.96
	(0.004)	(12.45)***
Per capita income	(0.000)	0.05
	(0.000)	(0.01)***
Percent nonwhite	0.13	26.84
	(0.07)*	(172.44)
Five-year change in population	0.19	−616.07
	(0.17)	(518.71)
Percent age ≤18	−1.11	−2,162.98
	(0.30)***	(1,332.62)
Percent age ≥65	−0.34	−3,132.41
	(0.32)	(1,337.52)**
Federal aid, five-year lag	0.0001	0.27
	(0.00005)***	(0.14)*
State aid, five-year lag	0.000	−0.14
	(0.000)	(0.19)
Constant		5,723.23
		(1,726.32)***
R-squared (within)	0.56	0.34
Observations	3,022	3,025
# of clusters	49	49

Notes: In model (1), the dependent variable is jurisdictional overlap in 2002.
In model (2), the dependent variable is general own-source revenue per capita in 2002.
Standard errors, clustered by state, are reported in parentheses. All models include state dummies (not reported).
*significant at 10%, **significant at 5%, ***significant at 1%.

nonwhite residents all had more overlapping jurisdictions, although the last relationship is significant at only the 10 percent level. The overall R^2 of the first-stage model is 0.56, with most of the explanatory power being attributable to the lagged value of jurisdictional overlap. Finally, in model (2) of Table A.12, I use the 1972 value of jurisdictional overlap directly instead of the contemporaneous value of overlap in a model of own-source revenue in 2002. Jurisdictional overlap in 1972 is a highly significant predictor of taxation in 2002, although, as expected, the coefficient is smaller than the one obtained when using the contemporaneous variable. The strong explanatory power of historically predetermined levels of jurisdictional overlap—in both 2SLS and OLS models—strongly suggests that the effect of jurisdictional overlap on local taxes and spending is not simply the result of contemporary demand shocks.

A.2.3   Results from Chapter 6

Fully Interacted Model. The main focus of Chapter 6 was on the interaction between party organizational strength and jurisdictional overlap in shaping local taxing and spending decisions. There, I presented several models using interactions between Mayhew's (1986) TPO score and my measure of jurisdictional overlap. In this section, I present a fully interacted model, allowing the slopes of *all* the coefficients to vary between TPO and non-TPO states. The results are shown in Table A.13. Two findings are noteworthy. First, the estimated main effect of jurisdictional overlap and its interaction with the TPO dummy variable are not notably changed in the fully interacted model, compared to model (3) of Table 5.2 in Chapter 5. Second, none of the other variables demonstrate a significant interaction with party organizational strength, with the exception of the FPI. Each dollar of the FPI is associated with about $0.95 in additional revenue in weak-party states but only about $0.75 in strong-party states. The differential effect of the FPI suggests that counties in TPO states spend less money providing the same functions as counties in non-TPO states, which is consistent with Mayhew's argument that party organizational strength is a constraint on government spending.

Party Organization and TELs. In Section 6.4.2, I presented several tests for differences in fiscal constraints between TPO and non-TPO states, finding none. In Table A.14, I show a regression of the number of TELs in a state against the TPO dummy variable and a set of year indicators. The coefficient is positive, indicating that TPO states had, on average, 0.72 more TELs in place than non-TPO states, but the difference is not statistically significant.

A.3   SUMMARY STATISTICS

Table A.15 presents summary statistics for the variables used in Chapters 4 and 6. Table A.16 presents summary statistics for the variables used in Chapter 5. Table A.17 shows the state TPO and SPO scores used in Chapter 6.

Table A.13. *TPO versus non-TPO States, Fully Interacted Model*

	(1)
Jurisdictional overlap	172.59
	(40.17)***
Strong party state * Jurisdictional overlap	−159.42
	(54.26)***
FPI	0.95
	(0.04)***
Strong party state * Functional performance index	−0.20
	(0.07)***
ln(population)	−23.20
	(41.71)
Strong party state * ln(population)	161.60
	(87.00)*
Per capita income	0.02
	(0.00)***
Strong party state * Per Capita income	0.00
	(0.01)
Percent nonwhite	−247.57
	(167.14)
Strong party state * Percent nonwhite	19.80
	(397.47)
Five-year change in population	−259.99
	(96.70)***
Strong party state * Five-year change in population	−70.84
	(200.72)
Percent age ≤18	−460.41
	(557.45)
Strong party state * Percent age ≤18	250.66
	(775.92)
Percent age ≥65	−1,051.62
	(593.38)*

(continued)

Table A.13. *(continued)*

	(1)
Strong party state * Percent age > 65	1,337.96
	(1,078.42)
Federal aid, five-year lag	0.02
	(0.03)
Strong party state * Federal aid	–0.02
	(0.04)
State aid, five-year lag	–0.11
	(0.04)***
Strong party state * State aid	0.04
	(0.06)
Democratic presidential vote share	0.43
	(0.55)
Strong party state * Democratic presidential vote share	–0.27
	(1.25)
Constant	–1,154.16
	(400.83)***
(Jurisdictional overlap) + (Strong party state * Jurisdictional overlap)	13.17
	(36.48)
R-squared (within)	0.34
Observations	21,196
# of clusters	3,032

Notes: The dependent variable is general own-source revenue per capita. All dollar values are CPI-adjusted to year 2002 dollars. Standard errors, clustered by county, are reported in parentheses. County fixed effects, year dummies, and year * TPO interaction terms (not reported) are also included.
*significant at 10%, **significant at 5%, ***significant at 1%.

Table A.14. *Test for Differences in TELs between TPO and Non-TPO States*

	(2)
Dummy = 1 if strong party state	0.72
	(0.76)
Constant	2.61
	(0.35)***
R-squared	0.22
Observations	21,756
# of clusters	50

Notes: The dependent variable is total number of TELs. Standard errors, clustered by state, are reported in parentheses. Year dummies (not reported) are also included.
*significant at 10%, **significant at 5%, ***significant at 1%.

Table A.15. *Summary Statistics for Chapters 4 and 6*

	Mean	Standard Dev.	Minimum	25th Percentile	Median	75th Percentile	Maximum
Dependent Variables							
Own-source revenue	$1,298	$822	$47	$770	$1,151	$1,615	$21,230
Common-function spending	$1,751	$731	$98	$1,269	$1,628	$2,072	$16,508
Common-function spending minus education	$676	$478	$1	$398	$582	$837	$15,414
Current expenditures	$1,837	$770	$94	$1,301	$1,692	$2,208	$10,859
Capital expenditures	$266	$272	$0	$120	$205	$336	$11,898
Property taxes	$670	$496	$16	$331	$569	$873	$13,614
User charges	$339	$355	$0	$118	$224	$428	$7,141
Other revenue	$289	$359	$4	$135	$218	$340	$19,524
Percent own-source revenue from user charges	0.25	0.16	0.00	0.13	0.20	0.34	0.96
Independent variables							
Jurisdictional overlap	4.24	3.99	1.00	2.00	3.13	5.00	74.00

(continued)

Table A.15. (continued)

	Mean	Standard Dev.	Minimum	25th Percentile	Median	75th Percentile	Maximum
ln(jurisdictional overlap)	1.20	0.65	0.00	0.69	1.14	1.61	4.30
FPI	$1,818	$402	$339	$1,491	$1,748	$2,140	$3,003
Income per capita	$17,856	$6,284	$5,400	$13,565	$16,460	$20,915	$87,688
ln(population)	10.153	1.333	5.704	9.279	10.021	10.895	16.094
Five-year log change in population	0.04	0.09	-0.64	-0.01	0.03	0.08	1.34
Percent nonwhite	0.13	0.15	0.00	0.02	0.06	0.19	0.96
Percent <18	0.28	0.05	0.09	0.25	0.28	0.31	0.64
Percent >65	0.14	0.04	0.01	0.11	0.14	0.16	0.35
Federal aid (five-year lag)	$78	$140	$0	$17	$51	$99	$13,549
State aid (five-year lag)	$763	$370	$25	$507	$696	$927	$5,182
Total TELs	4.5	3.0	0	2	3	6	15
Party competition index	61.10	9.96	45.07	53.06	57.80	68.57	89.61

Notes: Each row has 21,198 county-year observations covering 1972, 1977, 1982, 1987, 1992, 1997, and 2002. All dollar values are in year 2002 dollars per capita. Jurisdictional overlap is the number of overlapping jurisdictions (special districts, school districts, territorially non-exclusive townships, and county) per municipality (cities and territorially exclusive towns).

Table A.16. *Summary Statistics for Chapter 5*

	Mean	Standard Dev.	Minimum	25th Percentile	Median	75th Percentile	Maximum	Observations
Dependent Variables								
Local revenue per capita	$ 18.26	$ 16.22	$0	$ 7.50	$ 14.14	$ 23.94	$ 187.50	106,203
Total expenditures per capita	$ 22.35	$ 17.76	$ 0.31	$ 10.74	$ 17.72	$ 28.38	$ 352.23	106,959
Capital expenditures per capita	$ 1.48	$ 4.42	$0	$0	$0	$ 1.05	$ 292.74	105,430
Books per capita	5.41	4.43	0.12	2.65	4.16	6.66	92.27	106,574
Employees per 10,000 capita	6.06	4.90	0	3.24	4.97	7.45	127.80	106,641
Percent librarians among employees	0.56	0.30	0	0.31	0.50	0.88	1.00	107,484
Employee wage/average county wage	0.73	0.21	0.01	0.59	0.72	0.86	2.34	64,812
Percent "other" expenses	0.21	0.08	0	0.15	0.20	0.25	0.85	64,303
Visits per capita	4.77	3.38	0.03	2.45	3.97	6.13	35.56	106,213
Circulation per capita	7.68	5.15	0.07	4.00	6.55	10.06	72.47	106,716
Expenditures/circulation	$ 3.34	$ 2.67	$ 0.04	$ 1.91	$ 2.78	$ 4.07	$ 401.06	106,868
Expenditures/visits	$ 5.37	$ 3.59	$ 0.14	$ 3.12	$ 4.52	$ 6.59	$ 155.87	106,288
Independent Variables								
Dummy = 1 if special district	0.10	0.29	0	0	0	0	1.00	106,203

(continued)

229

Table A.16. (continued)

	Mean	Standard Dev.	Minimum	25th Percentile	Median	75th Percentile	Maximum	Observations
Dummy = 1 if nonprofit	0.11	0.32	0	0	0	0	1.00	106,203
Dummy = 1 if multiple outlets and multiple administrative offices	0.01	0.12	0	0	0	0	1.00	106,203
Dummy = 1 if multiple outlets	0.19	0.39	0	0	0	0	1.00	106,203
Log(service area population)	8.86	1.60	2.94	7.67	8.81	9.92	15.18	106,203
Log(duplicated population)	2.69	2.94	0	0	1.79	5.18	13.78	106,203
County per capita income (1000s)	$ 24.27	$ 7.55	$ 4.14	$ 19.16	$ 22.82	$ 27.48	$ 89.33	106,203
County percent BA degrees	0.17	0.08	0.04	0.11	0.14	0.22	0.53	106,203
County percent under 18	0.26	0.03	0.15	0.24	0.26	0.28	0.46	106,203
County percent over 65	0.14	0.04	0.01	0.12	0.14	0.17	0.34	106,203

Notes: For each dependent variable, I drop observations with a value that is greater than 1.5 times the 95th percentile value or less than 0.5 times the 5th percentile value (see text). As a result, the number of observations used in the analyses differs for each dependent variable. Summary statistics for the independent variables are based on the sample used in model (1) of Table 5.2.

Table A.17. *State TPO and SPO Scores*

State	TPO Score	SPO Score
Alabama	1	55.0
Alaska	1	—
Arizona	1	10.0
Arkansas	2	21.2
California	1	16.4
Colorado	1	4.0
Connecticut	5	65.8
Delaware	4	26.9
Florida	1	11.5
Georgia	2	11.3
Hawaii	1	37.8
Idaho	1	5.2
Illinois	5	28.7
Indiana	5	64.6
Iowa	1	8.7
Kansas	1	10.9
Kentucky	4	17.1
Louisiana	3	33.7
Maine	1	18.7
Maryland	5	15.0
Massachusetts	1	15.5
Michigan	1	22.2
Minnesota	1	24.0
Mississippi	1	23.0
Missouri	4	49.2
Montana	1	39.4
Nebraska	1	—
Nevada	1	—
New Hampshire	1	20.8
New Jersey	5	28.3
New Mexico	2	—
New York	5	57.5
North Carolina	1	26.0
North Dakota	1	—
Ohio	4	35.5
Oklahoma	1	11.2
Oregon	1	—

(continued)

Table A.17. *(continued)*

State	TPO Score	SPO Score
Pennsylvania	5	61.1
Rhode Island	5	44.8
South Carolina	1	—
South Dakota	1	—
Tennessee	2	7.2
Texas	2	12.0
Utah	1	30.6
Vermont	1	38.9
Virginia	2	—
Washington	1	14.2
West Virginia	4	5.6
Wisconsin	1	6.2
Wyoming	1	22.2

Notes: TPO scores are from Mayhew (1986). SPO scores represent state averages of the mayoral SPO scores from Clark and Hoffmann-Martinot (1998).

References

Advisory Commission on Intergovernmental Relations (ACIR). 1964. *The Problem of Special Districts in American Government*. Washington, DC: ACIR Publications.

    1981. *Measuring Discretionary Authority*. Washington, DC: ACIR Publications.

    1987. *The Organization of Local Public Economies*. Washington, DC: ACIR Publications.

    1993a. *State Laws Governing Local Government Structure and Administration*. Washington, DC: ACIR Publications.

    1993b. *Local Government Autonomy: Needs for Constitutional, Statutory, and Judicial Clarification*. Washington, DC: ACIR Publications.

    1995. *Tax and Expenditure Limits on Local Governments*. Washington, DC: ACIR Publications.

Aldrich, John. 1995. *Why Parties: The Origin and Transformation of Political Parties in America*. Chicago: University of Chicago Press.

Alesina, Alberto, Reza Baqir, and William Easterly. 1999. "Public Goods and Ethnic Divisions." *Quarterly Journal of Economics* 114:1243–1284.

Alesina, Alberto, Reza Baqir, and Caroline Hoxby. 2004. "Political Jurisdictions in Heterogeneous Communities." *The Journal of Political Economy* 112(2):348–396.

Alesina, Alberto, and Roberto Perotti. 1999. "Budget Deficits and Budget Institutions." In *Fiscal Institutions and Fiscal Performance*, James Poterba and Jurgen von Hagen, eds. Chicago: University of Chicago Press.

Arellano, Manuel. 1987. "Computing Robust Standard Errors for Within-Group Estimators." *Oxford Bulletin of Economics and Statistics* 49(4):431–434.

Aristotle. 1998. *Politics*. Indianapolis: Hackett.

Arrow, Kenneth. 1951, rev. ed. 1963. *Social Choice and Individual Values*. New Haven, CT: Yale University Press.

Axelrod, Donald. 1992. *Shadow Government*. New York: Wiley.

Bache, Ian, and Matthew Flinders. 2004. *Multi-level Governance*. New York: Oxford University Press.

Bailey, Stephen J., and Stephen Connolly. 1998. "The Flypaper Effect: Identifying Areas for Further Research." *Public Choice* 95:335–361.

Banfield, Edward C. 1961. *Political Influence*. New York: Free Press.

    1970. *The Unheavenly City: The Nature and Future of Our Urban Crisis*. Boston: Little, Brown.

References

Baqir, Reza. 2002, "Districting and Government Overspending." *Journal of Political Economy* 110:1318–1354.

Baum, C.F., M.E. Schaffer, and S. Stillman. 2003. "Instrumental Variables and GMM: Estimation and Testing." *Stata Journal* 3:1–31.

Beck, Nathaniel, and Simon Jackman. 1998. "Beyond Linearity by Default: Generalized Additive Models." *American Journal of Political Science* 42(2): 596–627.

Benhabib, Jess, and Roy Radner. 1992. "The Joint Exploitation of a Productive Asset: A Game-Theoretic Approach." *Economic Theory* 2(2): 155–190.

Berry, Christopher. 2008. "Piling On: Multilevel Government and the Fiscal Common-Pool." *American Journal of Political Science* 52(4): 802–820.

Berry, Christopher, and Jacob Gersen. 2009. "Selective Participation and Election Timing." Working paper, University of Chicago.

Berry, Christopher, and Martin West. Forthcoming. "Growing Pains: The School Consolidation Movement and Student Outcomes." *Journal of Law, Economics, and Organization.*

Bertrand, Marianne, Esther Duflo, and Sendhil Mullainathan. 2004. "How Much Should We Trust Differences-in-Differences Estimates?" *The Quarterly Journal of Economics* 119(1): 249–275.

Besley, Timothy, Torsten Persson, and Daniel Strum. 2006. "Political Competition and Economic Performance: Theory and Evidence from the United States." NBER Working Paper No. 11484.

Besley, Timothy, and Harvey Rosen. 1998. "Vertical Externalities in Tax Setting: Evidence from Gasoline and Cigarettes." *Journal of Public Economics* 70(3): 383–398.

Bhattacharyya, Arunava, Thomas R. Harris, Rangesan Narayanan, and Kambiz Raffiee. 1995. "Technical Efficiency of Rural Water Utilities." *Journal of Agricultural and Resource Economics* 20(2): 373–391.

Blake, Peter. 2006. "Colorado Will Teem with Special District Elections Tuesday." *Rocky Mountain News*, April 29.

Bollens, John C. 1957. *Special District Governments in the United States.* Berkeley and Los Angeles: University of California Press.

Bollens, John C., and Henry J. Schmandt. 1970. *The Metropolis: Its People, Politics, and Economic Life*, 2nd ed. New York: Harper and Row.

Bowler, Shaun, and Todd Donovan. 2004. "Evolution in State Governance Structures: Unintended Consequences of State Tax and Expenditure Limitations." *Political Research Quarterly* 59(2): 189–196.

Boyd, Donald. 2008. *Layering of Local Governments and City-County Mergers.* Report to the New York State Commission on Local Government Efficiency and Competitiveness.

Bradbury, John C., and W. Mark Crain. 2001. "Legislative Organization and Government Spending: Cross-Country Evidence." *Journal of Public Economics* 82(3): 309–325.

Brazer, Harvey E. 1959. *City Expenditures in the United States.* New York: National Bureau of Economic Research.

Brennan, Geoffrey, and James Buchanan. 1980. *The Power to Tax: Analytical Foundations of a Fiscal Constitution.* Cambridge: Cambridge University Press.

Broder, David. 1972. *The Party's Over: The Failure of Politics in America.* New York: Harper and Row.

References

Brulhart, Marius, and Mario Jametti. 2006. "Vertical versus Horizontal Tax Externalities: An Empirical Test." *Journal of Public Economics* 90:2027–2062.

Buchanan, James. 1967. *Public Finance in Democratic Process*. Chapel Hill: University of North Carolina Press.

Bureau of the Census, U.S. Department of Commerce. 1994, *Census of Governments*, vol. 1, no. 1: *Government Organization*. Washington, DC: U.S. Government Printing Office.

Burns, Nancy. 1994. *The Formation of American Local Governments*. New York: Oxford University Press.

Carr, Jared B. 2006. "Local Government Autonomy and State Reliance on Special District Governments: A Reassessment." *Political Research Quarterly* 59(3): 481–492.

Chicago Tribune Editorial Board. 2008. "Your New Stroger Tax." *Chicago Tribune*, editorial, March 5.

Chicoine, David L., and Norman Walzer. 1985. *Governmental Structure and Local Public Finance*. Boston: Oelgeschlager, Gunn & Hain.

The Civic Federation. 2003. *A Call for the Elimination of the Suburban Cook County Tuberculosis Sanitarium District*. Available at http://civicfed.org/articles/civicfed_63.pdf.

Clark, Terry N., Lorna C. Ferguson, and Robert Y. Shapiro. 1982. "Functional Performance Analysis: A New Approach to the Study of Municipal Expenditures." *Political Methodology* 8:187–223.

Clark, Terry N., and Vincent Hoffmann-Martinot. 1998. *The New Political Culture*. Boulder, CO: Westview Press.

Cook County Board. 2008. *Citizens' Budget Summary*. Available at http://www.co.cook.il.us/2008_budget1new.htm.

Cornes, Richard, and Todd Sandler. 1996. *The Theory of Externalities, Public Goods, and Club Goods*. Cambridge: Cambridge University Press.

Coughlin, Peter J. 1992. *Probabilistic Voting Theory*. Cambridge: Cambridge University Press.

Coughlin, Peter, and Shmuel Nitzan. 1981. "Electoral Outcomes with Probabilistic Voting and Nash Social Welfare Maxima." *Journal of Public Economics* 15(1): 113–121.

Cox, Gary, and Mathew McCubbins. 1993. *Legislative Leviathan: Party Government in the House*. Berkeley and Los Angeles: University of California Press.

Cremer, Jaques, and Thomas Palfrey. 1999. "Political Confederation." *American Political Science Review* 93(1): 69–83.

Cutler, David M., Douglas W. Elmendorf, and Richard J. Zeckhauser. 1993. "Demographic Characteristics and the Public Bundle." *Public Finance* 48(suppl): 178–198.

Dahl, Robert. 1956. *A Preface to Democratic Theory*. Chicago: University of Chicago Press.

DelRossi, Alison, and Robert Inman. 1999. "Changing the Price of Pork: The Impact of Local Cost Sharing on Legislators' Demands for Distributive Public Goods." *Journal of Public Economics* 71:247–273.

DiLorenzo, Thomas J. 1981. "The Expenditure Effects of Restricting Competition in Local Public Service Industries: The Case of Special Districts." *Public Choice* 37(3): 569–578.

References

Downs, Anthony. 1994. *New Visions for Metropolitan America*. Washington, DC: Brookings Institution.

Dranove, David. 1988. "Pricing by Non-Profit Institutions: The Case of Hospital Cost Shifting." *Journal of Health Economics* 7(1): 47–57.

Driscoll, John C., and Aart C. Kraay. 1998. "Consistent Covariance Matrix Estimation with Spatially Dependent Panel Data." *The Review of Economics and Statistics* 80(4): 549–560.

Dunne, Stephanie, Robert Reed, and James Wilbanks. 1997. "Endogenizing the Median Voter: Public Choice Goes to School." *Public Choice* 93:99–118.

Eberts, Randal, and Timothy Gronberg. 1990. "Structure, Conduct, and Performance in the Local Public Sector." *National Tax Journal* 63:165–173.

Ellcessor, Patrick, and Jan E. Leighley. 2001. "Voters, Non-Voters and Minority Representation." In *Representation of Minority Groups in the U.S.*, ed. C.E. Menifield. Lanham, MD: Austin and Winfield.

Emanuelson, David N. 2008. "A Comparative Analysis of Illinois, Ohio, Colorado and South Dakota Park Districts and Parks and Recreation Departments to Wisconsin, Iowa, Missouri, Kansas, Indiana, and Michigan Parks and Recreation Departments." Paper presented at the annual meeting of the Midwest Political Science Association, Chicago, April 5.

Enelow, James M., and Melvin J. Hinich. 1989. "A General Probabilistic Spatial Theory of Elections." *Public Choice* 61:101–113.

Epple, D., R. Filimon, and T. Romer. 1983. "Housing, Voting, and Moving: Equilibrium in a Model of Local Public Goods with Multiple Jurisdictions." In *Research in Urban Economics*, Vol. III, J.V. Henderson, ed. Greenwich, CT: JAI Press.

1984. "Equilibrium among Local Jurisdictions: Toward an Integrated Treatment of Voting and Residential Choice." *Journal of Public Economics* 24:281–308.

1993. "Existence of Voting and Housing Equilibrium in a System of Communities with Property Taxes." *Regional Science and Urban Economics* 23:585–610.

Epple, D., and G.J. Platt. 1998. "Equilibrium among Jurisdictions When Households Differ by Preferences and Income." *Journal of Urban Economics* 43:23–51.

Epple, Dennis, and Allan Zelenitz. 1981. "The Implications of Competition among Jurisdictions: Does Tiebout Need Politics?" *Journal of Political Economy* 89(6): 1197–1217.

Erie, Steven. 1988. *Rainbow's End: Irish-Americans and the Dilemmas of Urban Machine Politics, 1840–1985*. Berkeley: University of California Press.

Esteller-More, Alejandro, and Albert Sole-Olle. 2001. "Vertical Income Tax Externalities and Fiscal Interdependence: Evidence from the U.S." *Regional Science and Urban Economics* 31:247–272.

2002. "Tax Setting in a Federal System: The Case of Personal Income Taxation in Canada." *International Tax and Public Finance* 9(3): 235–257.

Ferreira, Fernando, and Joseph Gyourko. 2009. "Do Political Parties Matter? Evidence from U.S. Cities." *Quarterly Journal of Economics* 124(1): 399–422.

Filippov, Mikhail, Peter Ordeshook, and Olga Shvetsova. 2004. *Designing Federalism: A Theory of Self-Sustainable Federal Institutions*, New York: Cambridge University Press.

Fischel, William. 1981. "Is Local Government Structure in Large Urbanized Areas Monopolistic or Competitive?" *National Tax Journal* 34:95–104.

2001. *The Homevoter Hypothesis: How Home Values Influence Local Government Taxation, School Finance, and Land-Use Policies.* Cambridge, MA: Harvard University Press.

Flickinger, Ted, and Peter M. Murphy. 1990. "Special Districts." In *Illinois Local Government: A Handbook,* James F. Keane and Gary Koch, eds. Carbondale: Southern Illinois University Press.

Flochel, L., and Madiès Thierry. 2002. "Interjurisdictional Tax Competition in a Model of Overlapping Revenue Maximizing Governments." *International Tax Public Finance* 9:121–141.

Flowers, M.R. 1988. "Shared Tax Resources in a Leviathan Model of Federalism." *Public Finance Quarterly* 16:67–77.

Ford, Liam, and John Keilman. 2008. "Cook Tax Increase Has County Border Towns Steaming." *Chicago Tribune,* March 5.

Foster, Kathryn. 1997. *The Political Economy of Special-Purpose Government.* Washington, DC: Georgetown University Press.

Frey, Bruno S. 1996. "FOCJ: Competitive Governments for Europe." *International Review of Public Economics* 16:315–27.

2001. "A Utopia? Government without Territorial Monopoly." *Journal of Institutional and Theoretical Economics* 157:162–175.

Frey, Bruno S., and Reiner Eichenberger. 1999. *The New Democratic Federalism for Europe: Functional, Overlapping, and Competing Jurisdictions.* Northampton, MA: Edward Elgar.

Frug, Gerald E. 1980. "The City as a Legal Concept." *Harvard Law Review* 93:1059–1154.

2002. "Beyond Regional Government." *Harvard Law Review* 115:1763–1837.

Fuchs, Ester R. 1992. *Mayors and Money: Fiscal Policy in New York and Chicago.* Chicago: University of Chicago Press.

Galvan, Sara C. 2007. "Wrestling with MUDs to Pin Down the Truth About Special Districts." *Fordham Law Review* 75(6): 3041–3080.

Gardner, Roy, Noel Gaston, and Robert T. Mason. 2003. "Tolling the Rhine in 1254: Complementary Monopoly Revisited." Paper presented at the European Economic Association meetings, Stockholm, August.

Gilligan, Thomas, and John Matsusaka. 1995. "Deviations from Constituent Interests: The Role of Legislative Structure and Political Parties in the States." *Economic Inquiry* 33: 383–401.

Giuffrida, Greg. 2003. "Man Loses Uncontested Race, Says Polling Place Closed." Associated Press State and Local Newswire, September 18.

Goodspeed, Timothy J. 2000. "Tax Structure in a Federation." *Journal of Public Economics* 75:493–506.

Gordon, Roger H. 1983. "An Optimal Taxation Approach to Fiscal Federalism." *Quarterly Journal of Economics* 98(4): 567–586.

Guild, Frederic H. 1918. "Special Municipal Corporations." *American Political Science Review* 12(4): 678–684

Hajnal, Zoltan L., Paul G. Lewis, and Hugh Louch. 2002. *Municipal Elections in California: Turnout, Timing, and Competition.* San Francisco: Public Policy Institute of California.

Hajnal, Zoltan L., and Jessica Trounstine. 2005. "Where Turnout Matters: The Consequences of Uneven Turnout in City Politics." *The Journal of Politics* 67(2): 515–535.

References

Hallerberg, Mark. 2000. "The Role of Parliamentary Committees in the Budgetary Process within Europe." In *Institutions, Politics, and Fiscal Policy*, Rauf Strauch and Jurgen von Hagen, eds. Dordrecht: Kluwer.

Hallerberg, Mark, and Jurgen von Hagen. 1999. "Electoral Institutions, Cabinet Negotiations, and Budget Deficits in the European Union." In *Fiscal Institutions and Fiscal Performance*, James Poterba and Jurgen von Hagen, eds. Chicago: University of Chicago Press.

Hamilton, Bruce. 1983. "A Review: Is the Property Tax a Benefit Tax?" In *Local Provision of Public Services: The Tiebout Model after Twenty-five Years*, George Zodrow, ed. New York: Academic Press.

Hanushek, Eric A. 1986. "The Economics of Schooling: Production and Efficiency in Public Schools." *Journal of Economic Literature* 24(3): 1141–1177.

Harberger, Arnold C. 1964. "The Measurement of Waste." *The American Economic Review* 54:58–76.

Hardin, Garrett. 1968. "The Tragedy of the Commons." *Science* 162:1243–1248.

Hastie, Trevor, and R.J. Tibshirani. 1990. *Generalized Additive Models*. New York: Chapman and Hall.

Hawley, Willis D. 1973. *Nonpartisan Elections and the Case for Party Politics*. New York: Wiley.

Hayashi, Masayoshi, and Robin Boadway. 2001. "An Empirical Analysis of Intergovernmental Tax Interaction: The Case of Business Income Taxes in Canada.." *Canadian Journal of Economics* 34(2): 481–503.

Heikkila, Tanya, and Todd L. Ely. 2003. "A Comparative Analysis of the Effect of State Institutions on the Proliferation of Special District Governments." Paper presented at the Third Annual Conference on State Politics and Policy: Causes and Consequences of American State Institutions on Political Behavior, cosponsored by the University of Arizona Department of Political Science and *State Politics and Policy Quarterly*, March 14–15.

Helsley, Robert. 2004. "Urban Political Economics." In *Handbook of Urban and Regional Economics*, vol. 4, V. Henderson and J. Thisse, eds. Amsterdam: North Holland.

Hettich, Walter, and Stanley L. Winer. 1999. *Democratic Choice and Taxation: A Theoretical and Empirical Analysis*. New York: Cambridge University Press.

Highton, Ben, and R.E. Wolfinger. 2001. "The Political Implications of Higher Turnout." *British Journal of Political Science* 31(1): 179–192.

Hines, James R., Jr., and Richard H. Thaler. 1995. "Anomalies: The Flypaper Effect." *Journal of Economic Perspectives* 9:217–226.

Holtz-Eakin, Douglas. 1988. "The Line Item Veto and Public Sector Budgets: Evidence from the States." *Journal of Public Economics* 36:269 – 292.

Hooghe, Liesbet, and Gary Marks. 2003. "Unraveling the Central State, But How? Types of Multi-level Governance." *American Political Science Review* 97(2): 233–243.

Hoyte, William H. 2001. "Tax Policy Coordination, Vertical Externalities, and Optimal Taxation in a System of Hierarchical Governments." *Journal of Urban Economics* 50:491–516.

Illinois General Assembly, Commission on Intergovernmental Cooperation. 2003. *Legislator's Guide to Local Government in Illinois: Special Districts*. Available at http://www.ilga.gov/commission/lru/SpecialDistricts.pdf.

References

Johnson, William R. 1988. "Income Redistribution in a Federal System." *American Economic Review* 78:570–573.

Jones, Bryan D. 1983. *Governing Urban America: A Policy Focus*. Boston: Little, Brown.

Kam, Cindy D., and Robert J. Franzese. 2007. *Modeling and Interpreting Interactive Hypotheses in Regression Analysis*. Ann Arbor: University of Michigan Press.

Karnig, Albert K., and B. Oliver Walter. 1983. "Decline in Municipal Voter Turnout: A Function of Changing Structure." *American Politics Quarterly* 11(4): 491–505.

Keen, Michael. 1998. "Vertical Externalities in the Theory of Fiscal Federalism." *IMF Staff Papers* 45(3): 454–485.

Keen, Michael J., and Christos Kotsogiannis. 2002. "Does Federalism Lead to Excessively High Taxes?" *American Economic Review* 92(1): 363–370.

Kettleborough, Charles. 1914. "Special Municipal Corporations." *American Political Science Review* 8(4): 751–759;

Kiewiet, D. Roderick, and Mathew D. McCubbins. 1991. *The Logic of Delegation: Congressional Parties and the Appropriations Process*. Chicago: University of Chicago Press.

Knight, Brian. 2004. "Parochial Interests and the Centralized Provision of Local Public Goods: Evidence from Congressional Voting on Transportation Projects." *Journal of Public Economics* 88(3–4): 845–866.

———. 2006. "Common Tax Pool Problems in Federal Systems." In *Democratic Constitutional Design and Public Policy: Analysis and Evidence*, Roger D. Congleton and Birgitta Swedenborg, eds. Cambridge, MA: MIT Press.

Kogan, Vladimir, and Mathew D. McCubbins. 2008. "The Problem with Being Special: Democratic Values and Special Assessments." Working paper, University of California at San Diego. Available at http://ssrn.com/abstract=1277522.

Kontopolous, Y., and R. Perotti. 1999. "Government Fragmentation and Fiscal Policy Outcomes: Evidence from OECD Countries." In *Fiscal Institutions and Fiscal Performance*, James M. Poterba and Jurgen von Hagen, eds. Chicago: University of Chicago Press.

Kramer, Larry D. 2000. "Putting the Politics Back into the Political Safeguards of Federalism." *Columbia Law Review* 100(1): 215–293.

Krehbiel, Keith. 1991. *Information and Legislative Organization*. Ann Arbor: University of Michigan Press.

Kreps, David M. 1990. *Game Theory and Economic Modeling*. New York: Oxford University Press.

Ladd, Helen, and Nicolas Tideman, eds. 1981. *Tax and Expenditure Limitations*. COUPE Papers on Public Economics. Washington, DC: Urban Institute.

Laffer, Arthur B. 2004. "The Laffer Curve: Past, Present, and Future." Available at http://www.heritage.org/Research/Taxes/bg1765.cfm.

Langbein, Laura I., Philip Crewson, and Charles N. Brasher. 1996. "Rethinking Ward and At-Large Elections in Cities." *Public Choice* 88:275–293.

Ledyard, John O. 1984. "The Pure Theory of Large Two-Candidate Elections." *Public Choice* 44(1): 7–41.

Leigland, James. 1990. "The Census Bureau's Role in Research on Special Districts: A Critique." *The Western Political Quarterly* 43(2): 367–380.

Levhari, David, and Leonard J. Mirman. 1980. "The Great Fish War: An Example Using a Dynamic Cournot–Nash Solution." *Bell Journal of Economics* 11(1): 322–334.

Liebmann, George W. 2002. "The New American Local Government." *Urban Lawyer* 34(1): 93–130.

Little Hoover Commission. 2000. *Special Districts: Relics of the Past or Resources for the Future?* Commission Report No. 155. Available at http://www.lhc.ca.gov/lhcdir/report155.html.

Loucks, Christine. 1996. "Finance Industry PAC Contributions to U.S. Senators." *Public Choice* 89:210–219.

Lowi, Theodore J. 1967. "Machine Politics—Old and New." *Public Interest* 9:83–92.

Lyons, W.E., and David Lowery. 1989. "Governmental Fragmentation versus Consolidation: Five Public-Choice Myths about How to Create Informed, Involved, and Happy Citizens." *Public Administration Review* 49(6): 533–543.

MacManus, Susan A. 1981. "Special District Governments: A Note on Their Use as Property Tax Relief Mechanisms in the 1970s." *Journal of Politics* 43:438–444.

   1983. "State Government: Overseer of Municipal Finance." In *The Municipal Money Chase*, Alberta Sbragia, ed. Boulder, CO: Westview.

Marks, Gary, and Liesbet Hooghe. 2004. "Contrasting Visions of Multi-level Governance." In *Multi-level Governance*, Ian Bache and Mathew Flinders, eds. New York: Oxford University Press.

Martin, Dolores Tremewan, and Richard E. Wagner. 1978. "The Institutional Framework for Municipal Incorporation: An Economic Analysis of Local Agency Formation Commissions in California." *Journal of Law and Economics* 21(2): 409–425.

Martin, Lowell A. 1998. *Enrichment: A History of the Public Library in the United States in the Twentieth Century*. Lanham, MD: Scarecrow Press.

Maskin, Eric, and Jean Tirole. 2001. "Markov Perfect Equilibrium I: Observable Actions." *Journal of Economic Theory* 100(2): 191–219.

Matsusaka, John. 1992. "Economics of Direct Legislation." *Quarterly Journal of Economics* 107:541–571.

Mayhew, David. 1986. *Placing Parties in American Politics*. Princeton, NJ: Princeton University Press.

McGinnis, Michael, ed. 1999. *Polycentricity and Local Public Economies*. Ann Arbor: University of Michigan Press.

Miller, Gary J. 1981. *Cities by Contract: The Politics of Municipal Incorporation*. Cambridge, MA: MIT Press.

Miranda, Rowan A. 1994. "Containing Cleavages: Parties and Other Hierarchies." In *Urban Innovation: Creative Strategies for Turbulent Times*, Terry N. Clark, ed. Thousand Oaks, CA: Sage Publications.

Moe, Terry M. 2006. "Political Control and the Power of the Agent." *The Journal of Law, Economics, and Organization* 22(1): 1–29.

Mueller, Dennis. 2003. *Public Choice III*. Cambridge: Cambridge University Press.

Mullins, Daniel R., and Bruce A. Wallin. 2004. "Tax and Expenditure Limitations: Introduction and Overview." *Public Budgeting and Finance* (Winter): 2–15.

References

Munger, Michael C. 1989. "A Simple Test of the Hypothesis That Committee Jurisdictions Shape Corporate PAC Contributions." *Public Choice* 62:181–186.

Musgrave, Richard, and Alan Peacock, eds. 1958. *Classics in the Theory of Public Finance*. London, New York: Macmillan.

Nechyba, Thomas J. 1997. "Existence of Equilibrium and Stratification in Local and Hierarchical Tiebout Economies with Property Taxes and Voting." *Economic Theory* 10:277–304.

Nelson, Michael A. 1987. "Searching for Leviathan: Comment and Extension." *The American Economic Review* 77(1): 198–204.

———. 1990. "Decentralization of the Subnational Public Sector: An Empirical Analysis of the Determinants of Local Government Structure in Metropolitan Areas in the U.S." *Southern Economic Journal* 57:443–457.

Newey, Whitney K., and Kenneth D. West. 1987. "A Simple, Positive Semi-Definite, Heteroskedasticity and Autocorrelation Consistent Covariance Matrix." *Econometrica* 55(3): 703–708.

Niskanen, William. 1971. *Bureaucracy and Representative Government*. Chicago: Aldine.

Oakerson, Ronald. 1999. *Governing Local Public Economies: Creating the Civic Metropolis*. Oakland, CA: ICS Press.

Oakerson, Ronald, and Roger Parks.1989. "Metropolitan Organization and Governance: A Local Public Economy Approach." *Urban Affairs Quarterly* 25:18–29.

Oates, Wallace. 1972. *Fiscal Federalism*. New York: Harcourt Brace Jovanovich.

———. 1985. "Searching for Leviathan: An Empirical Study." *American Economic Review* 75: 748–757.

———. 1989. "Searching for Leviathan: A Reply and Some Further Reflections." *American Economic Review* 79:578–583.

———. 1990. "An Essay on Fiscal Federalism." *Journal of Economic Literature* 37(3): 1120–1149.

———. 1991. *Studies in Fiscal Federalism*. Brookfield, VT: Edward Elgar.

———. 1998. *Economics of Fiscal Federalism and Local Finance*. Brookfield, VT: Edward Elgar.

———. 1999. "An Essay on Fiscal Federalism." *Journal of Economic Literature* 37(3): 1120–1149.

———. 2001. "Fiscal Competition of Harmonization? Some Reflections." *National Tax Journal* 54(3): 507–512.

O'Connor, Diana. 2004. "Public Library Districts in Texas: A Case Study." *Public Libraries* (September/October): 275–279.

Oliver, J. Eric, and Shang E. Ha. 2007. "Vote Choice in Suburban Elections." *American Political Science Review* 101(3): 393–408.

Olmstead, Rob. 2008. "Cook County Board Hikes Taxes." *Chicago Daily Herald*, March 1.

Orfield, Myron. 1997. *Metropolitics*. Washington, DC: Brookings Institution Press.

Osborne, Martin J., and Ariel Rubinstein. 1994. *A Course in Game Theory*. Cambridge, MA: MIT Press.

Ostrom, Elinor. 1990. *Governing the Commons*. Cambridge: Cambridge University Press.

References

Ostrom, Elinor, Roy Gardner, and James Walker. 1994. *Rules, Games, and Common-Pool Resources*. Ann Arbor: University of Michigan Press.

Ostrom, Vincent, Robert Bish, and Elinor Ostrom. 1988. *Local Government in the United States*. San Francisco: ICS Press.

Papke, Leslie E., and Jeffrey M. Wooldridge. 1996. "Econometric Methods for Fractional Response Variables with an Application to 401(K) Plan Participation Rates." *Journal of Applied Econometrics* 11(6): 619–632.

Patty, John W. 2002. "Equivalence of Objectives in Two Candidate Elections." *Public Choice* 112:151–166.

Peltzman, Sam. 1998. *Political Participation and Government Regulation*. Chicago: University of Chicago Press.

Persson, Torsten, and Guido Tabellini. 2000. *Political Economics: Explaining Economic Policy*. Cambridge, MA: MIT Press.

2003. *The Economic Effects of Constitutions*. Cambridge, MA: MIT Press.

Petersen, Mitchell A. 2007. "Estimating Standard Errors in Finance Panel Data Sets: Comparing Approaches." *Review of Financial Studies*, forthcoming.

Peterson, Paul. 1981. *City Limits*. Chicago: University of Chicago Press.

1995. *The Price of Federalism*. Washington, DC: Brookings Institution Press.

Pettersson-Lidbom, Per. 2006. "Does the Size of the Legislature Affect the Size of Government? Evidence from Two Natural Experiments" (January 30). Available at the SSRN Web site: http://ssrn.com/abstract=988346.

Plott, Charles. 1967. "A Notion of Equilibrium and Its Possibility Under Majority Rule." *American Economic Review* 57:787–806.

Polsby, Nelson W. 1983. *Consequences of Party Reform*. New York: Oxford University Press.

Porter, Douglas R., Ben C. Lin, Susan Jakubiak, and Richard B. Peiser. 1992. *Special Districts: A Useful Technique for Financing Infrastructure*. Washington, DC: Urban Land Institute Press.

Porter, Kirk H. 1933. "A Plague of Special Districts," *National Municipal Review* 21(11): 544–547, 574.

Postan, Michael M. 1966. "Trade and Industry in the Middle Ages." In *The Cambridge Economic History of Europe*, 2nd ed., M.M. Postan and H.J. Habakkuk, eds. Cambridge: Cambridge University Press.

Poterba, James. 1995. "Capital Budgets, Borrowing Rules, and State Capital Spending." *Journal of Public Economics* 56(2): 165–187.

1997. "Demographic Structure and the Political Economy of Public Education." *Journal of Policy Analysis and Management* 16(1): 48–66.

Poterba, James, and Jurgen von Hagen, eds. 1999. *Fiscal Institutions and Fiscal Performance*. Chicago: University of Chicago Press.

Primo, David M., and James M. Snyder. 2007. "Party Strength, the Personal Vote, and Government Spending." Working paper, University of Rochester.

Qian, Yingyi, and Barry R. Weingast. 1997. "Federalism as a Commitment to Preserving Market Incentives." *The Journal of Economic Perspectives* 11(4): 83–92.

Rhode, Paul W., and Koleman S. Strumpf. 2003. "Assessing the Importance of Tiebout Sorting: Local Heterogeneity from 1850 to 1990." *The American Economic Review* 93(5): 1648–1677.

Ricciuti, Roberto. 2004. "Political Fragmentation and Fiscal Outcomes." *Public Choice* 118(3/4): 365–388.

References

Riker, William H. 1964. *Federalism: Origin, Operation, Significance*. Boston: Little, Brown.

——— 1980. "Implications from the Disequilibrium of Majority Rule for the Study of Institutions." *The American Political Science Review* 74(2): 432–446.

Rodden, Jonathan. 2005. *Hamilton's Paradox: The Promise and Perils of Fiscal Federalism*. New York: Cambridge University Press.

Romer, Thomas, and Howard Rosenthal. 1978. "Political Resource Allocation, Controlled Agendas, and the Status Quo." *Public Choice* 33:27–43.

——— 1979. "Bureaucrats versus Voters: On the Political Economy of Resource Allocation by Direct Democracy." *Quarterly Journal of Economics* 93:563–587.

Rose-Ackerman, Susan. 1983. "Tiebout Models and the Competitive Ideal: An Essay on the Political Economy of Local Government." In *Perspectives on Local Public Finance and Public Policy*, J.M. Quigley, ed. Greenwich, CT: JAI Press.

Rosenthal, Howard. 1990. "The Setter Model." In *Advances in the Spatial Theory of Voting*, James Enlow and Melvin Hinich, eds. New York: Cambridge University Press.

Ross, S., and J. Yinger. 1999. "Sorting and Voting: A Review of the Literature on Urban Public Finance." In *Handbook of Regional and Urban Economics*, vol. 3, P. Cheshire and E.S. Mills, eds. Amsterdam: North-Holland.

Rusk, David. 1993. *Cities without Suburbs*. Washington, DC: Woodrow Wilson Center Press.

Sacks, Seymour. 1990. "'The Census Bureau's Role in Research on Special Districts': A Necessary Rejoinder." *The Western Political Quarterly* 43(2): 381–383.

Samuelson, Paul A. 1954. "The Pure Theory of Public Expenditure." *The Review of Economics and Statistics* 36(4): 387–389.

Schmitter, Phillippe. 2000. *How to Democratize the European Union ... And Why Bother?* Lanham, MD: Rowman and Littlefield.

Shefter, Martin. 1985. *Political Crisis, Fiscal Crisis: The Collapse and Revival of New York City*. New York: Basic Books.

Shepsle, Kenneth. 1979. "Institutional Arrangements and Equilibrium in Multidimensional Voting Models." *American Journal of Political Science* 23(1): 27–59.

Shepsle, Kenneth, and Barry Weingast. 1981. "Structure-Induced Equilibrium and Legislative Choice." *Public Choice* 37(3): 503–519.

——— 1987. "The Institutional Formations of Committee Power." *The American Political Science Review* 81(1): 85–104.

Smith, Robert G. 1974. *Ad Hoc Governments: Special Purpose Transportation Authorities in Britain and the United State*. Beverly Hills, CA: Sage Publications.

Spengler, John. 1950. "Vertical Integration and Anti-Trust Policy." *Journal of Political Economy* 58:347–352.

Stetzer, Donald Foster. 1975. *Special Districts in Cook County: Toward a Geography of Local Government*. Chicago: University of Chicago.

——— 2004. "Special Districts." In *The Encyclopedia of Chicago*, James R. Grossman, Ann Durkin Keating, and Janice L. Reiff, eds. Chicago: University of Chicago Press.

References

Stigler, George. 1971. "The Theory of Economic Regulation." *Bell Journal of Economics and Management Science* 2:3–21.

1972. "Economic Competition and Political Competition." *Public Choice* 13:91–106.

Stratmann, Thomas. 1992. "Are Contributions Rational? Untangling Strategies of Political Action Committees." *Journal of Political Economy* 100:647–664.

Suozzi, Thomas R. 2007. "Special District Election Date Study: A Crazy Quilt." Available at http://www.nassaucountyny.gov/agencies/countyexecutive/News Release/2007/07-23-2007.html.

Teaford, Jon C. 1979. *City and Suburb: The Political Fragmentation of Metropolitan America, 1850–1970.* Baltimore: Johns Hopkins University Press.

1984. *The Unheralded Triumph: City Government in America, 1870–1900.* Baltimore: Johns Hopkins University Press.

Tiebout, Charles. 1956. "A Pure Theory of Local Government Expenditures." *Journal of Political Economy* 64:416–424.

Tirole, Jean. 1988. *The Theory of Industrial Organization.* Cambridge, MA: MIT Press.

Thompson, James Westfall. 1931. *The Economic and Social History of Europe.* New York, London: The Century Co.

Thompson, Lyke. 1997. "Citizen Attitudes About Service Delivery Modes." *Journal of Urban Affairs* 19(3): 291–302.

Tocqueville, Alexis de. 1835. *Democracy in America.* London: Saunders and Otley.

Townley, Arthur J., Dwight P. Sweeney, and June H. Schmieder. 1994. "School Board Elections: A Study of Citizen Voting Patterns." *Urban Education* 29(1): 50–62.

Tullock, Gordon. 1959. "Problems of Majority Voting." *Journal of Political Economy* 67:571–580.

1969. "Federalism: Problems of Scale." *Public Choice* 6(1): 19–29.

Verba, Sidney, Kay Lehman Schlozman, and Henry E. Brady. 1995. *Voice and Equality: Civic Voluntarism in American Politics.* Cambridge, MA: Harvard University Press.

Vigdor, J.L. 2002. "Interpreting Ethnic Fragmentation Effects." *Economics Letters* 75(2): 271–276.

Volden, Craig. 2005. "Intergovernmental Political Competition in American Federalism." *American Journal of Political Science* 49(2): 327–342.

von Hagen, Jurgen, and Ian J. Harden. 1995. "Budget Processes and Commitment to Fiscal Discipline." *European Economic Review* 39(3–4): 771–779.

Wallis, John, and Barry Weingast. 2005. "Equilibrium Federal Impotence: Why the States and Not the American National Government Financed Economic Development in the Antebellum Era." NBER Working Paper 11397.

Weimer, Debbi. 2001. "Data Brief 5." Education Policy Center, Michigan State University.

Weingast, Barry R. 1979. "A Rational Choice Perspective on Congressional Norms." *American Journal of Political Science* 23:245–262.

1989. "Floor Behavior in the U.S. Congress: Committee Power Under the Open Rule." *The American Political Science Review* 83(3): 795–815.

1995. "The Economic Role of Political Institutions: Market-Preserving Federalism and Economic Development." *Journal of Law, Economics and Organization* 11(1): 1–31.

References

Forthcoming. "Second Generation Fiscal Federalism: The Implications of Fiscal Incentives." *Journal of Urban Economics.*

Weingast, Barry, Kenneth Shepsle, and Christopher Johnsen. 1981. "The Political Economy of Benefits and Costs: A Neoclassical Approach to Distributive Politics." *Journal of Political Economy* 89(4): 642–664.

Weitzman, Howard S. 2005. "*Nassau County Special Districts: The Case for Reform.*" Nassau County, NY: Office of the Comptroller.

Wellisch, Dietmar. 2000. *Theory of Public Finance in a Federal State.* Cambridge: Cambridge University Press.

White, Halbert. 1980. "A Heteroskedasticity-Consistent Covariance Matrix Estimator and a Direct Test for Heteroskedasticity." *Econometrica* 48(4): 817–838.

Wilson, James Q. 1973. *Political Organizations.* New York: Basic Books.

Wilson, John. 1999. "Theories of Tax Competition." *National Tax Journal* 52(2): 269–304.

Wittman, Donald. 1995. *The Myth of Democratic Failure: Why Political Institutions Are Efficient.* Chicago: University of Chicago Press.

Wood, Simon N. 2006. *Generalized Additive Models: An Introduction with R.* Boca Raton, FL: Chapman & Hall.

Wooldridge, Jeffrey. 2002. *Econometric Analysis of Cross Section and Panel Data.* Cambridge, MA: MIT Press.

2006. "Cluster-Sample Methods in Applied Econometrics: An Extended Analysis." Working paper, Michigan State University.

Wrede, Matthias. 1997. "Vertical and Horizontal Tax Competition." *Finanzarchiv* N.F. 53:461–479.

1999. "The Tragedy of the Fiscal Common?: Fiscal Stock Externalities in a Leviathan Model of Federalism." *Public Choice* 101:177–193.

Zax, Jeffrey. 1989. "Is There a Leviathan in Your Neighborhood?" *American Economic Review* 79:560–567.

Zodrow, George, and Peter Mieszkowski. 1986. "Pigou, Tiebout, Property Taxation, and the Underprovision of Local Public Goods." *Journal of Urban Economics* 19:356–370.

Index

Advisory Commission on
Intergovernmental Relations
(ACIR), 114, 176, 204, 206, 218
Aldrich, John, 152
Alesina, Alberto, 50, 96–97
American Library Association, 132
Anzia, Sarah, 131n
Aristotle, 9

Banfield, Edward C., 150
Baqir, Reza, 13, 50, 96–97
Benhabib, Jess, 12
Besley, Timothy, 18, 169–70
Bhattacharyya, Arunava, 146
Bish, Robert, 6
Boadway, Robin, 18
Bollens, John, 45, 90
Bowler, Shaun, 48
Bradbury, John C., 13
Brasher, Charles N., 13
Brazer, Harvey E., 106n.15
Brennan, Geoffrey, 6
Brulhart, Marius, 18
Buchanan, James, 6
budgets and budgeting
  common-pool problems in, 12–14
  of special districts as part of local
    government, 38–40
  tax and expenditure limits (see tax
    and expenditure limits)
  Tiebout competition and, 78–83
    (see also Tiebout competition/
    model)
  total government spending, number
    of special districts and, 49

See also fiscal effects of
  jurisdictional overlap
Bureau of Economic Analysis,
  Regional Economic Information
  System, 134
Burns, Nancy, 48–50, 86n.27, 90n.1

California
  Little Hoover Commission, report
    on turnout for special district
    elections, 65
  teacher salaries, timing of school
    board elections and, 68
Canon, Joseph, 65
Carnegie Corporation, 131
Carr, Jared B., 48
Census Bureau, U.S.
  Census of Governments (*see Census
    of Governments*)
  Census of Population and Housing,
    98
Census of Governments (COG; U.S.
  Census Bureau)
  as data source, 29–30, 98,
    197–98
  geographic area of special-purpose
    jurisdictions, limited information
    regarding, 116
  governmental entities, definitions of,
    26–27
  jurisdictional overlap, data
    regarding, 90
chain-of-monopolies problem, 16–17,
  152n
Chicago. *See* Cook County, Illinois